START

OVER

EVERY

MORNING

Harvey Jackins

RATIONAL ISLAND PUBLISHERS
Seattle

Library of Congress Card Number: 89-38416
International Standard Book Number: Cloth Binding: 0-913937-36-3
Paperback: 0-913937-35-5

Jackins, Harvey.
  Start over every morning / Harvey Jackins — 1st ed.
    p. 407

  1. Re-evaluation counseling. I. Title.
BF637.C6J328 1989 158'.9—dc20 89-38416

Manufactured in the United States of America

If I could have but one wish granted
it would be
>*to live in a universe like this one*
>*at a time like the present*
>*with friends like the ones I have now*
>*and be myself.*

There is always at least one elegant solution
for any real problem.

"Morning has broken, like the first morning."

Table of Contents

Foreword

This volume contains many of the important insights that developed during 1987-89 in the world-wide Re-evaluation Counseling Communities.

The only requirement for participation in the Re-evaluation Counseling Communities is that one takes part in *re-emergence*, that is, that one uses Re-evaluation Counseling insights to recover one's occluded intelligence and helps others to do the same. Our ability to do this is improving rapidly in the current period, and some of the decisive new developments on this level are chronicled in these pages.

As our experience accumulates, Co-Counselors are more and more participating in three other activities. The first of these is usually termed *liberation*. This is the ending of the various oppressions (of workers, of females, of young people, of people of color, of disabled people, etc.) which the society has forced upon us in order to disunite us and keep us submissive and conforming. Probably at least a majority of present Co-Counselors are committed and active in resisting and eliminating these various oppressions. We do this both by refusing to accept such oppressions of ourselves and as allies to other people who have endured different oppressions than we have experienced.

Increasingly, Co-Counselors are seeking to *take charge* of the situations around them, to "reclaim their power" and to change the world. We seek to eliminate the wars, pollution, destruction of the environment, and the mistreatment of humans by humans that characterizes these last stages of this presently-collapsing society.

The diffusion of these precious insights and the *growth* of the community of people sharing them constitutes an additional activity that Co-Counselors are carrying out with more and more awareness and enthusiasm.

If this book is your first contact with the ideas of Re-evaluation Counseling, and you are interested in participating and in putting these ideas to *use*, you may write to me at 719 Second Avenue North, Seattle, Washington 98109, USA for knowledge of whom to contact for information in your country or locality.

This book is number nine in the central development of Co-Counseling literature. The previous books, in the order of their publication are: **The Fundamentals of Co-Counseling Manual, The Human Side of Human Beings, The Human Situation, The Upward Trend, The Benign Reality, The Reclaiming of Power, The Rest of Our Lives,** and **The Longer View.** Some of these have been published in twenty-two languages other than English.

There are also eight other books on auxiliary topics within Re-evaluation Counseling. Thirty special journals are published for particular groups of Co-Counselors.

Harvey Jackins
July 15, 1989

START

OVER

EVERY

MORNING

Advances in
Theory and Policy

Give Up False Expectations and "Disappointment"

In private conversations and occasionally in open question evenings, I hear some expectations about, and disappointments with, Re-evaluation Counseling that I think are getting in the way of your best use of RC. I would like to try to clarify again, in the light of our increasing understanding, what Re-evaluation Counseling is and what it isn't.

Such expectations and disappointments are not limited to people in your professions. Some of the mail I receive expresses similar sentiments and every variety of the people involved in RC participate in this to some extent. I hear questions: "Where can I get *good* counseling?" "Why can't the Community handle my problems?" There are many statements: "I am disappointed in _____ (a leader)." "I had expected...." "RC offers such a beautiful vision of reality, but then it doesn't live up to it." "Why don't RCers act like RC?"

WHAT RC IS NOT

I'm quite sure Re-evaluation Counseling will never become some of the things it is often expected to be. The Re-evaluation Counseling Community is not the perfect family that you failed to have in real life, for example. Re-evaluation Counseling is not the mother that you deserved, but didn't get. Re-evaluation Counseling is not the religious body that you longed for when you became disappointed in other religious bodies, not the church which will offer inspiration, but also be rational and powerful. Re-evaluation Counseling is not a

From College and University Faculty Leaders' Conference, June 5, 1988. Appeared in **Present Time** No. 72, July 1988.

place you come to have somebody solve your problems. Re-evaluation Counseling is not a therapy or a source of therapy (although many therapists do a better job with the insights and skills which they can acquire by using Re-evaluation Counseling). A Re-evaluation Counselor is not a perfect lover. Re-evaluation Counselors are not a group of people who will always understand you, always be supportive of you, always be a counselor to you under all conditions. Re-evaluation Counseling is not that great milk cow in the sky whose capacious udder will spray cleansing, healing streams of warm emotional milk over you and wash your sins and your patterns away, if you will just bunt her udder hard enough (by complaining and projecting expectations and re-hearsing your remaining patterns at her).

WHAT RC IS

Can I say what Re-evaluation Counseling *is*? I can try. It is changing all the time and is not the same as it was even a short while ago. Re-evaluation Counseling is a group of useful insights, useful glimpses of reality in areas where reality has been largely occluded for all of us growing up in these societies and these cultures. Re-evaluation Counseling is also a set of proposed relationships between a group of people trying to ally themselves with each other to use these insights to emerge from the great mess of patterns and unreality which we find ourselves born into and surrounded by as we grow up.

NO PERFECTION YET

I think it's important for us to face, however uncomfortable it makes us feel, that all human beings that we have any knowledge of at the present time are still thoroughly enmeshed in a great heap of patterns, irrational beliefs, lack of information, misinformation, oppressions, and cultural patterns which are a mixture of useful lore and foolish nonsense repeated and repeated from generation to generation. All human beings are still caught in an enormous web of confusion that has been generated by distress patterns, by op-

4

pressive societies, by misinformation, and by accident over a long period of time. It's as if we're still up to our noses, or our shoulders, or our waists in this sticky mud. Our relations with each other are continually assaulted by the mud, or rigidified by crude scaffolding that we have built to try to lift us part way out of the mud. All human beings are still caught in this mess, deeply. This includes all the human beings who have heard about Re-evaluation Counseling and have associated themselves together in some of the ways that we collectively call the Re-evaluation Counseling Communities.

Our expressing disappointment with each other because we are not free of this mud is very understandable, but not productive. It tends to keep us caught in not taking initiative or in rehearsing powerlessness. It interferes with our seeing the situation around us accurately and it tends to inhibit us from taking initiatives that could move us farther out of the mud, instead of grievancing around and around in a particular mudhole.

All RCers at the present are still contaminated by this great mess of patterns, oppression, and misinformation, just like all the other human beings in the world. Some RCers have used the insights of RC to get farther out of this mud in some particulars, but the percentage of our re-emergence, even though it's much higher than that of people who have not used these insights and information, is still far from complete. When you criticize an RC leader or complain that she or he has not provided for your quick and easy re-emergence, you are making life difficult for someone who is still waging at least as complex a struggle as you are. This person has perhaps, in some ways at least, made more effort than you have to date and so deserves your admiration and support and cooperation, but never your unreasonable expectations or your disappointments or your criticism or your complaints. The most experienced of us are still struggling in the big mudhole. If some of us have made decisions and discharged to the point that we splash less mud less wildly and manage to breathe un-muddy air a little more of the time, the main contribution we can make to others is the example, the indication that it is possible. Such people cannot furnish magic, never-ending assistance that will take you out of your mud without your having to make the same kind of effort as they did.

GOOD-HEARTED HELP

It is true that "experienced" (still meaning "not very experienced") RCers will often offer considerable effort and energy in counseling a person who is new to RC and helping the person get a good start. These first big, good steps that are often made can be very inspiring if it is understood that they are demonstrations of what is possible, rather than any commitment to go on providing such unselfish assistance. It needs to be understood that comparable assistance is expected to be given back or extended to newer people or support to the whole project in other ways offered to make the relationship rewarding to the first donor of assistance.

No matter how hard we look at the present period, we will not find anyone in the Re-evaluation Counseling Communities (including myself) who "lives up to" the picture of what human beings are really like that we have been able to get clear enough to look at and be inspired by. We need to keep these precious insights and goals clear without pretending that they are already accomplished actuality.

We have said to new RC teachers that they should teach RC correctly and rigorously but in *their own way*. We remind them that the way they were taught RC is not *the* way RC should be taught because, of necessity, the teacher who taught them taught some of the insights and valuable information that constitute RC but also taught, at least by example, some of her own distress patterns. If the new teacher copies these patterns and, unwittingly, adds her own additional distress, the insights of RC will become diluted and distorted to an additional degree for her students.

There is no person in RC who can yet be an all-round model for you except yourself. If you will use the frontier commitment, "From now on, the *real* John Doe, and this means..." over and over, you will find that, as the discharge occurs, an image of yourself as a complete human comes to mind and you can pursue this.

There are many RCers who can be models for the rest of us in limited ways, of course. I personally treasure and take great pleasure in them (when I do not fall into the patterns which I am warning against here, of being disappointed in them or having unreasonable expectations of them).

SAMPLE INSIGHTS

What we *do have* in RC is extremely valuable. Let's look at a few of these precious insights, just a small sample of them. (1) There is a qualitative difference between the pattern and the person and the pattern is a dispensable parasitic phenomenon detachable from the real person. (2) All people are good except in the way the patterns drive them to act otherwise. (3) All forms of discharge are to be encouraged, not repressed. (4) Feelings are not as good a guide to action as is logic. (5) "Every single human being at every moment of the past, if the entire situation is taken into account, has always done the very best that she or he could do and so deserves neither blame nor reproach from anyone including self. This in particular is true of you." (6) "There is at least one elegant solution to any real problem."

We have organizational forms which we have found useful in keeping us from patterned, "muddy" behavior with each other: the session, the support group, the class, the topic group, the workshop, the "think-and-listen," the Wygelian leaders' group. These are very useful, but it takes real decision, determination, and work to make them function fully in our interests. If we are not aware and responsible with each other, the patterns will creep in and the organizational forms will not work. If we allow our patterned behavior to intrude into our relations with other RCers when we are seeking to cooperate for each other's benefit, we do ourselves harm, but we also make it difficult for the other RCers.

FIRST PERSON SINGULAR RESPONSIBILITY

The re-emergence of ourselves, the recovery of our real natures and our real functioning is very much an individual responsibility. The process works much better if we are cooperative about it, but responsible cooperation is necessary. The amount of dependency that we can usefully lean on another person is very strictly limited by what the rules for being a good client in a session allow. Any less responsible behavior arises out of our distress patterns themselves and will not work.

Distress patterns come from at least three kinds of hurts. (1) Accidents: an accident hurt us and, if we did not get a chance to discharge thoroughly, it left a rigid pattern of irrational behavior and feelings upon us. (2) Contagion: as a child, frightened or hurt by the patterned behavior of parents, teachers, ministers, police officers, or employers, we acquired a distress recording that includes the patterned behavior of the perpetrator. We can be restimulated into acting out the perpetrator's role in the pattern, rather than our own victim's role in the pattern, as a seemingly "more comfortable" way of enduring it, and so hurt someone else. (3) Oppression: the oppressive society systematically installs hurts, fears, abuses upon us in an effort to require us to fit the rigid roles in the society demanded by its own rigid, oppressive nature.

We do have many insights on how to relate to each other in ways that make our cooperative behavior helpful. We can use these and help each other emerge from the mud, rather than sinking each other or taking advantage of each other or splashing mud in each other's faces. Some of these insights are assembled in the **Guidelines**. These are not rigid rules, not a "constitution" or "by-laws." They are exactly a summary of what we have learned will work well in our relationship of being "Community members."

THE LITERATURE

We also have a fairly rigorous, carefully-filtered picture of what RC is and what a re-emergent person can be like in one place. This is in the literature. You can get a fairly clear picture of how a re-emergent person can function by reading the fifteen books, the more than one hundred issues of the journals, the more than thirty pamphlets, and the more than forty video-cassettes and audio-cassettes that are available for observing and listening. The written word or the recorded image can be examined and edited repetitively. Applying this process with a great deal of care has succeeded in producing a workable, trustable picture of what "being an RCer" can be like.

This literature needs far more systematic use, far more persistent absorption. Because of its contradiction of patterns, RC literature needs to be not just read, heard, and viewed, but re-read, re-heard, and re-viewed.

It also needs far more systematic distribution, *including to non-RCers*. The failure of most RCers to regularly sell **Present Time** subscriptions to their friends is a ridiculous weakness in our work to date (but it can be corrected).

We also need to publish more literature more often. We need to somehow find the resources to translate much more of the literature into the twenty-two non-English languages into which translation has begun, as well as the 600 or so languages into which we have not yet begun to translate.

To English-speakers, the printed literature and the video- and audio-cassettes already constitute a treasure trove to which you can make persistent application to your benefit. Here are the models of what RC is, of what RC can be like, of how RC works when it is systematically applied.

Here are the answers to your disappointments at the muddy failures and weaknesses of those of us who have tried to play a leading role in the Community so far. Forgive us our failures. Don't waste time reproaching us. Take the insights that *are* available and begin modeling them for us.

Give up your understandable, but completely unrealistic expectations of "RC" and "RCers." Take these valuable insights *that do exist*, one of which is your complete freedom of decision and another of which is your complete power to have the universe respond to you in the way you wish it, and be a model *for me*. Be a model for the rest of the world, which is yearning to break out of the great mudbath of patterns, confusion, and oppression into which it has been diverted.

Start Over Every Morning

Actual reality is not the same as the pseudo-reality which distress recordings present to us. The actual situation may sometimes be very difficult, threatening, or even deadly, but it can be faced and, almost always, coped with well if it is seen for what it is. It is the false pictures offered by the distress patterns and their encrustations in the oppressive cultures that dismay us, and defeat us if we allow them to.

The distress recording, in effect, presents a projection of some past disaster or danger as if it were the reality of the present. This often keeps us from accurately estimating and handling whatever real difficulties are present. Acting *en masse* on us from their accumulations in the cultures, distress recordings and their social accumulations have even insisted that the past *determines* the future.

This is completely untrue. It was one of the great achievements of RC to clarify that the moving line of present time absolutely divides the determined past and the free-choice future. We know now that each instant can be seen as the beginning of a brand-new future, uncompelled by the past, open to our free decision as to what viewpoint to adopt towards it, what goals to pursue within it, how rational, how inspiring, how decisive to make it.

In discussing this with others, I have been able to envisage a future me making a fresh beginning with a fresh viewpoint every instant. A computer company has recently circulated a calculation that each human being, each second that he or she is awake, is processing eleven trillion items of information. Certainly if this vast a capacity were fully liberated, a fresh start with a fresh viewpoint every instant would not seem to be beyond our capacity.

Some of my very dear friends and co-leaders in the Re-evaluation Counseling Community write as if their annual or semi-annual contact with me at a teachers' and leaders' workshop marks a point of determined refreshing of their perspective. I would like to do it oftener than that.

What about the time of awakening each morning?

Waking to a new day has traditionally been seen as a dramatic break with the past, an opportunity for a fresh start, a time for thinking afresh. Can we organize our awakenings, discharge the distresses that may have accumulated around them, turn them into clean fresh beginnings for many "rests of our lives"?

Restimulation persisting through, or originating in, the time of sleep, will of course pull the other way. I have noticed that I have a habit pattern of tending to review the difficulties of the past day or week as a beginning activity for the new day. This must be some kind of a habitual surrender to a chronic pattern. It must have been inhibiting me from optimum dealing with my new days. It must have been acting to confuse me about my own goals and my own agenda for the future.

I now decide to change this patterned habit by decision, action, and discharge.

As I creep out from the patterned past into the sunlight of reality (occasionally interrupting the creeping with a small leap), I become clearer and clearer and remember more and more effectively that the future *is* completely within my province to decide about and to handle as I wish. In my interactions with people with whom I play a leadership role, I find more and more that to remind them that they are free at any moment to make any choice they wish to make, to act in any way they wish to act, to choose any viewpoint they wish to choose, and to operate from the present moment as a starting point for a future that can be completely different from the past, makes all my other efforts on their behalf more effective.

I have learned to be on guard against the pull to be restimulated during at least most of my waking hours. I now decide not to yield to restimulation while I am asleep.

I can understand the possibility that in the past "the little boy downstairs," the part of my rational intelligence that functions below my awareness, has tried to force some discharge of the old distresses by bringing them up in my sleep. So I used to frequently find myself waking with feelings of discouragement, isolation, or "being overwhelmed."

I've already found a number of ways to begin to counterattack this. One is to keep a copy of **Present Time** or other RC literature by my bed and begin the day by reading some of the inspiring thinking in those pages. Another is to turn on great classical music, recorded or broadcast. Another is to place drafts of thoughtful articles beside my bed each evening to be edited or proofread on waking as a way of starting the morning in an elegant direction.

I now promise, in addition, that I will decide and re-decide and re-decide as many times as necessary that each awakening shall mark the beginning of a brand-new perspective for the future. I shall in the future remind myself at least once a day that "morning has broken, like the first morning," that the start of a day is an excellent symbolic time to start a new career with a new attitude. Regardless of whatever has happened in the past seventy-three years, I am still, every morning, in the marvelously fortunate position of being able to start over afresh.

I serenely recommend to my friends and fellow-explorers of the future that we, each and all, start over every morning.

A PROPOSED NEW FRONTIER COMMITMENT

Since *thinking* is necessarily *fresh thinking*, I hereby decide that I will never again let anything from the past influence the way I act in the present or future

and

I will repeat this decision as many times as necessary to achieve the clear-cut results that I want.

A Report on the Anti-Racism Workshop

I want to talk about the workshop we had in January for anti-racism leaders. This workshop was for whites. We set out to have a panel of five people of color, and two of them couldn't come. Barbara was there, and Tommy Woon, and Emma Ramos-Diaz. They were there just to keep an eye on us, and the workshop was limited to white leaders of anti-racism work.

It has sounded real good, that the RC Community has had a lot of workshops for whites to get rid of their racism. We've had a lot of leaders. We had about fifty leaders there in January from all over the country, many of whom make their livings, or a large part of their livings, by doing anti-racism workshops. The Big City School Board hires them to work with all the teachers to get rid of their racism, or they do work on campuses between black and Jewish students to eliminate that cross-fire. These people have great reputations because they take some RC in there, and they explain oppression, and it's illuminating, and they're very popular, and they're called back. They're very successful, and they're highly honored. But, inside RC, the atmosphere is still racist. Overwhelmingly, RC is white in the countries where it's established, in the United States, in the British Isles, in The Netherlands, Sweden, and so on.

Last year at the Teachers' and Leaders' Workshop here in the Midwest, comparable to the one that was just over yesterday, we were very encouraged. Eileen wrote a letter to **Present Time** afterwards saying how encouraged she was at the great variety of people of color there. Every one of them was worked with in a demonstration, and the atmosphere was one of gain,

From the Black Leaders' Conference, Chicago, Illinois, USA, June 24-26, 1988. Appeared in **Black Re-emergence** No. 5, 1988.

gain, gain. The atmosphere this year had slumped as Charlotte found out. She showed up and she said, "Thank God the people are here from Kenya, but I'm the only U.S. black here at this workshop." The situation had gone backwards. Now part of the reason, a small part, was that blacks were saving their money to come here, or for the workshops that are going to start Sunday night here. But that wasn't enough of a reason, by far. We'd simply slipped back.

Well, some New York City people had been pushing for this anti-racism work. Two or three of them kept raising the issue until I said I would do a workshop, and we met in November. We had fifty white leaders of anti-racism work, celebrated and cheered and well-paid, in many cases, for doing their work. In trying to think about what was wrong in the area, the light broke through, and I was able to take a very firm position as the workshop started.

I think I scared Barbara and Tommy and Emma a little bit. Afterwards I saw them reassuring the whites that they really liked them and appreciated what they'd been doing (laughter) which, of course, didn't hurt any. They needed it at that point.

We looked at the situation. All these people were leaders of anti-racism work among whites. They're doing better than any-body else, there's no question of that, because they're getting across the basic theory of liberation. We took a census. We asked, who among you has intimate friendships with people of color? Who among you has close friendships with people of color? Who among you has at least as large a proportion of friends of people of color as there are people of color in the population? Who among you that are Area Reference Persons have populations in your Area that have as big a proportion of people of color as the community around you does? Who of you that are leading Regions have this? There were about five out of the fifty that could make some kind of a claim that they had some friends of people of color. R— probably has twenty close friends of people of color, but everyone else had less, and often, none.

I challenged them, "How can you possibly claim to know anything about working against racism when you don't know any people of color?" Well, the distress here is universal. As I was saying to you this morning, you have to face the fact that whites in this country are dipped in racism from the moment we're born. There's just enormous pressure on us to succumb to racism. Then later, as we become a little enlightened, we tend to put a kind of varnish over it of "liberal" anti-racism.

I had found that for myself to use the "three-step technique" for whites to discharge our racism, was awkward. I can make it work for somebody else. (It turns out to be a "two-step technique." It's on the second step that you get the discharge.) But it's so slow and cumbersome. In practice when I have had to work fast, I've found that all I have to do is look at the person of color, see them for who they are, fall in love with them, and act like it. You can't possibly love somebody and be racist. I swear to that. You can't do it.

D—, we've got lots of uneasinesses to work out between us, but I think we were pretty close by the time we'd been around each other for two days, weren't we? (She told me she decided to come and sleep in my doorway because it was the only place in the workshop she felt safe, being one of two blacks in a huge workshop.) All I did was take a look at her, see who she was, and love her to pieces. And I still do. You can't really look at D— and not love her. She was scared, but she discharged bountifully. She took a couple of swats at me first, just to prove that she wasn't easy. (laughter)

The whole business of racism has to be stupid. It has to be. In effect it's treating a person as not quite human because you're scared of him or her. Most of the racism you run into, all of it in a sense, is just the terror the whites carry. It's put into us when we're little. We're terrified when it's done to us, and so we're scared to death. The fear takes every form. It takes the form that you blacks are after our jobs. It takes the form that you blacks resent all the mistreatment you've endured and you're going to kill us for it the first chance you get to do it quietly. It takes the form that you can't really like us, that if we try to be friendly you will reject us. Fears, fears, fears.

In RC we've gone on too long being "pleased" with our anti-racism work when the people who were doing it didn't really know a damn thing about it in practice. We agreed on two proposals, two policies, that I want to say here. One, that no-one claims to understand anti-racism work, or do any RC workshops on anti-racism (they can do them outside to earn a living), until they have lots of close and intimate friendships with people of color.

My impression is that forty-five or forty-seven out of the fifty were tremendously uncomfortable the first day. They were so glad that Tommy and Barbara and Emma told them they still liked them. But RCers are good people, even the white ones. Inside our distresses we're completely human. They had sessions, and they shook, and by the end of the workshop they were welcoming the policy. I don't know how much momentum we got going. We'll have to find out. But they were relievedly planning to do just this, and to quit pretending that they knew anything about the anti-racism situation until they had close friendships with people of color. They were relieved at that point. Since then I've been preoccupied with health. It's been a tough period for me, and I haven't checked up on things very much. I don't know what your impression is, but I think we got something started.

We agreed on a second point of policy. This is that every white RCer, not just the leaders, not just the ones that claim to be experts on anti-racism, but every white RCer is enjoined to make close friends of people of color, no matter what effort they have to make. We went over their fears with them, such as that they're going to be coldly rejected. In the article in the current **Present Time** we tried to go into detail on this. There is a common fear that all people of color have resented our racism so much that as soon as we go off guard and act friendly, the people of color are going to slap us across the face with a wet herring and tell us they don't want to be our friend.

I said to them, "If they do, it's understandable. They may tell you to 'Get the hell out of my part of town, get out of my yard, take your fakey whiteness somewhere else.' That's fine. They're communicating with you. (laughter) Hang in there. They're being client in a good way. Listen to it. Let the thing develop."

It's a crucial point that white RCers are not doing this in order to be saintly helpers of people of color with the oppression of racism. No. We're doing it to clean up our own lives, because as long as we're racist, whites are miserable. At a deep level we hate ourselves, and we hate ourselves for hating ourselves. Many don't know what to do to get out of it. Racism, for whites, narrows our lives, makes them bleak and bare and unsatisfactory. Unless we have warm friendships with the majority of the people of the world, our lives are blah. It's for ourselves that we're going to do it.

Will people of color welcome us as real friends? I assured the whites that they would. They might have to tell us to go to hell first, and hit us across the face with a wet herring a few times, but of course, for a person of color to have a white friend who dependably acts human necessarily makes the world seem more tolerable, just to think that a white could be human. Haven't there been many days when you wished you could believe that? (*Audience, "Mm hmm."*) Can a close white friend be a good ally in handling other whites' difficulty? Of course they can. It's just amazing to me, how willing people of color are to forgive and forget and establish a human relationship. I understand it's because they're smart. It's because they understand the issues much better. As the victim of racism, you understand it much better than the perpetrators, who are glassed in with fear and shut down, who don't know what's been going on since they were three years old and it first got pounded into them.

I can say with confidence to other whites that people of color will eventually welcome us and treasure us, if we learn to be human.

What we're proposing to all white RCers is action. Up until now, most of what we've done has increased our sense of guilt, and we get more shut down than you realize. This is a proposal, a policy, that we're to actively seek people of color and establish close, warm, loving relationships with them. I've been out of circulation since the workshop and I don't know what's happened. *(From audience: The places where I have been, New York and a couple of other places, there are a number of people who report that they've taken the policy, and they're working with it, and that it's making an enormous difference for them.)*

Now, this is not a policy or a burden that I'm putting on you. This is a job for whites. But, as I said before, you're probably going to have to play the role of gadfly, and remind us that you want us to get out of our stuckness faster. I don't think you'll mind; I think you'll enjoy it once you get used to prodding us the right way. (laughter)

(Question: They're looking outside of the RC Community, they're not after us, right?) (great laughter) Good point, and that point was made then, and it was made at the other workshops where I've dealt with this policy. We don't go after a "tame" RCer of color. *(Q—: I just wanted to make sure.)* Well, it will happen, of course. No matter how clearly we say it, the shut-down white is going to start looking for an RCer of color where they feel a little safer, and you will have to say, (growls) "Go get a wild one." (shrieks of laughter) That's the sort of thing I think you'll have to do.

That's what I wanted to communicate. We have this better, two-pronged policy for white RCers now. How long until we make it work, I don't know. How much you will have to do to goose it along to make it work, I don't know. But at least our policy is correct. It wasn't correct before. We were tolerating

RCers claiming they were anti-racist and not having any friends of people of color, or claiming they went against their racism by saying, "Oh, how do you do? It's so nice to have one of you here! Heh, heh, heh!" (laughter)

The new **Present Time** has the report. It should have been out before. My apologies. It will get out at every workshop that I lead. The Regional Reference People have had special letters about it.

The patterns are always far more difficult than we imagine, but I think white RCers are going to start modeling this, and perhaps competing. There are going to be conversations like, "Are you going to do anything about it?" "Well, I did." Which is strong motivation. It's a patterned motivation, but what the hell. Ride a pattern into battle.

A Proposed Revision of the
Postulates of Re-evaluation Counseling

The *theory* of RC has grown out of, and followed upon, successful *practice*. In this we have been very fortunate. It is not the usual state of affairs in the so-called "social sciences," although it is, of course, the practice on which the physical and biological sciences are based. When the same kind of phenomenon occurs repeatedly in our Co-Counseling or some element seems to be common to all or most of our counseling experiences, we have generalized from the many different examples to the commonality which seems to be true and made it an item of our theory. In this, we've followed the *inductive logic* process which is followed in all the physical sciences; we observe or extract as large a number of examples as possible of the phenomenon that we are seeking to understand (and handle predictably) and then generalize from these many examples to one conclusion, one "principle." This guides us in attempting other experiences, handling other situations, conducting other experiments to see if the generalized principle that we extracted from our previous experiences will also fit (be confirmed by) those. To the extent that this principle seems to guide us accurately and lead to predictable occurrences, it becomes a dependable part of the *theory*. Our theory has grown this way. The fact that it is buttressed by more and more experiences in more and more cultures is reassuring and satisfying.

We've also assumed that the universe is *consistent*, that no fact in one part of the universe contradicts a fact in another part of the universe. Whenever we have made these inductive generalizations into a principle, we have been careful to see

Appeared in **Present Time** No. 74, January 1989.

that each such principle is consistent with our other inductive generalizations. This notion of consistency is a necessary and powerful guide in expressing and summarizing these principles into theory.

In an effort to reinforce the consistency of our theoretical structure, I attempted in the early 1960's to create a parallel structure of deductive logic. In this we would first state a number of *assumptions*. (These would be based, of course, to begin with, on our observations of what seemed to be going on in reality but in this new structure would be simply taken as assumptions: not proven, not verified, but only assumed.) From these assumptions we would deduce other conclusions. Such a deductively logical structure is the kind most in use in mathematics. A mathematical structure is assumed to be completely abstract (even though the basis for creating it does lie in observations of the reality around us). A certain number of consistent assumptions are made and then other conclusions (theorems) are deduced very carefully from the assumptions. One can then be quite sure that if the assumptions that one started with are true, then the conclusions deduced from them are also true. This is a useful check on consistency.

In 1964 I wrote and published the Postulates of Re-evaluation Counseling which are reprinted below. They have played an encouraging role in the development of theory and they have been a useful check on consistency. Not all of this checking has been done overtly or awarely. (The logicians and philosophers who have come into Re-evaluation Counseling have, in the main, been preoccupied with their own re-emergences rather than the application of their discipline to the theory.) Yet the statements of the Postulates have been widely "internalized" and have had significant influence.

THE 1964 POSTULATES

Re-evaluation Counseling is a theory of human behavior and set of procedures for solving human problems. It is a complex theory, still growing, containing a large amount of information in its details and techniques. Its main assumptions can be summarized at present (1964) in the following twenty-four points:

1. Rational human behavior is qualitatively different from the behavior of other forms of life. (It is not *just* more complicated.)

2. The essence of rational human behavior consists of responding to each instant of living with a *new* response, created afresh at that moment to precisely fit and handle the situation of that moment as that situation is defined by the information received through the senses of the person. (All other living creatures respond with pre-set, inherited response patterns—"instincts.")

3. This ability to create new, exact responses may be defined as *human* intelligence. It operates by comparing *and contrasting* new information with that already on file from past experiences and constructing a response based on similarities to past situations but modified to allow for the differences.

4. Each human with a physically undamaged brain has a large inherent capacity for this rational kind of behavior, very large as compared to the best functioning of presently observable adult humans.

5. The natural emotional tone of a human being is zestful enjoyment of life. The natural relationship between any two human beings is loving affection, communication, and cooperation.

6. The special human capacity for rational response is interrupted or suspended by an experience of physical or emotional distress. Information input through the senses then stores as an unevaluated and rigid accumulation, exhibiting the characteristics of a very complete, literal recording of all aspects of the incident.

7. Immediately after the distress experience is concluded or at the first opportunity thereafter, the distressed human spontaneously seeks to claim the aware attention of another human. If the human is successful in claiming and keeping this aware attention of the other person, a process of what has been called *discharge* ensues.

8. *Discharge* is signalized externally by one or more of a precise set of

physical processes. These are: crying or sobbing (with tears), trembling with cold perspiration, laughter, angry shouting and vigorous movement with warm perspiration (tantrum), live, interested talking; and in a slightly different way, yawning, often with scratching and stretching. Discharge requires considerable time for completion.

9. During discharge, the residue of the distress experience or experiences are being recalled and reviewed. (Not necessarily with awareness.)

10. Rational evaluation and understanding of the information received during the distress experience occurs automatically following discharge and *only* following discharge. It occurs only to the degree that discharge is completed. On completion, the negative and anti-rational effects of the experience are completely eliminated.

11. As a result of long-term conditioning of the entire population, the spontaneous attempt to claim the aware attention of another person and proceed to discharge and evaluation is almost always rebuffed. (Don't cry. Be a big boy. Get a grip on yourself. Don't be afraid. Watch your temper.) Applied to small children, these rebuffs begin and perpetuate the conditioning of the population which prevents discharge.

12. Undischarged and unevaluated recordings of distress experiences become compulsive patterns of behavior, feeling, and verbalizing when restimulated by later experiences which resemble them strongly enough. Under such conditions of restimulation the rational faculty of the human is again suspended and the new information of the current experience is added to the rigid distress pattern making it more far-reaching in its effect and more easily restimulated in the future.

13. This effect of an undischarged distress experience recording in "playing" the bearer through a compulsive, repetitive re-enactment of distress experiences is an adequate explanation for all observable irrational behavior in human beings, of whatever kind or degree.

14. Any human being, and human beings in general, can become free of the restrictions, inhibitions, and aberrations of the accumulated distress experience recordings by reinstating a relationship with some other person's or persons' aware attention and allowing the discharge and re-evaluation processes to proceed to completion.

15. Any infant can be allowed to remain free of aberration by protection from distress experiences and by allowing full discharge and re-evaluation on the ones that do occur.

16. Though a greater degree of awareness, rationality, understanding, and skill on the part of the person whose aware attention is used ("the second person," "the counselor") provides for more rapid and more complete discharge and re-evaluation, the process is workable if even a small degree of awareness is available and if even a roughly correct attitude is maintained by the second person.

17. By "taking turns," i.e., by exchanging the two roles periodically ("Co-Counseling"), two people can become increasingly effective with each other and can help free each other from accumulated distress patterns to a profound degree.

18. Distress patterns which have become too reinforced by repeated restimulation can become chronic, i.e., surround and envelop all behavior and activity. To discharge these requires initiative, skill, and resource on the part of the second person and considerable time for handling, but they are not different in origin or effect from lighter distresses, and can also be completely discharged and evaluated.

19. Distress experiences result from any unfavorable aspect of the environment. In our present state of civilization, the bulk of early distress experiences of any child result exactly from the dramatized distress recordings of adults which the adults received from earlier generations when they were children. We have a sort of transmission of aberration by contagion here—well-meaning adults unawarely but systematically infecting each new, healthy-to-begin-with child with their burdened distress patterns.

20. The irrationalities of society (enforcements, punishments, exploitations, prejudices, group conflicts, wars) are reflections of the individual human distress patterns which have become fossilized in the society and often enforced by the rigidities of the society itself.

21. No individual human has an actual rational conflict of interest with another human. Given rationality, the actual desires of each can best be served by mutual cooperation.

22. Nothing prevents communication, agreement, and cooperation between any humans except distress patterns. Given knowledge of their nature, these distress patterns can be coped with, handled, and removed.

23. Any individual or group can act rationally first without waiting for rational action on the part of someone else, and can take control of the situation by so doing.

24. It is always safe to be rational. Knowledge of the above information can be applied to all aspects of living and to all relationships with real profit and success.

Re-evaluation Counseling is a meaningful and useful description of the nature of human beings and the source of their difficulties. It is a rediscovery of the workable means for undoing human distress. It is a system of procedures for expediting this discharge and re-evaluation process. It is a promising and successful alternative to individual and social irrationality and distress.

Re-evaluation Counseling theory has advanced a long way in the last twenty-four years. We are currently assuming (with good reason) a number of important principles that were not obvious to us at the time the Postulates were first drawn up. I have been presenting these at workshops and conferences with some sort of covering statement such as ''There are many indications (or ''I am confident'') that this is true.'' For some such ''confident hunches'' (such as the possibility of re-attaining complete power) we have no examples as yet. I have in fact been relying a great deal on deductive logic and on ''consistency'' in making these statements.

I am now proposing an extension or expansion of the Postulates. These additions and changes will be printed in bold type in the version at the end of this article. I would like responses to these from as many readers as possible. I would like your opinions on:

—The consistency of these revisions with the original set of postulates;

—How important you think they are;

—Whether you think the taking of them as assumptions is justified by our experiences to date;

—Any other assumptions that you think we would be justified in making in the foundation of the deductively logical structure of Re-evaluation Counseling theory.

Please let me hear from you.

PROPOSED REVISED VERSION OF THE POSTULATES (1988)

Re-evaluation Counseling is a theory of human behavior and set of procedures for solving human problems. It is a complex theory, still growing, containing a large amount of information in its details and techniques. Its main assumptions can be summarized at present (1988) in the following twenty-eight points:

1. Rational human behavior is qualitatively different from the behavior of other forms of life. (It is not *just* more complicated.)

2. The essence of rational human behavior consists of responding to each instant of living with a *new* response, created afresh at that moment to precisely fit and handle the situation of that moment as that situation is defined by the information received through the senses of the person (other living creatures respond with pre-set, inherited response patterns—"instincts" **or with conditioned, equally-rigid modifications or replacements of the inherited response patterns, acquired through experiences of stress**).

3. This ability to create new, exact responses may be defined as *human* intelligence. It operates by comparing *and contrasting* new information with that already on file from past experiences and constructing a response based on similarities to past situations but modified to allow for the differences.

4. Each human with a physically undamaged brain has a large inherent capacity for this rational kind of behavior, very large as compared to the best functioning of presently observable adult humans.

5. **The complexity of our central nervous systems (now esti-**

mated to contain at least one-thousand billion individual neurons and a number of possible states of relationship between these neurons larger than the number of atoms in the known universe) has brought us not only human intelligence of a very, very high level but also has conferred on us the capacity to be aware; to notice what is going on while it is going on, to think about the rational processes while they are taking place. This ability or function of awareness is very hard to define or describe, but humans are completely aware when it is present in another person or not, and enjoy it fully in themselves when it is operating.

6. This complexity of our central nervous systems has also conferred upon us complete freedom of decision. Even though this freedom is denied unendingly and emphatically by the societies in which we live, it still persists and is completely available to us. This complete freedom of decision is not just freedom to make a good decision, to make a rational decision, to make a correct decision. It is an unfettered freedom. We are completely free to make wrong decisions, destructive decisions, irrational decisions as well. Our freedom of choice is unfettered, unlimited.

7. This complexity has also conferred *complete power* on each individual, if we define *power* as the ability to have the universe respond to us in the way we wish it to (not in the usual oppressive society's definition of power as "ability to enforce our will upon other intelligences, other humans").

8. The natural emotional tone of a human being is zestful enjoyment of life. The natural relationship between any two human beings is loving affection, communication, and cooperation.

9. The special human capacity for rational response is inter-

rupted or suspended by an experience of physical or emotional distress. Information input through the senses then stores as an unevaluated and rigid accumulation, exhibiting the characteristics of a very complete, literal recording of all aspects of the incident.

10. Immediately after the distress experience is concluded or at the first opportunity thereafter, the distressed human spontaneously seeks to claim the aware attention of another human. If he or she is successful in claiming and keeping this aware attention of the other person, a process of what has been called *discharge* ensues.

11. *Discharge* is signalized externally by one or more of a precise set of physical processes. These are: crying or sobbing (with tears), trembling with cold perspiration, laughter, angry shouting and vigorous movement with warm perspiration (tantrum), live, interested talking; and in a slightly different way, yawning, often with scratching and stretching. Discharge requires considerable time for completion.

12. During discharge, the residue of the distress experience or experiences are being recalled and reviewed. (Not necessarily with awareness.)

13. Rational evaluation and understanding of the information received during the distress experience occurs automatically following discharge and *only* following discharge. It occurs only to the degree that discharge is completed. On completion, the negative and anti-rational effects of the experience are completely eliminated.

14. As a result of long-term conditioning of the entire population, the spontaneous attempt to claim the aware attention of another person and proceed to discharge and evaluation is almost always rebuffed. (Don't cry. Be a big boy. Get a grip on yourself. Don't be afraid. Watch

your temper.) Applied to small children, these rebuffs begin and perpetuate the conditioning of the population which prevents discharge.

15. Undischarged and unevaluated recordings of distress experiences become compulsive patterns of behavior, feeling, and verbalizing when restimulated by later experiences which resemble them strongly enough. Under such conditions of restimulation the rational faculty of the human is again suspended and the new information of the current experience is added to the rigid distress pattern making it more far-reaching in its effect and more easily restimulated in the future.

16. **We have called the association of past distress feelings with the current scene and the resulting rigid, "inappropriate" behavior *"restimulation."* Although we originally assumed that restimulation was involuntary, we now assume that it was originally a decision, a decision apparently motivated by the hope that bringing up and "restimulating" the distress recordings would create a possibility of discharging them (if the attention of another person could be found or some other contradiction to the recordings could be achieved).**

Since, in general, this hope was not realized, the restimulation (which was a decision to begin with) became an addition to the distress recording. With many such experiences the restimulation seemed increasingly to be automatic, seemed to be involuntary, seemed beyond choice. It was a decision to begin with, however, and we have come to understand that it was a decision, and to realize that restimulation still is always a choice. This means that a decision to contradict this recorded decision can always be made and reviewed prior to the restimulating circumstances. The process of restimulation can not only be resisted but can be prevented, can be decided against. This can even be done in some situations after restimulation

has occurred. It is a dependably workable process to decide repeatedly "not to be restimulated," prior to the formerly restimulating events, and under non-restimulative circumstances. By repetition the compulsive, automatic, patterned functioning of the restimulation decision can be undone, with great profit to the person who undoes it.

17. This effect of an undischarged distress experience recording in "playing" the bearer through a compulsive, repetitive re-enactment of distress experiences is an adequate explanation for all observable irrational behavior in human beings, of whatever kind or degree.

18. Any human being, and human beings in general, can become free of the restrictions, inhibitions, and aberrations of the accumulated distress experience recordings by reinstating a relationship with some other person's or persons' aware attention and allowing the discharge and re-evaluation processes to proceed to completion.

19. Any infant can be allowed to remain free of aberration by protection from distress experiences and by allowing full discharge and re-evaluation on the ones that do occur.

20. Though a greater degree of awareness, rationality, understanding, and skill on the part of the person whose aware attention is used ("The second person," "the counselor") provides for more rapid and more complete discharge and re-evaluation, the process is workable if even a small degree of awareness is available and if even a roughly correct attitude is maintained by the second person.

21. By "taking turns," i.e., by exchanging the two roles periodically ("Co-Counseling"), two people can become increasingly effective with each other and can help free each other from accumulated distress patterns to a profound degree.

22. Distress patterns which have become too reinforced by repeated restimulation can become chronic, i.e., surround and envelop all behavior and activity. To discharge these requires initiative, skill, and resource on the part of the second person and considerable time for handling, but they are not different in origin or effect from lighter distresses, and can also be completely discharged and evaluated.

23. Distress experiences result from any unfavorable aspect of the environment. In our present state of civilization, the bulk of early distress experiences of any child result exactly from the dramatized distress recordings of adults which the adults received from earlier generations when they were children. We have a sort of transmission of aberration by contagion here—well-meaning adults unawarely but systematically infecting each new, healthy-to-begin-with child with their burdening distress patterns.

24. The irrationalities of society (enforcements, punishments, exploitations, prejudices, group conflicts, wars) are reflections of the individual human distress patterns which have become fossilized in the society and often enforced by the rigidities of the society itself.

25. No individual human has an actual rational conflict of interest with another human. Given rationality, the actual desires of each can best be served by mutual cooperation.

26. Nothing prevents communication, agreement, and cooperation between any humans except distress patterns. Given knowledge of their nature, these distress patterns can be coped with, handled, and removed.

27. Any individual or group can act rationally first without waiting for rational action on the part of someone else, and can take control of the situation by so doing.

28. It is always safe to be rational. Knowledge of the above information can be applied to all aspects of living and to all relationships with real profit and success.

Re-evaluation Counseling is a meaningful and useful description of the nature of human beings and the source of their difficulties. It is a rediscovery of the workable means for undoing human distress. It is a system of procedures for expediting this discharge and re-evaluation process. It is a promising and successful alternative to individual and social irrationality and distress.

"Re-evaluation Counseling" as a title, correctly denotes the collection of insights into the actual nature of reality which we have assembled as the result of our practice and thinking, in the areas of human thought and activities where this actual reality has been occluded or undiscovered as a result of lack of information, misinformation, distress patterns, and the operations of the oppressive societies. The people who practice Re-evaluation Counseling (often known as Co-Counseling) are collectively known as the Re-evaluation Counseling Community. This Community and the individuals in it, because of the power of these insights, are often mistakenly expected to be "problem-solvers for others," substitutes for parents and lovers, or an organization that will "provide justice for the oppressed," that will fill the recorded, frustrated needs of people who were neglected in some way in the past. These expectations are completely unreasonable and can lead only to unreasonable disappointment.

Actually, Re-evaluation Counseling consists almost entirely of this series of insights, accurate glimpses of reality in the many areas in which reality has been obscured for humans until now. Some of these insights are of how people can work well together, but it is up to the individual, the first-person-singular, to make them work in each case, whether individually or cooperatively. These insights into the actual nature of reality are by now numerous, profound, and very important. Their successful use depends on the individual.

Socializing: Tempting
But Unworkable

Dear Harvey,

*May I say firstly how much I appreciate having been intro-
duced to RC. In my personal life, introduction to being counselled and learning (painfully, at times) to discharge has had
an immeasurable impact. Professionally, as a social worker
and therapist, RC thinking has illuminated whole areas in
which my training was incomplete and inadequate. Naturalis-
ing RC in my work has had tremendous effect. Within the
Derby Community, I have learned to take a new kind of leadership (although the old distress creeps up on me occasionally, I now deal with it very much more effectively these days!)
and to teach "from the inside" rather than "academically."*

*I would like your clarification and any further thinking
upon one aspect of the "no socializing" principle. I know
this to be of concern to a number of other people as well, so
you may care to publish this correspondence, in whole or in
part, in* **Present Time***. My situation is that, after many years
employment by public and charitable bodies, I am attempting
to establish a private practice as a counsellor and trainer,
principally because of the greater professional freedom this
gives to me, but also because I wish to make RC information
available where I think it will be most effective, amongst
wide-world leaders and amongst those to whom other people
turn for help. Doing this was, and remains, a decisive step
forward in my re-emergence; it is important that I do it and
do it well. Although I have a small operation at present, I
could find myself, quite quickly, with more work than I could
cope with personally.*

Appeared in **Present Time** No. 74, January 1989.

I know of other people in RC who are in similar situations and of yet more who are contemplating such ventures. Amongst those with whom I have some direct contact, we all appreciate the wisdom of the no-socializing principle (blue pages) and the reasoning behind them; we all value our Co-Counselling relationships and do not want to risk damage to them; and we all value the support we derive from our association with RC, and neither wish to prejudice this, nor to cause dissension, nor to provide inappropriate models for new Community members. I would value very much your thoughts upon what levels or degrees of cooperation, between Co-Counsellors in similar professional situations, is possible. The kind of association that is at the forefront of my own mind is that of assisting, upon an ad hoc basis, with a particular class, workshop, or industrial project for a fee agreed between us. The arrangement about fees apart, this could be seen as analogous to asking another member of the Community to assist in teaching a fundamentals or ongoing class. Other forms of cooperation might be referring clients to each other when our own ability to do the work is restricted, or, possibly, sharing the use of office/consulting rooms and perhaps reception and clerical services whilst still maintaining separate practices. These are my thoughts only and it might be useful to examine the questions posed by full partnerships, etc., in the same context. What comes to mind is how these things are managed at Personal Counselors and how relationships were/are viewed at the Palo Alto Pre-School.

In my situation, it is a counsel of perfection to suggest that, as with the more obvious social relationships, one should seek to recruit from outside and to teach such recruits and/or to introduce them into RC. There is a certain minimum level of business that has to be achieved upon a consistent basis before that kind of step can be contemplated and, in the meantime, one can still find oneself with occasions when particular pieces of work are beyond one's own resources.

David Gardiner
Alvaston, Derby, England

Dear David,

Thank you for your letter. I'm glad to hear of your progress, and glad that you are trying to think firmly about tempting situations.

I would suggest that the cooperation you need from other people doing a similar kind of work is a support group for people in similar work, which of course is common and thoroughly encouraged, and that most of what you would hope for from association with other RC therapists would take place in the support group situation. As far as making referrals of clients to each other, I don't see any problem in that unless you expect some kind of a response beyond the satisfaction of having someone do the work that you couldn't do. As far as undertaking joint projects together, I would think in general that getting people to help you first and then recruiting them into RC would work much better. Otherwise, I think you will put unreasonable expectations on each other. The idea that there are advantages to having an RCer in a relationship as opposed to somebody else is illusory. There are just as competent people outside RC, certainly, as there are in.

There has been a major problem at such enterprises as the Palo Alto School and Personal Counselors, Inc., to keep each relationship distinctively separate. There is heavy pressure to turn client in these situations, and it is disastrous whenever it happens, so that it takes much, much more care to keep things rolling in these enterprises than it does in the ordinary relationship. This will turn out to be a burden, if you were to do it in the sort of thing you envisage, rather than an advantage. So that I would suspect that you need to find your own help, and then perhaps bring them into RC, once the relationship you want is firmly established first.

Harvey

Open Question Evening
in Copenhagen

Harvey: I bring you greetings from Co-Counselors in many parts of the world. Co-Counseling has been spreading quite rapidly into new places since I was last in Denmark. In particular, in November we've held workshops in four Latin American countries where Communities are starting. In January there was the first workshop in Hungary. In England, also in January, an owning-class workshop of sixty-eight owning-class people came together, terrified at first to be with a working-class leader of a workshop, but eventually becoming comfortable and enthusiastic, even indicating at the end of the workshop that they could see their way clear to supporting a working-class revolution.

Question: The three of us work at a psychiatric hospital and we would like your opinion on what is psychiatric illness? What is a psychosis?

Harvey: These are confusing terms that have been imbedded in the culture to disguise the oppressive role of the "mental health" system. The workers in the "mental health" systems are good people, trying to do what they can to help the people who are suffering from distress. But the systems themselves are oppressive, and are almost never helpful to any significant degree. The theories which the psychiatrists are trained in and the psychologists are taught are far away from the reality of what's actually happening with people. So, although the so-called "mental health" workers often manage to be helpful to the people they try to help, just by being human and in spite of their roles, the rules, the practices, and the theories are not helpful at

From February 1988. Appeared in **Present Time** No. 73, October 1988 and **Present Time** No. 74, January 1989.

all. The so-called "mental health" system is basically a weapon for oppression of the people. The person who is acting and sounding irrational is asking for help. If people were available who understood this and paid loving attention to the person and encouraged him or her, that person would soon begin to cry, shake, laugh, and yawn, would discharge their tension, would re-evaluate the distress which has had them enclosed, and fairly quickly begin to function very well.

When they are instead told that something is wrong with them, it is enormously invalidating and frightening to the person. It drives them deeper into the distress. When they are given drugs, it keeps their mind from functioning and makes everything worse. If they are given electric shock or insulin shock, it destroys part of their mind temporarily. If they are given so-called psychic surgery, lobotomies or leukotomies, it destroys their minds permanently.

The threat of being labeled insane is used by the society to require conformity from people who are rebelling against the irrationality of the society. The threat of being labeled insane is used to support the other oppressions, of sexism and racism, for example. The United States has made great propaganda against the Soviet Union, for their committing political dissidents to "mental health" hospitals as a weapon against them, and the point is well taken. But the United States also does this wholesale.

If a woman from a well-to-do family, for example, becomes involved in a fierce fight with her husband in a divorce action, male lawyers and male psychiatrists and judges will often co-operate with the husband to see that the woman is declared irrational and therefore gets very little in the settlement of the divorce action. In the United States not only the mental hospitals but the prisons are filled with blacks, Native Americans, and other people of color. If these people rebel fiercely against the racist society in the United States, they are declared insane and committed. And although the United States has a tradition of civil rights and legal rights for people accused of crime (which are sometimes observed), when the charge is mental illness all these rights are put by and people are imprisoned without a trial or any adequate safeguards at all.

"Mental health" is not a question of health at all, and the so-called medical model doesn't fit the actual situation. Large numbers of so-called "mental health workers," psychiatrists, psychologists, and therapists of various kinds are smart enough and human enough that they feel intensely that they are in an impossible situation. Quite a few of them have come into Re-evaluation Counseling for their own benefit. I'm asked to speak to societies of psychiatrists every so often, who complain to me bitterly how difficult their lives are, and are eager to learn how they can be listened to and get some relief themselves. Many of these workers have learned to Co-Counsel and have learned to organize support groups with the other members of the staffs at the hospitals and clinics they work in. Slowly a movement is growing underground in the "mental health" system to correct the worst abuses. In December, I led the second workshop for "mental health workers" near San Francisco, and the numbers and the clarity of the people were much greater than at the first one which was about five years ago.

Supporting this movement of RC "mental health workers" is a very large and powerful movement of survivors of the "mental health" system. They have their own magazine now, **Recovery and Re-emergence**, which S— can get you copies of. Not only within RC, but in contact with others outside RC, a powerful movement of protest against this abuse of people is building up. Some outstanding psychiatrists have joined this movement, and have written books exposing the abuses of people and the nonsense that goes on in the name of "professional help."

Question: I have a question about the raising of children. We talk a lot about, not education, but the upbringing of children. My son is five years of age. He is in a Rudolph Steiner kindergarten and that's the best place I have found for him so far.

(Harvey: It's better than many.) *I still have some scepticism about the very directed way the school is run. What do you think about this?*

Harvey: Well, the Steiner schools and the Montessori schools and many others were inspired efforts to improve the very bad education that was going on. They were improvements on what went on around them. They were attempts to think freshly about children. But Steiner in particular, and Montessori to a great degree also, became rigid in their innovations. The essence of being a good parent or teacher is complete respect for the child's intelligence. If the child's intelligence is respected, they will stay very smart indeed, and they will learn very fast if they are allowed to learn what they want to. If a child is allowed to choose what they want to learn and encouraged to do so, if information and equipment are made available to the child and if relaxed high expectations on how much the child can do are available to him, the child's intelligence just blooms. Over and over, three-year-olds who are just allowed to sit on a lap and look at a book while the stories are read to them, learn to read without any effort at all. This extends to all forms of knowledge. Children's minds are so much more effective than the society recognizes that even the best teachers and parents innocently invalidate their child repeatedly. This is not to put blame on the parents (or on the teachers) because the parents in this society are in an impossible situation.

The most important job in the whole society is producing new people. In a human sense this means producing new humans. Even from the society's point of view it's most important to produce new workers that can be exploited and profited from. That most important, most demanding, most exhausting job is decreed to be absolutely unpaid. Parents are supposed to work eighteen hours for the glory of it. If you complain as a parent you're told that you are privileged to be with your young people.

Well, it is a rare privilege, but that doesn't lessen the oppression at all. Parents are overworked so desperately, are so tired, that it's a wonder they do as well as they do. Whenever anyone says to me, "Don't you want to come to a family workshop and be with the young ones?" my fatigue pattern from my parenting days immediately becomes restimulated and I feel so tired I can hardly sit on my chair. The society loads parents up with guilt and fatigue. We have a commitment for parents in RC. If I'm working with a new parent I will ask them to repeat it after me. I ask them to say, "I promise always to remember that I am a good parent." *(Questioner: Ahha ahahah, I'm a terrible parent.)* They cry and if I keep insisting they are good parents they keep crying. Because, of course, they are good parents. They've always done the best they could in impossible circumstances. The whole commitment goes, "I promise always to remember that I am a good parent, that I've always done the very best I could do (this is true of everybody so it has to be true of parents), that I have passed on as few of the hurts that I endured as a child as I could possibly manage, and, someday, I'll get a little rest." This last lets them laugh a little.

Parents are coming from an impossible situation. There are no rational-enough schools ready for us. Schools to date have been devoted, not to educating children, but to training them to do what the society wants them to do. Working-class children are told that they are stupid, that they will be lucky to have a dull job. Owning-class children are tortured in special schools and taught to abuse each other terribly so that they will play the role of owning-class adults who are lofty and abusive and exploitative of the majority of the population while feeling terrified inside. There are no good-enough schools ready for us. There is no good-enough child care. The best child-care workers we can find were treated terribly when they were children and will be pulled by these old distresses to not treat children very well. There seems to be no money or leisure available to change things.

We have a parents' movement in RC. RC parents have their own magazine called **The Caring Parent**. I've been editing a new issue of it the last few days when I couldn't sleep for jet lag. Tim and Patty Wipfler and now twenty or thirty more people have become excellent leaders in this work. Patty Wipfler has taken the job of being International Reference Person for parents. There is a very excited parents' movement in RC in thirty or so countries, but we are just starting with a big job.

Question: I would like to know what I can do to help parents, as a non-parent.

Harvey: Take some time with their children. Give them some time to be listened to. Remind them that they're good parents. Counsel them by using the parents' commitment. Be positive and encouraging. Do not agree with their putting themselves down all the time. Help them organize parents' support groups where they can get together every couple of weeks and have a turn being listened to. Help organize child care so they can get to meetings occasionally. In general the attitude of non-parents in the society is, "You did it! You had the children! It's your business! I don't want to get involved!"

When I was young there used to be aunts and uncles and hired girls who could help parents a little bit, on the farms at least. But that was a long time ago. Now not many people live on farms, or work like that any more. So you have to deliberately and carefully organize support.

Sometimes the parents will say, "Oh, good! Here they are! Take them!" They will dump the children on you and you will feel abused. Don't accept abuse. Say, "I can do this much, but I can't take the job over from you."

Question: What will we be like when we have re-emerged from distress?

Harvey: I'm glad you asked that. We'll all be different. People speculate sometimes, well, if I were completely rational, and everybody else was completely rational, we'd all be just alike. No. Everybody is completely different from everybody else, not only in their distresses, but also in their interests, and in the way they develop. But I can give you a general picture, I think, because this is the direction people move as they discharge.

You will wake up in the mornings like you did when you were a child on the first day of summer. "Hah! The world is out there, waiting for me! I can't wait to get the grass between my bare toes." You will have lots of things waiting for you to do, that you want to do. And it will be fun to decide which you're going to do first. Because you know you have all the time in the world, there's no feeling of being rushed or hurried. You will look forward to being with people you love and who you know love you. You will enjoy finishing some work that is in progress, or taking a further step with it. And you will be continually learning something new. If you already play the piano well, you'll start the zither. You'll go to the library every once in a while and look for all the books that you never thought of reading, and start something completely new. You will not only be thinking of how to keep your dishes washed and your lawn mowed just right, but, without fear or worry, you'll be planning how to eliminate all nuclear arms from the world. You'll plan how to organize support groups and classes and various other structures around you, so that you can lead other people in the same direction. You will plan on what kind of a letter of introduction to write to the prime minister before you go talk to him personally. You'll be figuring out how to get all the political parties to agree on one thing, which is no more armaments. You will walk down the street with an expression on your face such that everybody who passes wishes they knew you. I don't know how far it will go, but there are a lot of RCers already functioning pretty much like this.

From about 1982 to 1985 the theory was clear enough for people to achieve the goals they had set when they came into RC, but they hesitated. They were improving a little bit here and a little bit there, but not moving decisively. In 1985 at the

Montreal World Conference, we challenged experienced RCers to immediately begin to build world-class communities around them as individuals. Most of them switched their hesitating to that. (A few dozen actually have done it.) But it had the surprising effect for thousands of RCers, that they went ahead and attained goals that they'd been hesitating on before. In the years since '85, I would guess at least 20,000 RCers have simply achieved all the goals that they had set when they first started RC. I get lots and lots of letters saying, "I've finally got my life just the way I want it. I'm making all the money I want. My job is completely satisfactory. My family is getting along lovingly and well. I almost always have good sessions when I Co-Counsel. My life is wonderful." (Of course I write back and say, "When are you going to eliminate nuclear weapons!?") People simply achieved the goals that they'd been hesitating on, once they were challenged to a more advanced one.

I haven't any real idea of what it will be like to be completely rational, because I'm not completely rational yet, and I don't know anyone who is. In a number of ways, I'm the most rational person I know. I've worked at it harder and longer than anyone else. But I'm not as good with children as Tim is, I'm not quite as devoted to the liberation of women as Diane Balser is, I'm not quite as effective with parents as Gwen Brown and Patty Wipfler are. I don't inspire men the same way that Charlie Kreiner does, although I model courage well. I don't have any clear notion of what it will be like to be completely clear of distress.

The young people who have had the best support in RC function differently than I do. They're very relaxed, they do well in school, but generally people don't notice them. Gill Turner, who is finishing her training as a physician this year, and has been our young people's leader since she was sixteen, just has a wonderful time, all the time. She'll finish a hard night of putting together four or five victims of a terrible automobile accident, in which maybe she couldn't save one or two of them, and just is cheerful and full of satisfaction, quite relaxed in knowing she did what could be done. If she gets a couple of hours' sleep she's ready to tackle some frontier counseling if I happen to be around.

So, I don't have a clear view, but we'll all be different. I think I can say that we won't be able to be intimidated. Nothing will intimidate us. That's already true of the little ones who went through the Palo Alto school. Tim says that once a child had had two years in that school, no-one could intimidate that child. Well, I'm not there yet. When somebody points a gun at me, I still get a little shaky. I think that in the future we won't be able to be intimidated. We'll know that we have complete power. We'll never forget that we have complete freedom of decision. We'll never blame ourselves or anyone else. We'll see the worst situation as simply a situation where something needs to be fixed, not something we have to get upset about. Does that make sense?

RC is different than meditation and diet and yoga exercises. Some RCers still don't understand this. RC is a deliberate, systematic attempt to find and use reality in the areas where society and patterns have covered up reality. RC next month is going to be different than RC today. This has been a real problem in RC, to have people face that. New teachers are always trying to teach RC the way their teacher taught them, but their teacher taught them some RC and a lot of their patterns. If they teach their teacher's patterns and some of their own, pretty quickly RC gets very diluted and patterned and confused. So we're continually trying to get a better picture of reality. The theory is growing and changing and improving all the time. We have the greatest research establishment the world has ever seen. People in fifty-six countries are experimenting in their lives, with each other, all the time. As soon as they learn something useful, they write in and we publish it in one of the twenty-nine magazines that we publish. So people are continually discovering reality better and exchanging the information with each other.

The decisive, breakthrough foundation of RC is simply that what the society says you must not do, which is to cry, shake, "rant," yawn, laugh, and talk and talk and talk and be listened to, this whole process which society suppresses, is exactly what people need to do! It's hard at first to help each other because we've been trained not to, but if you do help each other, marvelous things happen. That was how everything started.

Society tells you, "Don't cry. Don't be a scaredy cat. Don't laugh with your mouth full. Go to sleep if you're yawning, you must be tired." But the more we understand how crucial these things are, the more we realize that people are doing it all the time, anyway. What we're trying to do is to get it done efficiently, continually, and thoroughly. People talk to each other all the time, trying to be clients. They don't listen very well. But sometimes the person talking pretends the other person's listening, and it helps anyway.

We got some glimpses of how important this continual talking is, when we had professional clients come to Seattle, who had been isolated in the interior of Alaska for eight months during the winter. We were just learning to counsel and we wanted them to cry, because that was what most people had not been allowed to do, and it would always work. Well, we discovered that with these people, we had better just sit back and listen. They could not do anything but talk, talk, talk, talk, talk, talk, talk. For about two and a half days they would talk steadily, and then take a deep breath and be an ordinary client. Until they'd caught up on their talking, that was what they had to do. We got a glimpse of how important this continuing talking that we try to force on each other in ordinary living actually is, to keep us from collapsing.

Once you catch up, once you've discharged a lot, most things that you used to need a session about don't bother you any more. Most things that happen to me nowadays, I'm relaxed about. There are a few things that still get me, that remind me of the very terrible attitudes that my mother had towards me when I was born and the rest of her life. I haven't got the core of that out yet. I'm still working on it. But there are a thousand things that bother other people terribly that don't bother me at all. People at workshops will say, "What do you do if someone criticizes you?" and if I can get them to get up and criticize me, I can show them. I say, "Thank you. I needed that information," and the person says, "Hunh" and criticizes me some more and I say, "That's very thoughtful of you. Thank you very much!" They start to laugh. Step by step you become freer and freer. Nobody's made it all the way yet, but, boy, I'm so eager for it I can taste it.

Question: I have a child with an African man and I always try to push him back because I was suspicious of the way he wanted to hold me and grab me. Our mutual son loves him and me very much and he never has experienced us together. We are about to leave for Africa together. I know I want to go there because I want to be together with him with my son, but I don't want to have a relationship with the father because I can't handle it yet, and my child is needing us together very much. I was very happy yesterday. I was able to say, "Yes, I can lay in bed with him." But I'm worried. I'm going to another country.

Harvey: Well, you may not want a relationship with him as a lover, but you have to work out a relationship with him as a co-parent. It's a different relationship. Keep them separate. If he loves the child, appeal to his love for the child, and you can probably make it work. Help him find another lover, and you can counsel her. (Laughter)

Question: What is the difference between RC and, say, gestalt psychology? They also use kinds of sessions and....

Harvey: Well, I'm not an expert on gestalt or any of the other psychologies, and I will agree with anyone that the best of the humanistic psychologists were good men. Harvey Maslow, or Fritz Perls who started gestalt, or Carl Rogers who started several schools of psychology, were very human people, and their attitude toward humans was quite enlightened. They had many good things to say. They were not in general terribly helpful to people, but they wrote good books and they said good things. Their followers have not, in general, been very effective therapists, but they've also not been harmful in the way that many of the followers of the older theories have been. Some of the lower leaders in these humanistic psychologies have come into RC. The man who translated Carl Rogers' books into French is the leader of the French-speaking Community in Europe. Some of Perls' gestalt leaders are active in the California Communities of RC.

Gestalt people are taught to do one thing that I do not want Re-evaluation Counselors to do, I'll make that distinction. They propose certain set exercises, and then they have everyone do the same thing. This does not fit reality, because each client is at a different place, and needs to be dealt with specifically and uniquely. Former gestalt people would come into RC and ask everyone in their support group to take turns saying "Sex!" and feel that they were very successful because almost everyone has enough embarrassment on that topic that they could all laugh loudly together. It didn't do much harm. Everybody has distress about sex who grows up in this society, but each one has a unique distress that needs to be dealt with uniquely. This rigid doing the same exercises for everybody leads to some very stupid results. With gestalt leaders, the group often gets the impression that license and no-holds-barred is the only rational attitude to have about sex. Because it's different than the no-no attitude that they got when they were growing up, they feel it's liberating. But different is not necessarily rational. You can just get into another kind of a pattern. This would be a key point of difference between Perls' approach, or the gestalt approach, and RC.

Question: I might be the only one here who doesn't know, but I'd still like to know exactly what is Co-Counseling. What is the theory? What is it all about?

Harvey: Well, I have written several long books trying to tell people what RC is. So it will be a little hard to tell it all in three minutes. It is a continually changing and growing theory. It is a better and better approximation of the real nature of human beings and how they can really be helpful to each other. It is a set of assumptions about human beings. One is that almost every human being is enormously intelligent, even though he or she may not be acting like it. Another is that every human being is good, basically very good. When humans do evil things it's only because the scars of old hurts are forcing them to do that. Every human being has complete freedom of decision, even though most of them no longer believe it because they've been told so many millions of times that they don't. Every human being has complete power, if by power we mean the ability to have the Universe respond to you in the way you want it to. Hardly any humans believe that any more, because they've been told so many millions of times by the society that they have no power, that they must do as they're told. The flexible intelligence, the genius-sized intelligence, which humans start out with can be temporarily frozen into rigid, unintelligent behavior by the accumulation of hurt experiences. If a human being has been hurt in an area where she was formerly very wise and skillful and flexible, and not allowed to get rid of the hurt, she will, from then on, be compulsive, unintelligent, and often destructive.

If a human being has been hurt this way, and can find another human being who will listen to her, support her, and help her contradict the hurt, she will spontaneously do one or more of a series of processes that we call discharge, which are outwardly indicated by tears, trembling, laughter, angry storming, yawns, and talk. If she and her listener can follow this through sufficiently, the rigid hurt pattern will disappear. She will again be intelligent, powerful, flexible, successful, and happy, where she had been unhappy, rigid, and unsuccessful.

In the long-ago past, these hurt patterns were imposed on people by accident and by contagion. If I crawled over to the edge of the porch and fell off accidently, that could leave a hurt on me. They were imposed by contagion. The child who is beaten by his father, and grows up, will tend to beat his own child when his child's presence restimulates the old hurt. So hurts were and still are acquired by accident and by this kind of contagion.

At some time in the past (partly because of the hurts, and because of greed which undoubtedly arose out of hurts) human beings allowed themselves to be organized into oppressive societies. In the first place, it was always slave-owner and slave societies. Later these gave way to noble-serf societies, or feudal societies, and later these gave way to owning-class-working-class societies, usually called capitalist societies. These oppressive societies impose hurts deliberately and wholesale, in order to condition people to fulfill the rigid roles that the society assigns them. The slave-owner-slave societies and the noble-serf societies have collapsed in the past from their own internal contradictions, killing off large numbers of their members in the process. The present societies are in the last stages of their collapse (from their internal contradictions) and are in danger of killing off all the members of the present societies through their possession of atomic weapons.

The principal reason why people are not taking charge of this situation and eliminating the patterns and the oppression and the danger of nuclear holocaust, is the existence of large numbers of patterns on everyone. There is also a tremendous amount of misinformation, which is perpetuated by the oppressive society, and a lack of communication between people and a lack of leadership for them.

If people can just begin taking turns to listen to each other, the recovery process can begin, and if persisted in will accelerate, and all people of the world in all their different groups can come to a common agreement, can eliminate the oppression and the danger of war, and have a world that modern technology would allow us to convert and restore to a Garden of Eden very quickly.

We have a very real choice between a future Garden of Eden for our children on the one hand, and on the other the complete destruction of all complex life. The use of taking turns listening to each other, and the rest of what we call Re-evaluation Counseling, is the most hopeful way we've found so far for helping to make that choice in a good direction.

These are some of the assumptions that are part of Re-evaluation Counseling.

Re-evaluation Counseling is also an international movement. It began in Seattle thirty-seven years ago, acquired knowledge slowly but persistently for about twenty years, began to spread outside Seattle seventeen years ago, and in the time since has spread to most of the cities of the United States and Canada, and to fifty-six other countries.

Question: What is the difference between a child clienting with you, and a child coming to you and wanting to be with you?

Harvey: Well, if a person has distress, this is a very high priority in his or her needs, to be listened to so discharge can take place. So children naturally, if they find somebody who's interested, will put that at the top of their agenda. A child hurt at nine o'clock in the morning will judge that none of the people around during the day are good listeners, and won't say anything about the hurt, but as soon as someone comes home who they think will listen, they begin to discharge as if the hurt had happened just a moment before. He or she is just using good judgment.

As far as we can tell, all human beings hate and resent having hurts still inside them, and although control patterns get installed of top of this and hide it, all of us inside have been planning, all our lives, to find some way to get those hurts out. We've apparently become very controlled and very discouraged, but we still try to find some way to get the recovery process started.

Because I am often tired these days, and try to look after my rest, I wear an indifferent-looking mask in airports and on airplanes much of the time. I go around looking like this. (laughter) But when counseling was new, and I was very excited and not so tired, I would go around on ferry boats and trains and airplanes looking open, like this, and over and over again, complete strangers would come up to me and start crying within a few seconds.

I was riding a ferryboat from Bremerton to Seattle one day. It's a very beautiful ride, and it was a beautiful day. The mountains were clearly visible in all directions. It was lovely. As the ferry left Bremerton, I stood by the rail looking at the scenery, and a woman standing about six feet from me was looking at it too. I said to her, "Isn't it a lovely world?" She looked at me and said, "Yes, and a very sad one," walked over, put her arms around me, and started to cry very hard. I held her, and she cried, and cried, and cried, and cried. When the ferry boat blew its horn for landing, she drew back, wiped her eyes and blew her nose, and said, "Thank you very much. I'm (her name). I'm superintendent of nurses over at the Naval Hospital in Bremerton. I've just gotten word that my brother has died, and I'm on my way to take care of the family. I think I will handle it all right, but I don't think I could have handled it without that. Thank you very much." Six weeks later she wrote me a letter and told me that she had handled the family situation well, but would not have been able to do it without the chance to cry that day.

Another time, I was on a train in Minnesota. There were twenty empty seats on the car. A young woman got on and walked up and down looking over the whole car, finally sat down beside me, said "Can I talk to you?" and cried the next four hours to her station. I will always remember that there was a mother and daughter sitting about three seats in front of us. The daughter tried to keep the mother quiet, but the mother had obviously decided that I was a "white slaver" taking a victim away to a life of sin. She walked up and down the car, and every time she passed would shout "Humph!" at me, (which didn't stop the young woman from crying steadily all the way to her stop).

Every one of us is looking for a chance to do this. We're all wonderful clients. To learn to be as good counselors as we are clients, however, takes some work.

Question: You said that you can decide not to be a client unless someone agrees to and is able to listen to you.

Harvey: Yes. Always pay attention to them instead. That seems hard because you want so badly to be a client. But if you're both trying to be client, it doesn't work. It's just frustrating. If you decide to listen to them, and be a good counselor, there's great satisfaction in doing a good job. It's true that you want and need to be a client, but you have to train somebody well to be your counselor, in order to expect that. This has been a problem in the RC community, that everybody wants to be client and they forget that they have to learn to be good counselors part of the time.

In building your own world community this is the first step, to give up your old habit of trying to get everybody else to listen to you all the time. Never expect anyone to pay attention to you unless they know how to counsel and have agreed to be your counselor at that time. All the rest of the time, you pay attention to them, not expect them to pay attention to you. If someone obviously wants a long session, and you have to go to work, you say, "I love you a lot, but I have to go to work. I like that blouse you're wearing. Goodbye."

If someone is looking for you to listen to them all day, have a hundred ready excuses. "I can't take time right now! I'm sorry, I've got to go!" If none of the first ten excuses works, there's one that always works. Everyone has been "toilet trained." So if you say, "Sorry, I have to go to the toilet," they will respectfully say, "Go!" If you open the door a crack and they're waiting outside, close it and lock it and climb out the back window.

Question: Do I have a choice about what feelings I have?

Harvey: This has been one of the most difficult and confusing questions that Co-Counselors have faced. All of us started out being caught in feelings, apparently without much choice on our part. People around us would reproach us for feeling the way we felt. "Why are you so upset?" In beginning RC we theorized what we called "restimulation." We defined it as the *involuntary* coming up of past distress because of some similarity in the present. At first we found this very helpful, very comforting. When people said to us, "Why are you so upset?" we could say, "I was restimulated. I was just standing there with my hands in my pockets and restimulation came up." So it was a comfort; but it turned out to be a mistake. As people learned to Co-Counsel, they began to spontaneously correct the mistake. In the classes, students would begin to say that they "resisted restimulation." Later, some of them even said, "I decided not to be restimulated." The other students in the class intuitively applauded. They sensed that it was a good idea without noticing that it didn't fit the definition that "restimulation" was involuntary.

I remember a woman coming to a Co-Counseling class and saying, "Every time my mother-in-law came for a visit, I always had a terrible headache all week, because she found fault with everything I did. She would run her white gloves under the bed to see if there was dust there. She told me I wasn't feeding her wonderful son good enough food. I would have a headache all of the week while she was here."

"This week, when I knew she was coming, I decided not to be restimulated. Every time she started criticizing, I told her what a wonderful mother-in-law she was. I told her what a wonderful son she had raised. I thanked her for every criticism, and told her it was very helpful. She cried all week, and I didn't get a headache. (laughter) I decided not to be restimulated." Everybody in the class applauded and said, "Great!"

How can you decide something if it's involuntary? See? So after many years, we re-defined "restimulation." We now say, "Restimulation is the usually unaware, but nevertheless intentional, bringing up of past distress with the excuse of some similarity in the present, in the hope that someone will listen to us and we'll be able to discharge the distress."

That's how it turns out. Essentially we're saying that restimulation is a decision instead of an accident. It's true that often the decision was made a long time ago, and got covered with distress, so that we often don't realize that it's a decision that's being made again. It's been very helpful to realize that it is a decision, however, because *if you can decide to be restimulated, you can also decide NOT to be restimulated*. Even though it's very ha-a-a-rd once the restimulation has gripped you, to decide not to be restimulated at that point, it works very well to decide not to be restimulated ahead of time. You can decide over and over again in your session, not to be restimulated, and you will find that you will yawn and shake and cry in your session as you do this. Gradually, the thing that used to upset you automatically, becomes something you handle easily. It's complex, and it's been confusing, but our theory is clearer now than it used to be on that. You can decide ahead of time.

Question: If everybody is very intelligent, does this mean that there aren't any people whose physical conditions limit their intelligence?

Harvey: If you remember, I said "almost everybody." I once lived two houses away from a family with a little girl who had no forebrain at all. She was a very beautiful little girl. She was like a very young kitten. If you treated her like a partly helpless kitten, she was wonderful to be around. Something had happened during her prenatal existence, and the forebrain had never developed at all. The circuitry through which intelligence operates wasn't there. There undoubtedly are people who are physically limited in their intelligence; but we have enough experience by now to be suspicious of many such diagnoses, because children can become terribly frightened long before birth. An attempted abortion, for example, where your only supporter tries to murder you and does not succeed, leaves you very, very terrified when you are born. We suspect that many of the diagnoses of physical lack of mental capacity are made of people who really are mentally inoperative because they are just frozen with terror. We have had some success with counseling people who have been thoroughly labeled as "retarded," who, given enough safety and enough chance to shake and cry, turned out to be fully intelligent. In a decent society there would be enough resources that we could examine these people well. This society puts the priority on disposing of them in some way. I don't want to throw a lot of blame on the people who do this, because the society gives them very little choice. A psychiatrist in charge of a mental hospital, for example, is in an impossible situation. It's like being a police officer in a modern city as the society collapses. There is no possible way you can do a human job submitting to the system. Not at all. Theoretically we hold the reservation that we're quite sure that many of the cases labeled physically retarded are just simply very, very hurt and could recover.

When counseling was just getting started in Seattle, a variety of people heard about it and came to be counseled. I took the most promising of my early students and asked them to help me counsel some of these eager people. I also hired a psychologist who was a qualified psychometrist to measure the intelligence and personalities of these people before and after counseling.

In those days, psychologists were agreed that the IQ, the intelligence quotient, never changed. That was silly. Nowadays most psychologists wouldn't claim that; but in those days, that was accepted. A lumber worker came in to see us. He didn't have much money but he wanted counseling. One of my students, who was a Seattle policeman, agreed to work with him.

First the psychologist gave him the individual Wexler-Bellevue intelligence test, and he tested 99, just slightly below average.

The policeman was not a very smart counselor. He tried a number of things, but the lumber worker was too scared to discharge. Finally the policeman, who was a very big man, in desperation, leaned over the lumber worker and loudly shouted "Ho! Ho! Ho!" The lumber worker went "haha, haha, ha" and laughed wildly. For two weeks, the policemen went "Ho! Ho! Ho!" at the lumber worker, and the lumber worker laughed for four hours every day. Then the psychologist gave him another test, a variable form of the Wexler-Bellevue test. He tested 126, which is not a genius, but very, very bright. The psychologist was very excited. He had never heard of the IQ changing. So he went and told his fellow psychologists about it, and they told him he had become incompetent and his psychometry could no longer be depended upon.

Information is still so limited that there's much we can't decide on, but we have a healthy skepticism about many diagnoses that a physical limitation is limiting the mental ability of a person.

Certainly the urge to try to heal themselves is always there.

I had a student once who ran a home for retarded adults, and if I would go to see him, I would have to wait for a while in a room where these adults were. Immediately I entered the room ten or twelve of them would come and stand in a close circle and all talk to me at once, as loudly as they could. They were just wildly eager to be listened to. It's similar if you go to a park where children are playing. If you sit down near the children, with a pleasant look on your face, in fifteen minutes they'll surround you, all trying to talk to you at once.

Question: One of the things that interests me most at the moment is how to be a counselor for my child. I often experience that he comes to me for attention, and also he often starts in by crying. Sometimes I feel irritated about it and I tell him, "Go to your room until you are finished and then you can come back."

Harvey: You're never going to do that again!

W—: I know it's wrong.

HJ: They told you that, that's why you tell it to him. You never invent a bad thing with your children, you just repeat what was done to you.

W—: But I get confused because I ask him, "What's wrong? Tell me." And he says, "You're stupid!"

HJ: Well, you're stupid! (laughter) Come on, you be your little boy and I'll be you.

You sit down.

W—: No!

HJ: All right. (He sits on the floor.) Always be below your client if possible. Never stand over a child.

W—: You're stupid!

HJ: Thank you! (laughter) I have often been stupid. I want to apologize to you for that.

W—: What are we going to eat for dinner?

HJ: What would you like? (laughter)

W—: No vegetable!

HJ: What would you like?

W—: Cheese and bread.

HJ: Cheese and bread is good, isn't it?

W—: Ice cream.

HJ: Ice cream, too? I like ice cream, too.

W—: I don't want to eat any good thing.

HJ: What's good food?

W—: What you are doing, you are making vegetables.

HJ: Oh, vegetables, they're terrible! Blech!

W—: I don't want to eat.

HJ: Very good.

W—: I want to go and watch television.

HJ: Fine.

W—: I don't want to go to sleep.

HJ: I don't blame you. I hate to sleep, too. (laughter)

W—: I want to go over to my father-in-law's.

HJ: I wish you could, but you can't. He's not there.

W—: I don't like you.

HJ: I don't blame you. I don't like me either, sometimes. Why don't you like me? I like you. I like you a lot.

W—: You're stupid.

HJ: Yes. But I like you.

W—: But you are not playing....

HJ: I'm liking you.

W—: I don't like your hair.

HJ: It's terrible, I agree. (laughter) It's too short.

W—: I don't want to go in the bed now, I want to go outside and play.

HJ: Think any of your friends are out?

W—: No. (laughter)

HJ: I'll go out and play with you.

W: Now?

HJ: Ja. (Client talks to translator in Danish.) The only reason you do dumb things is because they did dumb things to you. You're just repeating the way they talked to you. You know that was terrible. You would never do that again. He just needs to be liked and listened to. (long silence) Okay, cry.

W—: (howls) I want you to stay, for you to stay with me all the time. You mustn't go home, you have to stay with me here tonight.

HJ: All right.

W—: I miss you. You have to stay here with me.

HJ: Okay.

W—: You have to sleep here with my father!

HJ: Well, your father doesn't like that, and I'm not too fond of it either. You can come home with me and sleep, though, next time. I love you. I love you.

W—: So when I say, "I will sleep with you," will he say, "Mother, you are the sweetest in all the world"? (laughter)

HJ: Sometimes. (laughter) You can sleep on the floor and just hold his hand. It worked, didn't it?

W—: He was happy! He was telling stories until half past twelve!

HJ: He's trying to teach you something, isn't he?

W—: Yes.

HJ: You're a good mother. I'm so glad I'm your son. (laughter)

Do I have your agreement that I shall take your greetings to Gothenburg and Stockholm?

All: Yes!

HJ: I will tell them that Denmark will not always stay behind, right? (laughter) Shall I tell the Norwegians that Denmark is getting going, and it's time Norway did? I'm tired of my native land hanging back!

Question: How can you be half Norwegian and half Indian and half U.S.?

Harvey: Don't forget my name is French. Jacquin. It came from Montbeliard in 1752.

Question: And the Indian blood?

HJ: It's a small part. I'm not even sure of the tribe. I think it's Penobscot. It's from Maine, anyway. Then there's lots of Irish and English and Scottish in there, too. The name was anglicized to Jackins. My mother's name is Moland from Tönsberg. She left there, I think, a hundred and five years ago, when all the starving Norwegians moved to Minnesota. Yes. Any more questions?

Question: I would like to have some "good and outs" for artists.

Harvey: Have you read the essay, "The Good and the Great in Art"? There's quite an artists' movement inside RC, too. The artists have their own journal called **Creativity**, and we've had many small artists' workshops and I've led one big artists' workshop. What I say in this pamphlet, and not all the artists agree with me, is that the artist is the prototype of the human being. What's human about a human being is their intelligence, and what intelligence does is come up with a new answer for every new situation. So the artist, in a sense, is doing the essence of what a human being does, which is being creative. Essentially, every human being is an artist. Certainly every good artist that I've ever known has said that all human beings are artists, if they just weren't discouraged from being.

The artist is also the prototype of a working-class person. The role of a working-class person in this society is to produce a great deal of value, and have most of that value taken away from him or away from her by the employer, by the banker, by the landlord, by the government, who all feed on what he produces, but leave him just a small amount as wages. The creative artist produces enormous value, which lots of other people profit by, but the artist gets very little. It's an extreme form of working-class oppression.

I once heard a lecture by a curator of one of the great art museums in the eastern United States. He was a very serious, knowledgeable person. (This is thirty years ago that I heard him lecture.) He described the situation in the art world for painters. Afterwards an artist stood up in the audience and asked, "How many painters in the United States are making a living from their painting, do you think? I don't mean from teaching art, I mean from their painting." The curator said, "I would say about twelve at this time." He said, "There are many, many more significant artists than that. I would say there are at least two thousand painters in the United States whose work will be honored in the future; but I would say only twelve are living off of their painting."

"Now," he said, "you should understand that lots of people are making a good living from these people's art. I draw a good salary as the curator of this art museum. There are dozens of art publications that support big staffs. There are thousands of gallery owners that are staying in business well. There are collectors who are making investments in today's art, that will pay off with enormous dividends in the future. So, there are thousands and thousands of people making very good livings out of the painting that's being done nowadays, but I would say that not more than a dozen painters are making a living from their painting alone. The rest are teaching art, giving lessons, or washing dishes in restaurants so that they can paint in their spare time."

So the artist is an extreme form of the worker.

In that essay I used Piet Mondrian, the Dutch artist, as an example. His rectangular array paintings were the basis for, oh, eighty percent of the architecture that's been done in the last seventy years. Billions of dollars of buildings have been built, based on Mondrian's artistic inventions, but only in the last few years of his life did Mondrian have even a little security.

The other main point I make in this pamphlet, and I think you'll enjoy it, is that it's possible for everybody to have some kind of a standard of what is good art and what is great art. (As I say, some artists disagree with this part. I think it's out of their fears, but they don't want anybody to make any judgment at all about art.) I suggest that there is "non-art," where an artist, just to make a living, copies something that's already been done. Much commercial art is like this. They don't want anything creative, they want something just like what worked last year. So that although it's called art, it's really non-art, it's not creative.

Then there is "poor art," where the artist is expressing distress in his or her art, and is presenting the distress as if it were reality. I call this poor art because it discourages people, it lowers their self-esteem and their expectations. Many artists fall into this in an effort to be successful commercially. They try to substitute novelty for creativity. I remember the Henry Gallery in Seattle had an exhibit of a group of San Francisco artists who had all glued muddy toilet paper over their canvases in clumps. Gallery owners were trying to promote it and sell it as art. But I would call the artists' work that presents distress as if it were reality, poor art.

Artists will often express painful emotion in their work, partly in an attempt to be client, to get the distress out there where they can see it as different from themselves. If they present it in such a way that one sees it as not human, sees that humanness is distinct from the distress, so that it ennobles and encourages people, I would call that "good art."

When artists create something that has no distress in it, that's brand-new and uplifting, I would call that "great art." Not everyone would agree with me, but I think almost everything Mozart wrote, for example, does this. It's easier to do that with music, of course, than it is with paint. That's a little bit of what I say in the pamphlet. I think you'll enjoy it.

Let me ask a question, all around, and then it's about time to go home. What did you like best about the evening?

(Everyone answers what they liked.)

Let me just say a word about RC in Denmark. It began quite a while ago, but we had some unfortunate, accidental circumstances here. Some people who were very eager to take leadership and aggressively did so, also had some patterns that were very destructive, and made life difficult for the people around them. We've depended on Sweden for the overall leadership of Scandinavia, and our leadership there is excellent in many respects, but does not take aggressive action to clean up problems when they show up. So some of the problems that became prominent with the early leaders in Denmark, almost destroyed the Community several times. A few brave people hung on. Susanne has been the bravest of the brave. After a while Leif joined her, and has contributed greatly. Birgit down at Haslev has persisted against many difficulties for a long time. Now, more recently, others have joined, and it's now a supportive group in Denmark. People have been re-emerging well. I think the workshop of the last two days may light a fire in a couple of new rockets, and RC will go a little faster. I am not anxious. RC has started and collapsed in many places, but it never stays collapsed, and when conditions finally get just right, it grows very fast.

England, Ireland, The Netherlands, the United States, even Germany, have a large number of Co-Counselors now. I think Sweden is about ready to accelerate growth; there at least I'm going to try to help them accelerate in the next few days.

RC has persisted well in Poland, under great difficulty, for many years now. RCers are playing key roles in Poland, in Hungary, even in Yugoslavia, and in troubled spots like Israel and in Northern Ireland.

The way to get involved is to give Susanne your name and address and telephone number. She has many other things to do, so does Leif and all the rest of the RCers, but I think they would be glad of classes that were a little larger than have been happening lately.

Don't join the class if you want to be taken care of. RC is not a place where you get taken care of. Many people come to RC with that attitude, and it makes things very difficult. RC is a place where you learn to take care of each other. You need to be prepared to give as good as you get. It doesn't work any other way. You are expected to become a great and powerful counselor, as well as a successful client. I'd like to issue a personal invitation to you, Benedikté, at this point, to become a leader of the RC community. I think I know some of the things that have held you back. I know you already have a very full and exhausting life, but I'd like to invite you to become a leader. You already have most of the qualities that make a strong leader. The rest of you, use your judgment, but encourage and assist Susanne and Leif, don't lean on them. That will work.

You don't need to be an RC teacher, you don't need to have a certificate, in order to teach another person how to Co-Counsel. Start teaching someone else right away. Even if you think you only know a little bit, teach them that little bit. When you think you would like to teach a class, even though you don't feel ready, tell Susanne you want to teach, and she will tell me to send you a credential. It will be a credential to teach one class series. If you make an absolute disaster of that class, we won't give you another credential right away. But you will have learned something. There are now about two thousand good RC teachers in the world. All of them learned to teach by teaching. It's the only way you ever learn to teach. You can discuss it forever and you won't learn until you start doing it.

Start a support group around you. You don't have to be a teacher to do that. Get two or three friends together every week or every two weeks. The simple rule is that each person has their share of the time to be listened to with no-one interrupting. It's a very simple thing, but it will make an enormous difference in your life to actually be listened to by several people. It is an amazing experience. You are all authorized to do that. You don't need to call it RC, just do it. If you try and try and it doesn't work, and Susanne just frustrates you, and Leif is no help, then write me a letter, and I will read your complaints. Maybe that's all I'll do (laughter) but it will help to complain.

I will tell the people from Gothenburg and from Bergen and Siljan and from Stockholm and Malmö that you are alive and well and they better hurry up or Denmark will be taking the leadership of Scandinavia away from them.

Thanks for having me in to talk to you.

The Frontiers of Theory
June, 1988

There are some key points of theory that have been evolving in this last year. As with all good theory, it's anti-pattern, so it's easily forgotten, and we need to refresh it and review it. I'll try to cover some of these key points, and then spend a good deal of this weekend concentrating on effective ways to discharge internalized oppression. That's the key to *using* a lot of our knowledge.

At the faculty leaders' workshop a couple of weeks ago, I realized that certain attitudes exist everywhere in the Community. It's a general problem. One of the articles in the new **Present Time** tries to deal with it. It's a little tricky.

One of the things we have to keep continually in mind and continually reminding ourselves of is, that in spite of all our patterns and in spite of all the oppression, we are still, we are presently, enormously intelligent. Our intelligence has been occluded but has not been destroyed or replaced. It's waiting to be uncovered. We are enormously intelligent. Each one of us has the intelligence of an Einstein and a Michelangelo and a Madame Curie and a Martin Luther King, all functioning together. We have far more intelligence available to us, with a little uncovering, than the best functioning great person of the past has ever been able to use at any particular time, even though some of them did pretty well. We have not lost it. We have not had it destroyed. It's just waiting to be uncovered.

From the Black Leaders' Conference in Chicago, Illinois, USA. Appeared in **Black Re-emergence** No. 5, 1988.

GOOD, AND AWARE

Each one of us is enormously *good*. The person who's doing the most evil act is having his arms and mouth jerked by a pattern. The person himself is completely good, completely innocent. Each of us, first-person-singular and second-person-singular when we're Co-Counseling, is that wonderful, good entity, completely good. Completely upward-trend.

Each of us has the ability to be aware, to notice what's going on. We treasure every evidence of this. In part it's been occluded, but it's not been destroyed. We can reach out to awareness. We can reclaim the habit of thinking about what's going on while it's going on, instead of tunneling our way through life as the hurts and the oppression have convinced many of us we have to do. We can actually operate awarely. This possibility is there.

DECISIVE

We have other great abilities that we have only recently become confident about. One is the complete freedom of decision. Each one of us is able to decide anything she wants to, any way she wants to, any time she wants to. This has been explored to some extent by a relatively small number of CoCounselors, and they've made outstanding progress when they started relying on this.

I generally mention three people: D— who's publicized well anyway, who basically relies on decision. She made a decision "Anything in the way of women's complete flowering is going to be eliminated." She functions like that, all the time. D— is easily the most influential women's leader who has ever lived. You look at all the famous women leaders in the past, and look at how many women actually followed them, and it's a tiny number compared to the number of women just in RC who support D, and she has a big following outside of RC.

A— says she relies on decision. She made a key decision to

go out and cover Micronesia. She shook day after day after day, and when she came home, everybody in Hawaii began pleading with her to come and be a consultant to them. She's just reached for it in every direction. She says she simply decided, acted on the decision, and then the discharge rolled off.

G—, a working-class intellectual woman down in Delaware, got fed up with what was on television for children. She went to her university and one of the public television stations and made a series of short "tips for parents." Other series have been made since. Several million people watch her "tips." After a few months they're spreading across the country, out of the Delaware Valley, as other public television stations and small chains borrow them. Her station gives them to other stations free. There's something in the last **Present Time** telling how to get them on your TV if you want them. Basically she just made a decision.

There are a few dozen more who've done that and are beginning to be widely influential. C— is hired by many non-RC men's organizations to come and inspire them, and does a good job inspiring.

POWERFUL

The latest big insight that we have has not, in general, been used yet. We're going to do a little bit of work on it here. It is the realization that we have complete power. Not the power to push other people around, which is the usual meaning of the word in the oppressive society, but power to have the universe respond to us in the way we want it to. That power is intact, it's just covered over with the millions of fierce, hurtful announcements in the past that we haven't any power at all, the orders to shut up and do what we're told. These have fallen on us by the million since we were born.

But the power is there intact. We need to keep this picture before us all the time, against the pressure of the patterns, against the rationalizations like, "Oh, we're doing pretty good, maybe someday something will be better," and all these other compromises with the distress.

It is clear that, right now, we have this enormous intelligence, this great good will and goodness, this awareness, this complete freedom of decision and complete power to have things go the way we want them to.

And yet (and this is the breakthrough clarification that we made at the faculty conference), we have distorted our interpretation of this clarity in a way that has held back the development of RC. (It has certainly held back the development of black RC as well.) We hear these insights. We get very excited by them. We read the Guidelines. (Some people find the Guidelines and cry about them for many sessions because they never dreamed there could be such rational suggestions for people's relating to each other. Most RCers have never read the Guidelines. You might try it.) We get this picture, these insights as to how we could relate, and these other great insights that make up RC. Then many of us make the assumption that other RCers *are already like this*, and that the RC Community that has such great ideas, is perfect; and we project that ridiculous expectation on RC and on RCers and on the RC Community. We then become "disappointed." Our patterns have found this roundabout way and excuse of getting back into negative non-functioning, instead of our taking the insights and using them.

UNREASONABLE EXPECTATIONS

I tried to talk to the academic people like this: that RC is not a group of wonderful, perfect people who always do the right thing. RC is not the mother that you never had because she had to go off to work. RC is not the perfect lover who will love you under all conditions. RC is not that great giant milk-cow in the sky, whose udder will spray you with warm, healing streams of milk that will wash all your patterns and sins away and leave you perfect if you will just bunt her udder hard enough. RC isn't any of those. And yet I see over and over again this kind of expectation, and then disappointment, "I'm dropping out of RC, it hasn't solved my problems." I think this has slowed us down enormously.

RC is none of those things. RC is a bunch of insights, a bunch of recovered glimpses of reality, in an area where reality has been obscured by all the patterns and the lack of information and the misinformation and the oppression. This great mass of mud, the misinformation, the patterns and the lack of information and the oppression, covers the whole human race. All human beings are struggling in this great mud-pile, trying to keep their nose above the mud enough to breathe a little bit and live somewhat rationally. All human beings are engaged in this continual struggle and are wrestling with distress all the time. This includes all the human beings who are "in" RC. Your fellow RCers, the people in the Community that you expect to act perfectly and get terribly disappointed because they don't, they're struggling with just about as much mud as you are. Maybe a particular person has done some right things, or made a more consistent effort and her head's a little bit more out of the mud, and so you can see some inspiration. I use Barbara as inspiration. When the going gets tough, the tough get going, as far as Barbara's concerned. When she comes up against a difficulty, she sails into it with a couple of war-cries and a big smile.

When I start sinking into "I don't know why Barbara doesn't counsel me better, because she's got so much pizzazz, why doesn't she use it to help me?" I've lost the whole point, I've lost the whole picture. I can use her as inspiration for what I can do, but if I start expecting her to stop and scrape my mud off, and forget that she's got darn near all she can do to keep her own chin above the mud, I have distorted the whole role of RC.

ALL HUMANS ARE STRUGGLING
All human beings are struggling in this great mud-pile, and

this includes the RCers. What we have is some precious pieces of knowledge, some precious insights, that enable us to get out of the mud a little faster if we use them. But the notions that these insights make RC a great nurse to take care of us, or make an RCer the perfect lover, or someone who's delighted to counsel us all the time no matter how we act, stuff like that, that is just nonsense. We're deep in a very difficult struggle. Most of humanity is about up to here in mud. Give them a little information and a little boost and tell them it's up to them. Try to keep your eyes clear so *you* can see where *you're* going because the pressure is to give up and go under, drugs or alcohol, and die fast. There's enormous pressure this way on humans in this collapsing stage of society.

Some wide-world people have grasped these insights. Some people did it just by sheer decision. We run into such people occasionally, who are leading good lives by sheer decision, and we can admire them. They never heard of RC, but they're parallel with it.

Some RCers have been able to get up to where they're out of the mud this far most of the time. If we project these unreasonable expectations on them, we'll leap on them, shove them under the mud, and then wonder why they've failed us. I think everyone here is an inspiration to some people. But you're to be used as an inspiration, not as something to clutch at and be disappointed in. If we realize that RC just consists of these glimpses we've got of reality, including the glimpses of how we can relate to each other effectively, how we can cooperatively re-emerge, we'll make it work. We'll make it work all the time like we have made it work occasionally up to now. If we go back into putting out these unrealistic expectations and being disappointed in each other, or in RC, then the whole thing slows down again.

We've crept a long ways. It's only been thirty-eight years since the first accidental breakthrough. It's only been eighteen years since RC left Seattle. Fifty-six countries in eighteen years "ain't bad." It was all word-of-mouth and person-to-person. But it's been slow, compared to what it can be. We can really move ahead. I think that the two clarifications, that we stop treating each other like disappointing saviors, and start treating each other like fellow strugglers out of the mud that we can learn from and give a hand to, will help a lot. Does that make sense?

THE WHITES ARE STRUGGLING

Now, in particular, and I hope Barbara will speak at length on this because she's spent a lot of time thinking about it: for black RCers being disappointed in the white RCers and the white RC Community is a favorite occupation. (laughter) Can we justify it? Sure. My god, RC is against racism, but every white RCer you meet is a racist. But what the hell did you expect them to be? They've been dipped in racism fifty times a day since they first drew breath. This is in this country. Not all of you are from this country, but the racism in England is getting to resemble the U.S. racism very closely. In this country, every white has been systematically coached and beaten into a racist attitude all through childhood for the last four hundred years or so. Heavy, heavy, heavy, heavy. Are white RCers going to be free of racism because they've said, "Ha! Racism is an oppression. I am opposed to it"? Does that get rid of all the distress? No. Of course the RC Community is racist. It consists mostly of whites. The majority of them live in the United States, in England, in The Netherlands, in nations that are thoroughly racist. The United States is an intensely racist society. Intensely racist. It is so intensely racist that whites in general don't remember any of the conditioning. Once they have thought, "Oh. Racism is wrong, I am against it," they assume that's done it, because they are still unaware of the great mounds of racism that cling to them, the great streams of mud that cascade from the society upon them.

And of course, blacks living in the United States internalize the racism to where most of the time they can't imagine the amount of racism that they accept and internalize, in the same way. It seems that you have to numb up to it. If you realize that you've been hurting all the time, you never get your dishes washed.

So, in particular, I would like to remind you that the RC Community, which is still overwhelmingly white, because it started in a largely white country and spread more quickly to largely white countries, is of course racist. Not intentionally so, it has goals of not being, it has made commitments. White RCers are racist, of course. They have been conditioned in the cruelest way. Once you get a white working on racism, really, you get back to a child who is just broken-hearted. They have to cry for hour after hour after hour at the loss they suffered when they gave in to the pressure of their loved adults and adopted a racist attitude. Once they get to it, they're just heart-broken. They're just as human as anybody else. That's difficult for a black to believe, of course, if you forget the conditioning.

In particular, the RC Community is a bunch of insights, and people who have tried to climb out of the mud. Grab the insights on how to climb out of the mud cooperatively, and use them, and never forget that every white has got a stream of racism cascading down his back or her back all the time until they get enough help to get up out of it. (Maybe you as a black can furnish motivation. It's not your primary job but it's a thing you can do, if you decide to.)

Never forget that the Community is not a perfect society of the future. The Community just consists of some insights on how to work cooperatively instead of alone on this stuff. Use those insights. But don't project the unrealistic thing so you can justify your disappointment. Take it for what it is. You knew damn well that every white was racist before you got into RC. How can you adopt the illusion that because somebody's an RCer they're no longer racist? It takes an enormous amount of work to get that mud off.

We've got some good projects going. I'll talk about them later. I think the Whites' Campaign Against Racism has finally got a clear policy and a couple of tools that will work. The news will be in the July **Present Time**. The policy was only worked out in January.

YOUR RE-EMERGENCE

Let's talk about your re-emergence, your counseling and clienting. I want to review some important insights that we've known for some years but have never been able to state clearly enough: Distress turns to discharge when it's "contradicted." What we mean by "contradiction" is anything that lets the victim of the distress, the client, see the distress as not present-time reality. Anything.

What makes the best session is a situation in which the client has organized himself or herself, or has been helped to organize, so that the client is contradicting the distress thoroughly and dependably in the session (which is a little hard for the client to do because of the confusing effects of the pattern), and the counselor is also contradicting the client's distress. There's two sets of inputs contradictory to the distresses.

As client, I remind you that you need to conclude that if nobody ever gave you any counseling, you could still completely re-emerge. If you assume anything other than that, you've backed into a helplessness or powerlessness pattern. I tried to communicate this years ago by saying that if you're cast away on a desert island, with nothing but a palm tree and a fiddler crab, you should still decide to completely re-emerge, instead of feeling, "Oh, I'm lost without a counselor." You can talk to the fiddler crab, you can put your arms around the palm tree and hug it. If you say to me, "I can't see my chronic pattern, I don't know how to contradict my chronic pattern," I say to you, just look at your tracks at the end of the day in the sand, and you will see your chronic pattern laid out. Then figure out the exact opposite of that, and you have a contradiction to your chronic pattern.

YOU CAN DECIDE

Under the worst circumstances, you can decide to completely re-emerge because you can mobilize your resources as a client against the distress. Individually we have to be responsible. Those of us who've moved very far ahead or have taken much responsibility in the Community find that this is realistic. You have to rely on planning your own re-emergence. We have to assume we can do it completely alone if necessary, because anything else is backing into the powerlessness or helplessness pattern.

Given that, it's obvious that to do it cooperatively is enormously better. Enormously better. Our own patterns can seem to be ninety-eight percent confusing to us, but if we get our attention off our own distress when we're counselors, and look at our clients, their distress is obvious. It's no effort at all to figure out a good contradiction to that! The client is often into heavy discharge because you paid a little bit of attention. Cooperative re-emergence from this mud-bath is obviously a lot better.

So we seek to improve our counseling because this is faster. We can say now that if we organize the session so that the client is contradicting his or her distress all the way through (and this usually takes some help from the counselor to do it because the patterns are so confusing to the client,) then, when the client is committed to contradicting and is contradicting the distress, the counselor can furnish additional contradictions, and you achieve an excellent session.

For a long time, we have done some very special counseling as demonstrations before workshops. It's clearly a notch above the usual counseling. But we didn't see why clearly enough to say it as well as I just did. Organize the client to contradict the distress. Once the client is committed to continue that (and the Framework, the Synopsis, and the many kinds of commitments are great tools for this), then add additional contradictions from you as a counselor. It's not beyond anybody's skills at all to do it.

So we use the RC insights to re-emerge cooperatively, because it's more efficient, much more effective. One of these crucial insights is that the difference between the two roles in the session is absolute. Being a client and being a counselor are two completely different roles. It's been five years now since we reached this insight. Counseling between leaders had previously been unsatisfactory, and it's improved since that insight. We realized that an "ancient habit-pattern" had grown on everybody in the world. All five billion people in the world, almost every minute of every day, have had their attention on their own old distresses and are going around trying to get somebody else to pay attention to them so they can discharge. Since everybody else is doing it too, it has practically never worked.

DESPERATE TALKING

I should qualify that a little bit. I've realized lately that this frantic talking to each other but not listening actually gets a certain amount of distress off of people. What we call counseling is not a strange process to anybody. Everybody's making it work a little bit the hard way all the time. (laughter) They pretend that the other person is listening. (laughter)

I realized this by looking back at some of our early experiences with professional clients in Seattle. We would get a person from the interior of Alaska who'd been out on the trap line for eight months of the winter, all by himself, never seeing anything but a dead mink. He would come for a week's intensive counseling at Personal Counselors. I remember M— used to be the one who worked with these people. At the time, we knew that everybody needed to cry and everybody had had their tears inhibited, so we figured we would be successful if we could get them to cry. M— would join us at lunch and say, "I can't get him to do anything but talk." We'd make all kinds of suggestions as to how she might get him to cry, and she'd go back and try it, and at the end of the day, she'd say, "He's still talking. Talk, talk, talk, talk, talk." And the next day, and the next day. Finally after about two and a half days he'd draw a deep breath and turn into an ordinary client. But until he'd talked that much, he couldn't touch anything else.

Think back to the way it used to be before telephones. When women had small children, they would get what they called "cabin fever," just dying for lack of contact with another adult. It makes me realize that actually, all this incessant talking, even without listening, has kept the mud down to shoulder level for most people. It does some good. Of course, we're looking for much more effective counseling than the compulsive talking to a non-listener that the population uses as much as they can.

Recognizing this ancient habit-pattern, we started carefully distinguishing the roles of counselor and client. The general recommendation now is part of the tools of building your world community and comes into everything else we do. You accept the role of client, you ask for other people's attention, only when the other person knows how to counsel and has agreed to be your counselor. This doesn't mean you have to move to the best-organized community of RCers. As Pat Barry and other counselors have shown, if you need a counselor badly, you can go up to a stranger and say, "Could you listen to me for a little while? You don't need to say anything, just listen to me and if I cry, put your arms around me." The stranger almost always agrees to try, and it works. You have a five-minute session, you thank the stranger, you go away feeling better, and the stranger goes away thinking, "What an interesting day." (laughter)

The two conditions have been met. The stranger knew how to counsel, because you gave him thirty seconds' worth of instruction. That's enough. And he *agreed* to be the counselor. It works. We give up trying to be client, except in those circumstances. By decision, all the rest of the time, we pay attention to other people.

Sometimes we counsel them. Sometimes we give them a long session. I remember the time a person came in for an interview and cried for fourteen hours. I learned something from it. But you don't necessarily counsel people. Just your attention enhances their survival. You can say, "It's good to see you. I like the colors of that blouse. How's your life going? I've gotta go," if you don't have time. You have all kinds of ways of protecting yourself from compulsive clienting. But your attention is always on the other person.

You will find, once you break the ancient habit of trying to always be client, of trying to grab their attention, (I hope you can break it, I haven't quite broken mine yet, but I'm better at it than I used to be) that you'll find great satisfaction in putting your attention on other people and enhancing their survival, in sometimes counseling those people. There's great satisfaction in doing a good job.

Once I made up my mind to quit "expecting" good counseling, it saved me an enormous amount of distress, because I would expect it and then be disappointed and sunk and have to dig myself out. Now, I have asked the whole Community to make this decision with me, to give up trying to get good counseling. It's a good decision. Until you do this, the ancient habit-pattern is pulling at you all the time to get you back into compulsive clienting.

(It pulls afterwards, too. I find myself compulsively clienting at the staff in Seattle. We have a meeting assigning jobs, and then I notice it's five minutes later and I'm telling them something "interesting." I catch myself, say, "I'm sorry, I didn't notice I slipped into it, I apologize." They say, "Oh, that's all right, we're getting paid anyway." (laughter) And it would have been all right if I'd asked for time, but I didn't. It slipped in.)

SEPARATE THE ROLES
So we separate the two roles of counselor and client, and we

only slip into the client's role when somebody knows how to counsel us and has agreed to counsel us. The rest of the time, our attention is on other people. We draw this sharp distinction between the role of client and the role of counselor because confusion between the two roles has slowed us down. I think we would have the world in hand by now if we'd known thirty-eight years ago, the importance of making this sharp distinction. Now we've got it, and we apply it.

TWO NOTEBOOKS

What Barbara xeroxed for you is the end of an article in **Present Time**, that proposes to use the power of the written word to organize our role as client, and organize our role as counselor, and keep them completely separate.

Keep two notebooks. If you have to have them in the same loose-leaf cover, put a big divider between so you don't get confused. In your client notebook, write down all the ideas that are helpful to you as a client: all the personal commitments, all the commitments against the internalized oppression of your group, all the frontier commitments that apply to everybody. Write down your Framework and your Synopsis. Keep a list of every direction that ever helped you discharge, of every book or television show that ever made you cry or shake, of every song that you used to play over and over again because it melted you, of every piece of poetry that grabbed you. You keep a record in your client notebook of everything that's ever enhanced your re-emergence. Write it down.

Before you go to a session as client, you will take out your client notebook and read it through, to refresh it, because you need to. Then after your session as client, before you forget, you haul out your client notebook and write up whatever you learned about being a client, whatever was effective that your counselor did, and so on.

On the different pages you keep as a client for your different counselors, you make note. "Never try telling Roy again how I was smitten with my brother-in-law. It upset him terribly. He can't handle that. On the other hand I discovered that Roy appreciates my deep love of flowers and helped me cry about the smell of lilacs in spring." Keep a page in your notebook for your different counselors. Keep a notebook for yourself as client. After every session, add to it, write in it. The manual that will re-emerge you is the one you will write yourself. Borrow all the information from the regular literature that you want, but keep writing, keep thinking for yourself. That's the manual that will guide you as client.

Before you go to a session where you'll be counselor, review your counselor notebook. Review all the things a counselor must remember. The four steps that lead to discharge.

Point Zero: remember the total goodness and brilliance and power and completeness of the client as a human being. If you don't know the client, refer to your basic theory assumption that every human being is like this.

If you do know the client, remember what's special about this one: how this one is close to the surface of humanness in some way. If I'm working with K— I remember that she has a brilliant way with words, she expresses herself extremely well; that she has insights into internalized oppression that are very valuable to other people. If I'm going to be working with A— I remember that she hustles, she starts things, she gets things going. She's always got a bunch of projects going. She's never too tired to get something else going, which is an essential human characteristic. If I'm working with L—, I remember his robustness, his ability to see humor in situations, bring it to the surface quickly. If I'm working with J—, I remember he persists in difficult circumstances. He will outlast the postal system. I remember where his humanness shows through. Point Zero.

Point One: I pay enough attention to the client to see

clearly what the distresses are. Now, I don't know K— real well, but I've seen enough of her in the last couple of days to know that it isn't easy for her to bubble happily all the time. Something's happened to her that gave her a kind of a suspicious attitude toward what's going on. If she waves this in the hope that I'll notice, the hope somebody will notice, and if I can notice this, I at least have my first guess as to what the distress is.

Point Two: Think of all possible ways to contradict that distress. It may not be easy, but I think of asking K— to say, "Someday I'll find a person I can trust." I'll try anything that goes in that direction.

Point Three: Contradict the distress sufficiently. So, I will try to get K— to promise that she will trust me. If she does, and discharges, maybe she'll discharge at the thought of it for the first three hours, but if it gets hard I'll take over the pattern that I think she's emerging from, and I will stand there looking suspicious and make it harder for her to fall back into the pattern.

So there are the four points. They'll be in your counselor notebook. Remind yourself of these four things that you need to do. Remind yourself that you have no distresses in your client's session. A counselor has no distresses. There's no such thing as a counselor with distress in a session, because both people's attention are to the client.

Use the written word in these two notebooks. Use these sheets that Barbara has Xeroxed for you, and start filling them out. Keep the two roles distinct. You will become an expert at both. Someone called it "strategizing your re-emergence." You will be actually planning in a definite way, so that each session brings you to a better level of functioning than before.

It seems real simple, doesn't it? Why did it take thirty-eight years to think of? Well, because patterns are confusing.

Why does this notion of the written manual, that you write, and rewrite, and keep up-to-date, contradict this so well? Well, we've known for a long time that a pattern has three "pseudo-abilities." Now of course an "ability" of a pattern is nothing but a groove in a recording, or some temporary short-circuits in the neural connections in our enormously complex central nervous system. But it has three "pseudo-abilities": That it can persist. If a pattern is "Dada de da da," as long as it exists at all, it is "Dada de da da." And if it gets real faint, it's (whispered) "Dada de da da." It persists. It is completely rigid. It gives the impression of persistence.

In general, we've not been real good at out-persisting patterns. The best counselors do, but clients give up very quickly on the persistence. It has in general, in the past, taken the counselor's persistence to contradict this pseudo-ability of the pattern. But the written word out-persists a pattern. So get it down in writing. Keep this notebook up-to-date. Review it. (You have to read the written word, of course, too.) Using the notebooks, you're out-persisting the pattern. So the pattern took over the last three sessions, and you're disappointed in RC, but you happen to eye the open manual. By golly, there's the written word contradicting it and you start to discharge. The written word will outlast the pattern. There were patterns four thousand years ago in ancient Egypt, but they're dead. But there are still some hieroglyphics carved on the walls in Egypt that can still be read, that outlasted those patterns. So you use the written word to outlast the pattern's pseudo-ability to persist.

The pattern can confuse you. Again and again I've sent out an intelligent client with a firm direction of "North! North! North!" And in five minutes it has shifted from, "North! North!" to "North! Nooorth! No-, no-, sorth! South! South!" (laughter) The pattern can confuse you. It has this pseudo-ability. I run into this one particular example over and over again with old physical distress. With old physical pain, it's crucial to not put attention on it. Unless it's an injury that just happened, putting attention on it reinforces it, restimulates it, makes it worse. The question comes up at workshops, "What do you do with an arthritic knee (or something like that), a restimulated pain?" I say, "Put attention away from it." Never put attention on restimulated physical pain. Have your client talk about the time when their knee was supple and they leaped over great hedges with a bound, how it was wonderful to run across the meadow, and topics like that, and they will start yawning. You will get discharge. You have to direct their attention away from the pain, in order to contradict it. I say this over that clearly when the question comes up. Often I get a phone call two weeks or a month later, saying, "We're in trouble. We've been working with this client on this old pain of hers, and it gets worse and worse and worse, and we've been working on it just like you said." And I say, "How have you been working on it?" "Oh, putting attention on it, just like you said." This happens over and over again. The pseudo-ability of the pattern to confuse is there.

The written word is un-confusing. If you're going to write an article for **Present Time**, not only are you going to read it over four or five times, to make sure it says what you think, but I'm going to read it over four or five times, and edit it to get it to say what I think you meant to say. I also get somebody else to edit it, and somebody else to proof-read it. Your written word can be read over and over again and any confusion eliminated. You can read the written word over and over and it's still there, even though you've originally projected all kinds of confusion onto it. The written word is a real weapon against confusion. So, writing your notebook as client and writing your notebook as counselor is an effective weapon against this pseudo-ability of the pattern as well, the pseudo-ability to confuse you.

The third pseudo-ability of the pattern is to make you forget. My favorite story about that is what happened when I was first able to formulate these three pseudo-abilities of the pattern at a California workshop. A week or so later I got a letter from one of the people there that said, "I remember you said a pattern could do three things. You said it could persist, and it could confuse you, but I can't remember what the third thing was." (laughter)

The written word is the weapon you use all the time against forgetting. You write out a grocery list, you write out a note on the door of the refrigerator, "Don't eat all the ice cream!" You told them that in the morning, but you wanted them to remember, so you used the written word. Writing your client notebook and your counselor notebook and keeping them up-to-date uses the written word. The written word is a powerful tool against all the pseudo-abilities of the pattern.

This is another key insight.

USE COMMITMENTS

Commitments have turned out to be a marvelous tool, extremely powerful. I'd like for you to master the use of them at this workshop. They began as directions.

When we were first counseling, we noticed that if we listened to somebody, they usually cried and got better. If you listened to them cry a few times, the thing that was spoiling their life often went away. That was nice. That was what we knew. But then, as we went on with more clients, we found that some clients cried a few times and their problems went away, and others cried and cried and cried and cried and cried, week after week after week, and their problems never went away. At least, the ones they most wanted to go away didn't. Little things improved, "I do notice that I am keeping my refrigerator cleaner, I'm feeding my children better, and I had dinner on the table when my husband wanted it. But this feeling that I'm totally worthless just seems to be there forever." They would cry about it. (Intuitively we would be contradicting the distress by looking at them lovingly or touching them, encouraging them.) They would cry and cry and cry, but they would come back the next week still feeling hopeless. It was a big breakthrough when we finally glimpsed the fact that sometimes patterns are chronic. You can discharge part of them in a session, but if you then go act them out the rest of the week they will gain back all the distress you discharged. You're just endlessly dipping out distress that runs back in.

So we came up with *directions*. Once we began to understand the nature of the chronic pattern, we would say to the client, "I want you to stand in front of the mirror each morning and say, 'I'm an extremely valuable person!'" There would be dramatized resistance, but finally, the client did go around saying, "I'm valuable. I'm a little valuable, at least. I'm valuable." She stopped losing ground between sessions. After a certain number of sessions (the chronic pattern would turn out to take a lot of discharge), she felt "just as valuable as anyone else. I'm at least as valuable as my husband."

So we began with directions, realizing we had to contradict a chronic distress in between sessions in order to gain on it. We used directions and directions and directions. (Sometimes they were pervertedly misused. People quit listening, because they were too busy giving directions that were great contradictions to their own distress but had nothing to do with their client. There is no possible mistake that we haven't made a thousand times.)

Somewhere along the line, we tied a promise into the direction, and the direction became a commitment. We crafted a commitment for each individual. It worked great, especially when they took it into their other sessions. We learned a lot. We began exchanging these individual commitments, which is a powerful tool that I want to revive.

Then, general commitments happened. They happened in England to start with. We had a meeting of Regional Reference People in a London hotel. S— was there, and she was having trouble discharging, and I had her tell the story of her life. That's what you do when you don't know what to do when you're counselor, you listen to the client. I heard something that had happened over and over again, as her life had unrolled. I decided to ask her to make a commitment. I asked her to make the commitment that "I solemnly promise that from this moment on, I will never again settle for anything less than absolutely everything!" And S— exploded with discharge. It was a great session.

Two weeks later I was back in the States working with another woman, and there was something familiar about her distress, and I thought, "I'm going to try S—'s commitment on her." I gave it to her, and she exploded with discharge. That encouraged me to try it with other women. By now thousands of women have tried S—'s commitment. Somewhere along the line we realized it was the Women's Commitment. It was a commitment not to ever accept second-class treatment. I don't know a woman that has ever used it without discharge.

That was interesting, why S—'s commitment worked for all women. I tried to think about it. Later G— was leading young people's workshops alongside my adult workshops, all the way from the north of England down to Sussex. In a session she was discharging about the disrespectful, condescending way young people are treated. So I put together a commitment and I asked her to say, "I solemnly promise that from this moment on, I will never again treat any young person, including myself, with anything less than complete respect." And G— cried and cried and cried. She had asked me to come visit her young people's workshop and work with them that morning. So it was time to go and we started over, and on the way she said, "Would you try that commitment with them?"

I think the youngest was seven, and the oldest was nineteen, a small group but very diverse. I said, "G— wants me to try this," and I asked for someone to do it, and she burst out crying, and the person next to her began to cry, and they reached for each other, and they all fell into each other's arms, and G— and I got in there, and we all held on to each other and we all cried together. By now, many young people have tried G—'s commitment, and it turns out to be the commitment against the internalized young people's oppression, the lack of respect and putting each other down unceasingly. If you're around young people you see that they continually invalidate each other as they pass on what's been done to them by the adults and the older young people.

Gradually, a whole stable of particular commitments against particular internalized oppressions were developed: the Jewish commitment, the working-class, the men's, and so on.

(demonstration)

Now we have five, in some ways six, general frontier commitments that have evolved out of all these particular commitments against internalized oppression: the Jewish commitment, the working-class, the men's, and so on. The first one is the commitment against pretense. It's very powerful. It cracks the shell that many people have built around their hurts, of pretending that the hurts are not there. You've often got three layers. At base, you've got this fine, wonderful, magnificent person. Then you've got the layer of hurts, the invalidations. On the outside of that you've often got the shell of pretense patterns. "I'm just fine." It keeps us from getting to discharge. People sometimes take leadership in RC on this basis. There are some leaders who operate almost completely on pretense. It's been great to use this commitment with them.

It is an important tool in some cases. It has two halves. The first half is admitting what you knew all the time, that you're covered with mud like everybody else, instead of pretending that you have a private shower that keeps you squeaky clean. The second half is, "However, fortunately or unfortunately, I happen to be the best person available." This goes against a pattern that's almost universal, of feeling that we're so inadequate that we have to wait for someone else to come along. We say, "I can't lead because other people could lead better." This brings you face to face with the fact that nobody else is ever going to lead your life, and discharges the patterns that keep you waiting for somebody else to do it for you. Nobody's ever going to do it for you, so you start living at a more responsible level.

The second one is very profound and very universal, and it never wears out. "From this moment on, the real me!"

(demonstration "The real X—.")

The commitments are not the only tool, but they're a very powerful tool for organizing the client's participation in the session. They keep the client contradicting the distress. Once they get into doing it, you don't need to remind the clients very much. Once they get excited, "From now on the real X—," he may talk for an hour and a half without ever repeating. Insights fly out, and lots of discharge. As counselor you can do all kinds of additional things to contradict the distress and keep it going. It's a very useful, powerful tool.

The frontier commitments are:

AGAINST PRETENSE:
I am obviously completely incompetent and completely inadequate to handle the challenges which reality places before me.

However, (fortunately or unfortunately), I happen to be the best person available.

TO BE ONE'S REAL SELF:
From now on, the REAL me, and this means _____.

TO RECLAIM POWER:
From now on I will see to it that everything I am in contact with works well, and I will not limit or pull back on my contacts.

AGAINST IDENTIFYING ONESELF WITH PATTERNS:
No recording of past distress has any power of its own at all.

It only contrives to give the appeareance of power and influence to the extent that I slavishly submit to letting it use *my* power and *my* influence.

(If I think of it as a piece of recorded tape, it has, at most, a trifling historical significance, unless I insert it into the tape recorder that is myself and allow it to play me, an action which I am completely free to decide to do or not to do.)

Therefore, I now decide to deny past distress any credibility in the present, or any influence or operation in my life.

And I will repeat this decision as many times as necessary to free my life completely from the influence of past distress.

TO THE UNITY OF ALL HUMAN ASPIRATIONS:
From now on I will inspire, lead, and organize all people to eliminate every form of humans' harming humans.

94

Demonstration on Discharging Internalized Oppression

P—: (laughter) I've always wished I was blonde. (more laughter, then repeats phrase again, more laughter, etc.)

Harvey: Hi.

P—: I hate being black. (laughter)

HJ: Talk about it.

P—: In what I think was a support group, somebody was talking about having her hair straightened, and it's this long curling-paper process (laughter)...oh god (more laughter).... I was so happy when I met this woman who's Jewish, who said she used to iron her hair to try to get it straight, and (uproarious laughter), thank god it's not just us blacks. (more laughter)

HJ: White women iron their hair to try to put a curl *into* it.

P—: No, this one was trying to straighten it. My mother used to threaten me with an afro. I never understood. Then when I got one I thought, "What have you been keeping me from all these years?!!!" No problem. (more laughter)

HJ: Long and straight blond hair? (laughter from client) You know where whiteness came from? People migrated from the tropical areas of the earth up to the north of Europe. The supply of sun was so low there that most of the people died off because they got such a small amount of Vitamin D through their dark skins that the women got rickets and couldn't bear children. Only a few freaks who mutated to lighter skins could soak up more Vitamin D from the sun to survive in the tough region. That's really true. The natural lovely dark skin...gave way to a pale, sickly mutation in order

From the Black Leaders' Conference, 1986. Appeared in **Black Re-emergence** No. 4, 1987.

that people could get enough Vitamin D. That's where we whites came from. (laughter from listeners)

P—: That is grim. (listeners' laughter) I don't know what I thought, but the first thing to come out of my mouth is, "It's all right. I'll comfort you."

It's better than it used to be.

HJ: How did it used to be?

P—: It was hell. Growing up in an all-white community and them having everything. Your popularity was based on your looks, and everything that looked good was the antithesis of what I am. You know, blond-haired, white women. They got all the attention and they were the cute ones and the pretty ones. I was cute for a while, 'cause all little girls are cute, but then I grew out of being cute, and then I was ugly, like everybody else. Then looks started mattering more and more. That's what people worried about, right? (laughter)

HJ: Sexism began being involved.

P—: It starts with little dresses and shiny shoes. Then all hell breaks loose. (laughter) It was awful. I had to start wearing clothes. Now, the black people around me won't tolerate me wearing junky clothes. Then, it didn't matter, because none of the white people cared about what I looked like anyway, since I wasn't blonde and blue-eyed or even a brunette. It's blue eyes and brown hair or green eyes and blond hair or something like that. Anything I wanted to do that was important, like running for office in high school was always a popularity contest and there were always the same girls who got in. (laughter) It was really pathetic. (laughter)

HJ: Tell me everything.

P—: I thought I was the ugliest thing on earth years ago (laughter) in high school. We put the "ugh" in "ugly." (laughter) I'm ugly. (laughter)

HJ: (to the workshop audience) Now, pick up on what I'm doing for contradictions here, at this point. Notice my facial expression, my tone of voice, how clearly I love and admire P—.

P—: Mmm. I'm ugly. I get ugly. (laughter, more laughter) But I'm less ugly now that that big gap between my teeth closed up. (laughter) The wisdom teeth came in, thank god. (laughter) Something about women, black women, was hooked on a big gap between their teeth. You got the image that, at least, if you're going to be black, you shouldn't look that *way. (laughter, listeners join in.)*

HJ: Anyone in the audience have those feelings? It's awful quiet out there...(followed by tremendous laughter and inaudible exchanges).

P—: There's a gap there (screams of laughter) any more?

Listener: Here's mine, just big enough to spit water about twelve feet.

P—: Oh boy, am I ugly. (laughter) The first night at the workshop, last night, I was admiring how many people actually did look beautiful. (laughter) You look through magazines and see the ads, and the women are made up fancy. Even **Ebony** *does it, although* **Ebony** *is getting better. You'll see black women in it. You don't see only white, straight-nosed, thin women.*

HJ: I'll give you a true statement. I want you to say it to me. Try and assume that it's true, because it is; say it over and then give your thoughts in between. "You think I'm beautiful!"

P—: You think I'm beautiful? No, you don't. (laughter) I'm not going to tell you what thought I had. Oh god. All the women you say you fall in love with don't look like anybody here. (begins sobbing)

HJ: I'm in love with a number of women here.

P—: But you never brag about it. (more sobbing)

HJ: Tell me about it.

P—: (heavy sobbing) I used to get so mad at you when you liked Sonya, because Sonya is the classic pretty face, you know.

HJ: Classic stereotype face?

(Client roars and sobs, Harvey speaks at length but inaudibly.)

P—: I feel like all these leaders that I see, that are white, never seem to have black people around them, who they look up to. It always seems like there's some white standby over here. (roars and sobs)

HJ: (after sobs subside) Tell me again.

P—: You think I'm beautiful. (laughter) No, you don't. (more laughter)

HJ: Say it again.

P—: You think I'm beautiful. (laughs)

HJ: I sure do. (Elaborates inaudibly)

P—: You're supposed to say that. (laughs)

HJ: It seems to me to be true.

P—: I'm supposed to think it's true; it's supposed to be honest. (inaudible exchange) You think I'm beautiful. (continues laughing)

HJ: I sure do. Say it again.

P—: (laughing) Oh, that's all right. Even if you don't think I'm beautiful, I can see you're interested in a lot of beautiful people. (laughing)

HJ: You *can* have any differences you can imagine and still be beautiful.

P—: (sobbing) Yeah, I was noticing how different we all look, like there's no such thing as one way of being black, we're so different.

HJ: Every one of you.

P—: I see more white faces that look alike than black faces. (sobbing heavily, pauses to roar and resumes sobbing) Mmmm, Harvey thinks I'm beautiful. (laughs)

HJ: You can see why. (There's more, but it's inaudible, and is addressed to the listeners. P— begins sobbing again as he talks.)

P—: My mother has Cherokee heritage. I think it's her

great-grandparents on both her mother's and her father's side, but before the Cherokee and after the Cherokee came two British slaveowners, so my mother's hair is kind of fine, you know, it's not as coarse as mine. I think she used to make an issue out of that to us, not overtly, but slyly. She used to tell us all the time that if her hair would get kinkier she'd probably stop liking her hair, that it wasn't that it was better than ours but.... I don't think she ever got the response she wanted. I don't think it ever registered even with her what she was saying.

HJ: Come again.

P—: Harvey thinks I'm beautiful.

HJ: (to the group) Is she? (Group agrees that she is.) I had a professional client once, a black woman, who told me that every morning she got out of bed and the first thing she did, she went to the mirror and looked at it and said, "Oh, look at you, you ugly monster. Look how horrid you are. Aren't you ashamed to be alive? Why don't you get off the face of the earth?" (P— begins sobbing.) She started every day driving herself into the ground. She didn't have any idea that she hadn't invented that herself, hadn't any idea that it came from outside. Every day she pounded herself into the ground as the first thing to start her day. That's internalized oppression. (As P—'s sobbing subsides...) You're beautiful. Just plain and utterly beautiful.

P—: That makes me feel stupid. (Group laughs.)

HJ: Well, in this one area you haven't been entirely intelligent, at least recently, since the hurt went in. Nobody's very smart where they're hurting. (Laughter, sniffling, more unintelligible exchange.) Bryan thinks you're beautiful.

P—: Yeah, he takes drugs. (Group laughs.)

HJ: Say, "Harvey, you think I'm beautiful, Harvey!" (unintelligible) Over and over.

P—: Just keep saying that? You think I'm beautiful, Harvey.

HJ: I sure do.

P—: You think I'm beautiful, Harvey.

HJ: Now your thoughts on that.

P—: Oh. Nothing important.

HJ: Say it again.

P—: (sighs) You think I'm beautiful, Harvey.

(Unintelligible exchange, laughter, then P— repeats again.)

HJ: Give me a thought again.

P—: What I'm wondering is whether we should do something else for a second, 'cause I'm not following you.

HJ: What are you fighting? What makes you fight it? First thought?

P—: Well, I know it's terror.

HJ: Terror of what? (repeats, encourages) That vague impression, what is it? (P— begins laughing.) Yeah, that one, that one.

P—: (laughing) Oh no, I don't want to work on that now. Oh, come on, I don't want to look at that.

HJ: Quick, before you lose it.

P—: I'm not gonna lose it. (laughing, then sobbing heavily) Gross.

HJ: What was it?

P—: Eyuchk. Just some early sexual stuff.

*   *   *

HJ: "Am I really beautiful, Harvey?"

P—: Am I really beautiful, Harvey?

HJ: There are no single standards of beauty.

P—: I know. Intellectually, I know that. (laughs)

HJ: "I lack the good faith, but intellectually I know I'm beautiful."

P—: Intellectually I know I'm beautiful. Intellectually I know I'm perfect, I'm just fine, but emotionally, I mean, patterns....

HJ: What patterns? What does the pattern say?

P—: The pattern says, "You're awful, you're stupid, really, really stupid." (further inaudible)

HJ: Put it in the first person, translate it. Try to convince me that you're awful and stupid.

P—: I'm really awful and stupid. (laughing) Oh god, am I stupid. If you want to see a good example of stupid, and that's stupid. (more laughter)

HJ: It feeds on itself.

P—: I know it. All of them, they all have their own little cycle. (laughing)

HJ: (to the audience) Now, in this atmosphere, thinking as counselors, there's enough support here. There's a strong counselor that can be aware of anger. I don't have to worry—if I get her to just express it, she'll hear herself say it. So (to P—), give me the worst.

P—: The worst.

HJ: "I'm stupid, I'm ruined, I'm gross," whatever it is.

P—: (groans, Harvey encourages, roars) Oh, this is real black women stuff.

*   *   *

P—: (laughing) I'm stupid! (again, brightly) I'm stupid!

HJ: (cheerfully) What else?

P—: I'm gross and ugly! (laughs) I'm really stupid! Oh god, I know people who act like that, ugh, it's awful.

HJ: (to audience) Any place other than this there would not be enough contradiction for her to say these things and have me say words in apparent agreement (I'm contradicting them, of course, by my facial expression and tone of voice) and have her be able to discharge like this.

P—: I wouldn't stay here if you agreed with me and were serious. I'm stupid. And ugly and gross. (laughs) And awful. And a slut. (more laughter) And a whore. Oh boy, am I stupid.

HJ: Get them all out.

P—: Ugly! (laughs, then stops.) Oh, mmm, euh. It's foggy again.

HJ: Hello!

P—: Hi.

HJ: Hi in there. (P— shudders, Harvey encourages.) Try a phrase: "This stuff would scare some people, Harvey."

P—: This stuff would scare some people, Harvey. (shudders, then laughs) But not me. (repeats)

HJ: "I'm black, therefore I'm...."

P—: Therefore I am. (laughs, listeners laugh too.) I'm black, therefore I am. (more laughter)

HJ: You know, I think this is about as good a demonstration as I ever hoped to participate in. In all the years I've known you, I've never seen you look as gorgeous and high-toned as you do now. Let's go for a contradiction in words now.

P—: Okay.

HJ: "I'm black, therefore I am especially beautiful...."

P—: I'm black, therefore I'm brilliant, powerful, beautiful. (kissing sound) I'm (unintelligible) (laughs, inaudible remark from listener, more laughter)

HJ: "...therefore I'm...."

P—: I'm black, therefore I'm gorgeous, wonderful, intelligent, brilliant, powerful, and (kissing sound) the greatest. (laughs)

HJ: "...therefore I'm...."

P—: I'm black, therefore I'm gorgeous, wonderful, intelligent, brilliant, powerful, and (kissing sound) the greatest. (laughs)

HJ: One last time. Throw in "innocent and pure."

P—: "Pure as the driven snow." (laughter) (inaudible exchange, more laughter) I'm black, therefore I'm brilliant, powerful, beautiful, pure and innocent.

HJ: Again.

P—: Pure and innocent.

HJ: What would you rather say?

P—: Well, I mean, I don't think there are the words.

HJ: How about "wholesome"?

P—: Umm... (group laughter) What state are we in? (more laughter) I don't know; that's always felt kind of cold.

HJ: The whore/slut stuff, what's the best contradiction to that?

P—: I don't think the western European language has come up with something yet. I mean, it's either Mary Magdalene or Mother Mary. Either the virgin or the prostitute.

HJ: Okay, try the virgin business.

P—: Virginal. (Group laughs at inaudible remark from listener.) That was a very, very embarrassing song. (laughter)

HJ: Virginal.

P—: Virginal. (laughs) I'm black, therefore I'm proud, brilliant, strong, virginal, pure and innocent. (laughs)

HJ: You're getting more used to it than you were when we started. (laughter from P—)

P—: I'm black....

(Side of tape ends, other side begins with:)

P—: (laughing) Oh, no, anything but that!

HJ: (cheerfully) "I'm black, and therefore terrified."

P—: (laughing) I'm black, and therefore terrified.

HJ: If you've ever worked with Jews, you can assume that if they are Jewish, they're terrified.

P—: Yeah, I think so, too. My first real memory of being terrified was when Martin Luther King was shot. (sobs) But I remember the funeral. (more sobs) It's like being black meant you got shot. (sobs heavily, roars) I remember talking about how blacks train their children to not speak up and (sobs) not be visible. (sobbing) You open your mouth, you get killed.

(more sobbing) All you have to do is walk in the street. (sobs) So I thought I'd not make waves for the sake of my own survival. Many times I know what to do and want to do it, but draw back because of this fear. (laughs) Maybe from now on, I'll move a little more boldly, but I still will be careful. Beautiful and brave, that's me.

(Rest of tape is unintelligible.)

Leadership

A Favorable Situation
For Reaching Out

The overall situation we're in now seems to me very, very favorable. Any situation has positive factors and negative factors, but there's no question that progress has nudged us around a corner at this point. It's important that we take a fresh look at what's happened, and, just for our own morale, take a little pride in what we've accomplished. I don't think there's any question that the missile pact and the ongoing developments are in large part the result of peace activism. Overwhelmingly they are the result of pressure from the people. I don't think there's any question about that. These developments are taking place because of the mass pressure of the populations in many countries. The peace movement expressed this sentiment of the people well enough, in spite of all the mistakes and weaknesses, that this factor has prodded the situation 'round the bend and gives us new opportunities.

I'd like to remind you of some of the published White House notes about the Vietnam War. There's a little piece in there I remember well. This was when all the activists were feeling despairing and hopeless, were saying to their confidants, "No matter how much we do, we never have any effect." Of course the War Department and the White House were issuing bulletins four times a day saying, "You never have any effect." (laughter) (It's hard not to be influenced by them.) During a discussion the general staff were urging President Johnson to bomb Hanoi, to just flatten Hanoi out. He said, "Well, what do you think the results will be?" And the general says, "We will break their will completely, we'll be able to bring the troops home. It will take care of every-

From the January 1988 Peace Activists' Workshop. Appeared in **Present Time** No. 72, July 1988 and **Peace** No. 1, 1988.

thing," and a couple of other staff joined in supporting the general. President Johnson said, "Yes. And the people will tear down the White House fence and lynch their President." This little item makes obvious how often, when people are feeling they are having no effect at all, they are really striking right to the heart of the matter, and being enormously effective.

Our poor brothers and sisters who are caught in these roles of general or President or Chairperson of the Board, of playing the most oppressive, offensive roles in the collapsing society, have very little choice. They've been assigned these roles of making powerful noises, acting as if they have complete confidence and promising to stick to their guns, in order to keep you afraid and wondering if it will ever be possible to have any effect. The media pour out this message. We're so used to it that we don't notice it, but every newspaper article and every television program tells you peace activists in some way or other that what you're doing is useless, that you are ineffective. This comes at you several times a day. Actually the people in the oppressive, war-mongering positions are far more afraid than you are. Their roles are case-hardened on them. They don't feel they have any choice to get out of them, and they probably can't unless one of us asks the right questions so they can discharge. In general they are far more afraid than you are.

I learned this years ago in labor negotiations. We workers would be feeling near despair. It would seem that we had held out on strike as long as we could possibly hold out against the company's overwhelming strength and confidence, and then I'd get some word from a friend I'd made in the owner's family that the management were just sick with dread that we would hold out another day, because if we did that, they'd have to give in. The oppressors are always far more uneasy than people they oppress. I don't know if you believe me when I say that or not, but it's true.

ALWAYS IN OUR FAVOR

The balance of forces is always with us. The future is always on our side when we have a good program. It's understandable that we're so timid and slow and confused and often dump our internalized oppression on each other and fight each other harder than we fight the enemy. But reality is always with us, the future is always with us.

There's only one serious danger. This is lessening, at least, but there's the one big danger, that the patterns and the rigidities of the class society will bring about nuclear holocaust. Aside from that danger and the stupidities of the collapsing society, EVERYTHING is going our way. That may seem to be a little over-optimistic in terms of the usual peace rhetoric, but it seems to me that with present technology and communications, we can lay the nuclear threat to rest. The collapsing society can be allowed to collapse gently, without too much destruction of wealth and people. I would figure fifty years. (I really don't think it will take more than fifty years for the earth to become a Garden of Eden with just everything going splendidly. All the non-human parts of it can be returned to safety and health and humans can be rescued from the pile-up of irrational distress patterns. Even a lot of the animals that we've extinguished can be re-created with modern genetic engineering. We can bring back the mammoths that our predecessors on this continent extinguished eleven thousand years ago by taking some genes from the tapir and the elephant. Undoubtedly we can do things like that. The possibilities are just lovely.)

WHAT RC REALLY IS

But here we are. We're all RCers, or we're on the edge of being RCers. There's still a lot to learn in this area of reality that we call RC. I'd like to re-define RC this morning. What we call RC is the best approximation we have reached, so far, of reality in the area of the distress pattern where the oppressive society has offered unreality. All the things that we treasure so as RC knowledge, the real nature of human beings, the role of distress recordings, the role of discharge, is actually just the best approximation we've reached, so far, of reality in this area, where unreality has dominated for a long time. We've hinted at this by saying that the way to teach RC is not the way you were taught RC, because every RC teacher teaches his or her patterns to a great extent. The copying of these patterns, or saying RC was what I learned six months ago, or four years ago, has slowed us down a great deal. Because RC is very different in 1988 than it was in 1986 or '87. It continually grows. That's one of the nice things about it.

What individual RCers sometimes treat as a cult or magic information, is simply the best approximation that a group of accidentally interested but dedicated people have been able to reach in thinking through the mess of unreality with which human affairs have been covered. It is but an approximation, and it's continually changing.

It's improving. There's an area now that I'm asking everybody's help on. We know now that a decision preceding discharge roughly works better than discharge preceding decision. Whenever we can get the decision ahead of the discharge, we get more discharge, and we change things more quickly. I don't know that it's possible to simply make one big decision, act rationally from then on and let the discharge stream off as we do it. I like the thought, but in practice I'm not always able to help people do it, and it may be an unrealistic but inspiring picture I'm projecting. I'm asking people at workshops to join with me in thinking about this relationship. As I counsel people, I set up the decision first whenever I can, but I wind up often having to stop and help people discharge for a long time till they even get to where they're making a repetitive decision, let alone a final one.

This is an example of where we're still progressing, where we still don't know. Please help think about this one, because it's important to our effectiveness.

We do know a lot more than we did, and we know a lot more than anybody else does, so far. This is the positive side.

WE KNOW ENOUGH NOW

In my judgment, we know enough now, have enough clear theory and technique out in the open, in print or on video-cassette, in English at least, for complete re-emergence for any one of us. If we applied what we know, as well as we know how to apply it, or see it demonstrated, complete re-emergence would be a fairly easy thing.

We're still letting the patterns contaminate the use of what we know. That's what's holding us back, in terms of our individual re-emergence. I think the relationship of forces in the world, particularly since this last big nudge around the bend where Gorbachev and Reagan shook hands (laughter) puts us in a position where if we acted with the power that we theoretically accept that we have, if we moved on what we know, put the decisions ahead of discharge as far as we know how to, at least, the whole looming nuclear danger would collapse like a house of cards.

People say to me after they've learned a little bit about RC, "Oh, if you could only reach Reagan and counsel him!" Well, it wouldn't hurt the old man (laughter), but you have to realize that Reagan has no real power in that role. He might be a useful source of information for this or that. It doesn't hurt to recruit somebody in the apparatus, somebody who gets a bodyguard, but he has no power except to do what the oppressive society tells him. None of the others do either. They don't have real power.

The working class has real power. The industrial working class, if it ever united and decided firmly on everything it wanted, would be able to get it.

The objective factors are all with us. If we just could bring ourselves to do what we know to do, to apply and carry out the theories and the policies that we've already worked out (and which we're still improving), taking charge of the situation would be very easy. The main thing that's holding us back and keeping the world in danger, in my opinion, is a whole series of bad habits of not acting on what we know. We have the information now and we've revealed the opposition as our own and others' patterns. That's begun. That's encouraging.

FREEDOM OF CHOICE AND POWER, TOO

We're quite sure at this point that the enormous complexity of our central nervous systems brought us not only vast intelligence, brought us not only awareness, but also brought us complete freedom of decision, and brought us complete power (if we define power, not as the ability to dominate somebody else, but as the ability to have the universe respond to us the way we wish it to). We have, for a long time, possessed enormous intelligence, complete awareness, complete freedom of decision, and complete power. Now that we have this clear enough that I can at least say it to you, we still have a little problem in taking it seriously, because of some of the distress. The fact is that we have the information to put the world to rights very rapidly.

The question is, how to expedite the use of it? Here's where I need help. I can't *prove* yet that a person can make a decision, act on it, let the discharge stream off, and never stop. I think it's probably true, but I haven't been able to prove it yet. When I try to help one of my clients do that, I find myself having to stop, over and over, and help them discharge, discharge, discharge, before they can take the prospect seriously. The little bit we did yesterday, J—, it seemed from out here to the people watching, that you were at a point where if you just continued with that, terror would run off of you in great rivulets and you'd be free from the distress. I don't know how to encourage you to keep doing it. I tried a little last night.

I think this is the basic situation we're currently in as clients, or as Co-Counselors.

Question: What do you mean by run off? Discharge quickly?

Harvey: Act against the pattern, and let the discharge take place while you act rationally. Combine heavy discharge with functioning well.

This is happening more and more often. It's happening enough of the time that the possibility of doing it consistently is exciting. We're very close to a breakthrough here. The possibility of simply making a decision firmly enough to carry one through a breakthrough, is near hatching. You can hear the eggshell being pecked at from the inside.

The peace movement has certainly come a long way. I'm very proud of the influence that you people and many like you have had. I think the injection of RC information has made a great difference in the peace movement so far. More of it is needed. The internalized oppression is still too much of a brake on the effectiveness of peace people. Yet *we have the information* on how to combine solving the individual problems of the leaders and the followers and the group meetings, with the working out of a full-scale program.

REACH ALL OTHER ORGANIZATIONS

It seems to me that the peace activists now must tie their program in with every other program people are supporting. One of our frontier commitments, our fifth one, is: "From now on I will inspire, lead, and organize all people to eliminate every form of humans harming humans." This is a fundamental uniting principle. Our ethicists in RC say that it's enormously important. Half the people who hear it are enormously excited (half of them say "so what?"). Our ethicists say it's the first important advance in ethics since Aristotle. They say all the problems we're trying to solve between people always involve the question of how much shall we hurt someone here in order to keep from hurting someone here? Eliminate *every* form of humans harming humans.

I think we should sell our programs, should win hundreds of thousands of supporters to them, and make them become an active part of other people's programs, simply on the basis of how they affect the needs of other people. We want the end of spending money on armaments so that it can be spent on food. We want the ending of financing of armaments so that we clean up our pollution of the sea. We want the end of financing of armaments so the space program can soar aloft, so the space station can go into action, so we can explore Mars and Venus, and then set deep space vessels adrift for the stars. The end of armament and war preparation is necessary in order to carry out these people's programs. These appeals can reach everybody on earth.

Peace activists have to quit huddling with themselves. They have to be in all the precinct caucuses of the political parties. With their friends they have to be elected delegates to the party conventions, at the county, district, state, and national level. They have to be active in their trade unions. The peace activist's job is to see that *all* the people's organizations act for peace, including new ones that they will have to organize because there aren't yet any of the right kind available. Remember the message from Diane, "There is as yet no women's organization that is open to all women." We'll have to build some new ones. We certainly need to organize many new unions. The working class is terribly disorganized at this time.

These other organizations, the existing ones and the ones we will help build, will be speaking out on the issues of peace. As long as the peace movement has been the peace movement, by itself, it's had a lot of influence, but this is just a speck of influence compared to what it will have when each program is being endorsed by trade unions and political parties and PTA's and bankers' associations. There isn't any organization whose members' real needs will not be enhanced by the achievement of the peace program. People are open to hearing this.

The final economic crisis is deepening, creating lots of hardship. We can't have big RC workshops any more, because nobody can afford to come for very long. We started out with two-week workshops. People could come for two weeks. Now we've got four days here, and it's a strain. Many of the outreach workshops we have, we have to fund them in order to carry them through, and our outreach funds are being sapped. We'll need to raise some money in new ways.

ENORMOUS OPPORTUNITIES

At the same time, the economic crisis is creating enormous opportunities. Everybody is in trouble. (laughter) *Everybody.* The collapsing society is collapsing on the necks of a large number of people, not just the hopelessly discouraged permanent poor, who are supposedly trained to just die quietly. The damage is reaching all sections of the population. Peace activists, I think, starting from their key issues, must tie peace into all the other places people are hurting. Many of you obviously are. The reports last night show that there are many people here who know what they're doing in other fields, who also have a broad picture. I think *all* peace activists must be encouraged to challenge a broad range of issues.

We're out to change the world in every possible way that makes it safer for people to live. I don't think we'll have any trouble if we move boldly and confidently, using the tools that we've had a chance to learn, even though we've only learned them partially up to now. I don't think we'll have any serious problem at all, achieving all this.

The internalized oppressive patterns will try to drag us down, but so what? We know the tools to use against them.

We have to take the boldest, sharpest, broadest outlook, and at the same time keep wiping the mud off our trousers, get the distress off ourselves, make firm decisions against it so that we go ahead. We have to discharge. We can get that efficient. We have to do everything at once, but there's nothing contradictory about that. We have to do everything at once, but that's exactly what we'll enjoy doing.

The cleaning up of our acts, as clients, as counselors, as peace activists, as leaders of the world, is overdue. We know enough now to do it right. Let's land a mighty blow, here, against the confusion that has kept us from doing that well up to now.

I think we're in a very fortunate position, in some of the spontaneous events that have moved for our support. An amazingly flexible Russian leader popped up. He may have trouble staying there, but so far he has successfully. Reagan got his tail caught in Irangate. All this will help; but behind the spontaneous events, the patient work of this group of people, and a lot of other peace activists, has been gnawing away at the dead dangerous inertia of the society collapsing toward war.

My Ideas? Our Ideas

Dear Harvey,

Thank you for answering my letter so quickly. Your encouragement is very meaningful to me. You said that there is no big jump from a friendly relationship to RC, it's just doing what comes naturally. A few days after I wrote my last letter to you, one of my Ethiopian friends I was telling you about began a barrage of questions to me. I've been telling him a lot about how the human mind gets rigid and stuck and what needs to happen in order to relieve that problem. Finally he just outright asked me, "So what should we do with each other to get out of our patterns?" Now we counsel twice a week.

At this point, however, I have a question. I've taken very seriously your advice to present the theory as my own thinking developed by myself. Well, this guy I counsel with is getting very curious, and so I've been gradually letting it out that there is a large community of people out there doing what we're doing. If I tell him that that community was started and is sustained by me, he's going to know I'm a liar. You also suggest giving literature to people, but I can't do that and still be known as the originator of these ideas. So I guess my question is, just how far do I take this idea? It's been very useful to carry around in my head, and I think it's made people respond to RC theory more positively, but now it's getting in the way.

Appeared in **Present Time** No. 74, January 1989.

Thanks again for all your encouragement.

Chris Kurtz
Addis Ababa, Ethiopia

Dear Chris,

I'm glad things are going so well. Just relaxedly say that there are a bunch of you trying to think these things through and that you keep in contact with each other through a loose relationship that you call a Community and that some literature has been published if he is interested in it. Then let him read the literature and gradually get used to it. That part is fine. I think the big improvement in the way you present it has already been made.

Harvey

Getting Outside the Fear of
Mixing RC and Being a Physician

Harvey: Okay, try to state your reservations.

S—: About RC?

Harvey: About putting medicine and RC together.

*S—: Well, I can't afford the time out of the library.
(Laughter) But I never go to the library anyway, because it's
too distressing. (more laughter) It's true. I never go! Unless I
might kinda look like I'm going, but I never go in there. I just
get a candy bar.*

Harvey: Any other reservations?

*S—: It's not real. It's not really going to help me. What's
really going to help me is medical facts. I mean when the
chips are down they're going to say, "Well, what was in the
annals last month?" (Laughter, agreement from other partic-
ipants.) They're not going to say, "How are your distress
levels?" So, you know, that's finally going to be it, "You
didn't read the annals, Dr. S—, you don't belong here!" I've
never really read them! (All laugh long and hard.) The only
thing I know is what color they are. That's real important.
You've got to be able to say the green. If you just say "the
annals," they know you don't know them well enough to
know what color they are, because you never took them out
of their wrapper.*

Harvey: Keep talking.

*S—: Those are my biggest reservations. And we were talk-
ing today about journal club! All the times I've been to journal club I wanted to say, "Listen! I didn't understand this article; I couldn't read the first sentence. The words all blurred*

Transcript of a demonstration at the RC physicians' workshop, October
1983. Appeared in **Well-Being** No. 5, 1989.

together. That's as far as I got. I don't even know the title! I'm going to talk to you today about something more important." Those are my big reservations.

Harvey: Go ahead, "I'm gonna talk to you today about something more important."

S—: What shall I talk about? What do you want me to talk about?

Harvey: Something that's more important.

S—: More important? You mean RC?

Harvey: I don't know.

S—: Well, the weird thing is that it's like you're on this precipice, because you sort of know that there's probably something more important than the annals last month, but it's too frightening. It's like taking on everybody. It's like those white coats, those groups of stones over there. A rock pile that makes you think they know! It's like they know, and you don't know enough. I always used to think that was just how the women felt in this, but it's everybody. So you feel that you don't know enough and that somehow they know more; the reason they know more is because they read those stupid journals! And I couldn't read them because they're too distressing! Even if I want to read them, I can't read them. It's almost like I'm in this box. So first I think, "Hey, the reason I'm going to use RC is so I can read those journals." (All laugh.) That's going to be the key; that's what I'm going to use RC for; I'm going right to the top. But I don't want to be there. See, that's the other thing. I don't want to be like them. And yet I want to be like them so I can not be like them. That's the contradiction.

Harvey: Keep talking.

S—: It's like I want to be like them so I can say, "Hey, you guys are acting weird. And I'm just like you so I can say it." But you can't be both. That's the other thing: you can't be both. If you dedicate your life to being like them, your life will be full of distress and unhappiness. I'm convinced of it. I don't want to do that. But if you're not like them then you have to be as powerful as they are, and that's hard.

Harvey: Aaaaah! Ah ha ha ha! (and S— joining almost immediately with him.)

S—: So you have to be equally or more powerful than they are.

Harvey: Uh huh.

S—: That's tough. That's risky.

Harvey: So?

S—: Sure, we'll take a chance at it.

Harvey: (deep, relaxed voice) From this monent on, the *real S—.*

S—: From this moment on, heh heh, the real S—.

Harvey: No, you had a tentative ending there. (In deep voice.) The real S—.

S—: From this moment on, the real S—.

Harvey: Which means.

S—: Which means, heh heh heh.

Harvey: Say every thought.

S—: Uh, a lot of personal power. Good patient care in the face of not having read the journals! (All join her laughing.) Um, being able to read the journals. That'd be real nice, having that information. I mean, I'd like to be able to read a journal like I read a cookbook. You know?

Harvey: Sure.

S—: Or I'd like to do medicine like I run. This is fun. Gosh, it doesn't matter how far I'm going. This feels really great. That's the other big conflict. Is medicine real interesting? The information is fascinating. Everybody here would say that. It could be so much fun!

Harvey: Mm hmm.

S—: We could say, "Gosh, you've got a problem here. I'm not really sure how to solve it, but let's just think about it." If all that was acceptable it'd be fascinating. (Yawns and sighs from the group.)

Harvey: We're reaching people. I hear yawns already. Keep going.

S—: It would be fascinating! Because the problems are wonderful. Everybody here would say that. We do the work despite the horrible distress of it. We still try to get some pleasure out of it. But it would be wonderful to say, "Gee, we had this problem so we all got together and we weren't sure about it so we looked some stuff up." I mean looking stuff up?! Without distress? That would be wonderful.

So you have to include in that: the real S— really likes medicine. And does it with a certain ease. The amazing thing about it is this sort of ease, but she's also real good.

Harvey: Good. Well, I think she's got it, don't you?

S—: That's because we're not at the hospital.

Harvey: We'll get our steam up here and take the hospital with us when we come back.

S—: One thing that's real important is to see that information as helpful, not so charged. I mean the medical journal is something that might have something that interests you. If it doesn't, that's real nice. And if it does, you could be able to read it. That would be wonderful, to be able to sit down and say, "Gosh, I always wondered about that. Guess I'll just take a look at this article." And not think, "Oh my God, how many pages is this article?" You know, I don't think I could even get through the abstracts!

Harvey: I think we're finding our spokesperson. Keep talking.

*S—: That's because I know about these distress patterns with medicine. I have all these journals stacked up. I was thinking of cancelling my subscription to **The New England Journal of Medicine**. (All laugh) Listen to that! I'm cancelling my subscription to **The New England Journal**!*

Other workshop participant: That's going all the way.

S—: It's cluttering up my kitchen! I don't have enough room for my recipe cards! I want that journal out. If I want to read it, I'll read it in the library. I have the power to cancel *this subscription! I don't want it, and I don't want any lifetime subscription either, even if it is only $500! What a bargain that is, only $500 for a lifetime of distress. (All laugh long and hard.) That is a real bargain. Every week! I think if we all got together and cancelled our subscriptions they'd get the message that we don't like their journal. It's like the emperor's new clothes, finally somebody says, "Hey! I don't like this journal!"*

So the real S— could read about medicine without distress. That would be great, because it's fascinating. Health care's fascinating. Why does it have to be so painful?

Harvey: That's a good question. Do you think it does?

S—: Well, I guess it doesn't.

Harvey: As a consumer I'll support you for it.

S—: Yeah, well, yeah. Consumers would probably get better care. I mean it would it be nice to be treated by a physician that wasn't distressed. (All laugh.) What would that be like? What would that be like?

Harvey: (Carefree) From this moment on, the real S—.

S—: From this moment on, the real S—. The real S— is really personally powerful in medicine. Reads journals with ease. Never goes to the library and doesn't really care much about it either.

Harvey: Go on.

S—: She really loves medicine, and also does a lot of other things.

Harvey: Yes?

S—: Like RC and sports and swimming.

Harvey: Enterprise S— going where no humans have ever gone before. (Laughter)

S—: Singlehandedly in the face of distress. Among the senior physicians, all taller than she is and male, and who don't even recognize her as a person or a woman. She takes over! Seizes the microphone during grand rounds. (Shrieking laughter from all.) I couldn't really do any of this. Could you

*imagine me getting up in grand rounds? "Oh! This is Dr.
S—. I just wanted to seize the microphone. I'm awfully
sorry." Heh, I'm really no good at this. It could set RC back
for years.*

Harvey: (high voice, somewhat timidly) This is S— and I'm
tired of listening to you old fogies. And I just cancelled my
subscription. (All laugh.)

*S—: That's my other fantasy: for a woman physician to
say, "This has been real interesting, but we're going shopping." (All laugh.) "We need new shoes." I can't really do
any of this though.*

Harvey: Of course you can.

S—: I can?

Harvey: Of course you can.

S—: Tomorrow?

Harvey: Why not?

S—: Yeah, that's true, why not?

Harvey: There has to be some turning point, some decisive
turning point.

S—: Yeah.

Harvey: Someone has to say, "No" at some point.

*S—: Well, you know, I was talking about the fantasy of
women saying I'm going out shopping. But then I imagine
another beyond that where the women say, "We're just going
to stay late tonight and work on these cases because we really
love this." It'd be wonderful to move past the defiance.*

Harvey: Be my guest.

*S—: Hah hah. Past the defiance and distress into, "We
love this and we're here and talking about cases." I mean all
of us have put so many years into this and....*

Harvey: Tears are all right.

*S—: And we love this stuff. I mean not just the women, the
men, as well. We love this stuff. And it'd be wonderful to
say, "Yeah, we're gonna stay here, and there's no place else*

we'd rather be but here in this room talking about our patients." I don't like to emphasize the alienation too much. I feel it and it scares me that I feel it, because it makes me forget I love medicine.

Harvey: The real S—, getting the defiance out of her system.

S—: Yeah, I mean the real S— stays after work with the other people and talks about the difficult patients. And finds out solutions for them. Or goes to the bedside. With them.

Harvey: (Quietly) And asks the patient how to do it.

S—: Yeah, "Why do you think you're sick?" I ask my patients that a lot: "Why do you think you have this problem?" Some people handle it well, other people don't. (All laugh.) Some people decide to see another doctor. Yeah, why do you think? That's a good question, actually. Alienation scares me because it's so powerful for me. And it's such a painful thing. I spent so many years hating, I mean I spent all of medical school hating those people....

Harvey: And look how few minutes it took you to move past it.

S—: Well, yeah.

Harvey: We'll go back and clean up some more.

S—: I'd like to move past it.

Harvey: Good! the real S—.

S—: The real S— loves medicine. And stays after work. The real S— loves to go to work and share the information with the people she works with. The real S— works with a group of people who all consider themselves equal and wonderful. And takes care of people who happen to be sick. She just has a great time, and would never want to be anyplace else when she's at work. Never thinks, "I gotta get outa this place!" (All laugh.) Maybe thinks that occasionally, and then can go.

Harvey: Takes time when she needs it.

S—: Yeah, takes time when she needs it. And gets support

for difficult situations, personally and professionally, from the people she works with. And gives support equally. That's what I imagine it to be. That would be so wonderful.

Harvey: It would. I think this is a historical occasion. Can you talk about it some more?

S—: Let's see. I just keep saying the alienation is scary to me, because I don't want to go on being alienated, to the point of saying I'm going to give up this career. Am I going to give up fifteen years of my life of incredible determination? Why can't I be a great doctor? (sigh) I can be.

Harvey: You are.

S—: I am. I'm a great doctor. Heh heh. I'm the best doctor in the world! Hah hah hah. I am so good. Hah hah hah.

Harvey: You're the most impressive I've met.

S—: I know all the electron miscroscopy patterns of every real disease there ever was. (All laugh.) But that's not what it takes. At least I can't do it. If you're going to ask me about glomerular entritus right now, I'm sorry, because I don't know it. Does everybody know it but me? I don't know it. Maybe it's okay not to know it. If you took all the time you were distressed and you turned it into constructive time, you would be a better doctor. I'm not sure that would mean you'd have to memorize all the facts. See I think I'm really smart, and if I didn't have distress then I could be smarter. That doesn't necessarily mean knowing facts, but I could be smarter. And then my life could be better; I could be a better doctor.

Harvey: The real S—.

S—: The real S— is not distressed at work. She's personally powerful, and works with a group of people who are equal in ability. And they're supportive of her and she's supportive of them. And they solve amazing problems. And have a great time doing it. And they laugh. They laugh. They say, "Oh look at this problem, this is just great! This is another chance to solve a difficult problem. And there's feeling issues involved? Wonderful! Oh boy! Great! Send 'em in; we'll help them!" "Oh good. I love this! Isn't this great? Aren't we glad we went to medical school? It's wonderful." That's what I imagine it to be. Great! Good! Oh boy, what'll happen tomorrow?! Can't wait. That's what I imagine it to be.

Harvey: This is perfectly realizable.

S—: (sigh) Yeah. (tentative)

Harvey: Nothing but a little old powerlessness distress, and you've already got that marked.

S—: Yeah. It's real scary. I keep thinking I can't, you know I say these things here; I say a few of these things at work. But it's the daredevil; I come across as a daredevil. It's like me coming up and going, to this giant thing, this monster and going weak and then running away. Coming out again and going "ledleleldl" (wagging tongue). (All laugh.) Then running back in my cave, right? Throwing out a few New England journals. But I really want to do it. That's the real thing. So you feel like you can't be alienated and love it at the same time.

Harvey: But you have to express it and discharge it. Tell them where you're going at the same time.

S—: Yeah. It's real scary. I could sit and make cracks about medicine forever, but that's painful too, because finally I love it. And you say "I can't stay like this forever, because it's interfering with my work."

Harvey: I defy your rotten old system, and I'm gonna clean it up.

S—: Uhh, I defy your old rotten system, and I'm gonna clean it up and make it into our system.

Harvey: Just a little fear to discharge.

S—: Yeah, a lot.

Harvey: A little. Get outside it and it comes off as you walk.

The Improvement of Counseling

A Fourth Point

Clarifying the "Three Things Which a Counselor Needs to Do to Help the Client Discharge" has led to a major improvement in the general level of counseling everywhere. These have been stated as:

1. Pay enough attention to the client to see clearly what the distress is.
2. Think of all possible ways to contradict the distress.
3. Contradict the distress sufficiently. The client will always discharge.

Examining the *very best* counseling we see taking place and reviewing some discussion (particularly at the July meeting of Regional Reference Persons and International Liberation Reference Persons) have led to the conclusion that a *fourth point* should probably be added, preceding the other three, but not weakening their importance at all.

I propose that we call this point POINT 0 (borrowing computer practice) so that the list would now read:

FOUR THINGS A COUNSELOR NEEDS TO DO TO HELP THE CLIENT RE-EMERGE

0. **Review the counselor's goal as seeing to it that the client re-emerges decisively, remembering that the client is inherently a person of great intelligence, value, decisiveness, and power as well as needing assistance with emergence from distress, and, in particular, noticing and re-**

Appeared in **Present Time** No. 69, October 1987.

membering where this particular client is capable, treasurable, and already functioning, or close to functioning, elegantly and well.

1. Pay enough attention to the client to see clearly what the distress is.
2. Think of all possible ways to contradict the distress.
3. Contradict the distress sufficiently. The client will always discharge.

Efficient Co-Counseling

I want to talk this morning about *efficient* Co-Counseling. There is a wide variation in efficiency. There are Co-Counseling sessions that are a little negative. They should never have happened to anybody. The variation moves through Co-Counseling sessions that have had only the slightest effect in any way at all, to those that have been a little helpful, then those that have been more helpful. Every once in a while, we have a session that is absolutely decisive, where client and counselor are working together well and decisive changes are happening.

I don't think we've put enough aware thought into what the difference between sessions is, what makes the difference. I would like us to start thinking very rigorously about this job of ours, the job of Co-Counselor.

The analogy I think of is the work of professional golfers. Golf is a little calmer than some games. If you have watched a professional golf tournament on television, you know they are fun to watch because these men or women esteem themselves as professionals or "pros." What being a "pro" means to them is not just that they make a living at golf, which is one meaning of the word, but that they set themselves and work hard toward the goal of doing their very best at all times. They set out to make every game the best game that's

From the Teachers' and Leaders' Workshop, Santa Cruz, California, USA, August 1987. Appeared in **Present Time** No. 70, January 1988.

ever been played. They try for excellence in everything they do. Every drive, every chip, every putt is calculated to be just as good as it can be done. I think this is why great crowds of people come out to watch them. This is why you and I watch them on television. There is something inspiring about people reaching for excellence, trying to reach the ultimate.

I think we need to apply this attitude to our Co-Counseling. In a recent article in **Present Time**, "Who is in Charge of the Session?" I tried to summarize what I'd been able to think about the roles of people in their sessions.

In the article I point out that there are two completely distinct roles in a Co-Counseling session. One is the role of the counselor, and the counselor is in charge of everything in that role, and there's a good deal to it. The other role is that of the client, and the client is in charge of that. In a symphony orchestra there's one person who sets the beat. If everybody sets their own beat, we'd have a mess. The director is in charge of conducting or directing. The player who is the concertmaster is in charge of making that lead fiddle sing and nobody else is going to do that for him. He's in charge of that part of the performance. There are many different roles, and when a hundred players are all doing their roles well together in a symphony orchestra, you get a glimpse of what tremendous cooperation human minds are capable of.

The counseling session usually involves just two people; but it is an exquisitely delicate and complex inter-relationship, one of the most complex inter-relationships that human beings have. The relationships in a symphony orchestra are wonderful. If any of you have ever played in one, you know how great it is to be in the middle of the orchestra, contribute your part, and hear 99 other people contributing their parts, all just right. Boy! Because we're dealing with the inherently confusing situation of combatting patterns, the complexity of a Co-Counseling session is at least as great. It's more demanding of excellent thinking from both parties than one can easily imagine. Of course it's also enormously important. If a pro golfer sinks his putt he may win $120,000, but *we* Co-Counselors, if we sink our putts, people have their lives back, the only lives they'll ever have, which will otherwise be spent completely under the lid of patterns.

The significance of what we're doing is enormous. We're trained not to think of ourselves as significant, we don't think of our work as significant, but that's just patterns. The actual significance of this effort we make is huge! It may determine whether evolution has to start over after three and a half billion years.

What does the counselor's role consist of? Well, it consists, in part, of remembering important information. What's some of this important information? That every client is a tremendously intelligent person, every client in his or her essential nature is as good as the most holy saint that ever sainted. Every client is tremendously creative. Every client is whole and intact, underneath the scar tissue of the patterns. The client's intelligence has been occluded, not replaced by the patterns. The patterns only cover it. Is it important that the counselor remember that? I think so. You're not going to have a bold enough and clear enough attitude toward the Co-Counseling session if you don't have these factors clear in your mind. The client will find it very difficult to remember that because the minute the client tackles the pattern, the pattern is screaming loudly. The client can't remember which way is up, remember his or her own name, or much else. The pattern is screaming in the client's inner ear, "You're dirty and evil and vile." You can't expect the client, in the midst of that hubbub, to remember that he or she is a *wonderful* person with tremendous integrity and intelligence. No. That's the counselor's job to remember that. To remember it under all conditions.

Here is the client, this god-like person with this marvelous intelligence still intact, with this tremendous goodness, this tremendous desire to be human and good and cooperative and all the rest, who is covered with a writhing mass of fungoid patterns, which purport to be him or her—patterns that are evil, stupid, destructive, uncomfortable, nonsensical, tricky around the edges. This patterned mass has not much flexibility. Though the client is actually intact in all these fine ways, functionally the client is like someone whose back has been broken and whose one arm is dangling, whose mouth is wound around with barbed wire so that it can't speak when it wants, has a bear trap on every foot and a strait-jacket around himself or herself. In terms of the inhibitions and difficulties that the client has to contend with, they're that handicapped, at the same time that they are persons of god-like power and persistence. If the counselor doesn't have that picture clear in his or her mind, the job is going to fall short of what needs to be done.

You, as counselor, may think, Okay, I'll remember that this is a god-like, wonderful person and you say, "Try this phrase, please." And the god-like, wonderful person says, "Mmm-mmm, I can't mmmmmm." And you say, "Heck, god-like person, get on the stick and try it." Now sometimes that will work, but very rarely, because there is an invisible, patterned gag that has got the client so blocked so that he or she can't say the phrase and it's tied down with a knot that the client cannot reach. The client can't reach to untie it, but the counselor looks carefully, sees the knot, and says, "I see why you can't talk," slips the knot loose and says to the client, "You're free."

The counselor needs to remember all about counseling theory—have it all available. I just reviewed a couple of pieces. Another is, it's good to discharge thoroughly. That's so simple, but how many counselors forget that and eagerly settle for the client stopping discharge: "Whew, well, we got a little off, shall we quit?" And the client always says, "Yeah, yeah." Inside their "thought" was "I almost felt this extreme discomfort, let's quit. I'm used to having barbed wire around my mouth and a bear trap on each foot. I just want to get home and rest." The client can't usually tell you that they really want to keep going. If you let them rest for three minutes, they may say, "What should we try next?", signaling to you in the only way they can, "Let's get back and finish the discharge."

The counselor needs to have all the main tenets of Re-evaluation Counseling theory, the main information that we've dug out from under the occluding distress and oppression right there and clear in mind. One piece of information that the counselor needs to be very, very clear on: *there's only one client in the session.* This is more violated than anything else because of the "ancient habit pattern." The client says it was my Aunt Beulah and the counselor thinks, "It was *my* Aunt Tillie. I remember my Aunt Tillie did something almost similar like that..." and goes drifting away into clienting, violating the basic function of the session. Is that just something that happens very rarely and is amusing because of its rarity? Up until now, I would say at least 95% of all sessions have been seriously contaminated by the counselor drifting off into their paying attention to the counselor's own distress. Is there a means of combatting it? Yes. Will making the decision at the beginning of the session, "I will only pay attention to my client," help? Yes. It'll help, but it'll help a lot more to have a few sessions making the formal decision against the ancient habit pattern: "It is logically possible and certainly desirable to end this ancient habit pattern of paying attention to my old distress all the time and substitute for it a new, more effective posture or attitude of paying attention to interesting concerns *such as my client, when I am counselor.*" As you respect that, the role of the repetitive decision becomes clear. You become better and better the more you work at it. It's slow. We'd like to make a decisive breakthrough, but decisive breakthroughs always occur after a series of small gains. That's the nature of the universe. Qualitative, abrupt changes always alternate with a series of small quantitative changes.

If you come to the session as a client, what's your responsibility? Well, your responsibility is to discharge. Those of you who were here earlier when I was working with E— noticed that, in effect, I scolded E—. (I hope she'll take it kindly.) I scolded her because she was rehearsing certain patterns that she has fallen into, patterns which she shares with many clients, of getting discharge started and then immediately allowing the pattern to take her off to something else instead of recognizing from long experience, "Ah ha, I've discharged there, I'll come back to it, I'll come back to it, I'll come back to it." Can you do this as a client against the pull of the patterns to change the subject? Yes. I know some clients who do just this. Ahead of time, they may be at a loss as to what's going to bring discharge, but they have disciplined themselves so that when they hit discharge, they bring themselves back to it, back to it, back to it. They'll say to the counselor, "Don't let me get away from that." They add a little bit to the persistence role of the counselor and prop him up.

Is it your responsibility as client to plan your session ahead of time? Yes. It may go completely different than you've planned it, but if you don't have a plan then the random character of patterns and restimulations will come in and try to take the session over. Is it your business as client to remember what needs to be remembered about your progress as a client? Yes. Can you do it just by deciding to remember? No, not usually, because patterns have this extraordinary ability to make us forget. Patterns have three pseudo-abilities. One of them is to make you forget, make you forget, make you forget. So, you have to write yourself notes. You have to remember to bring your notebook along. You have to tie a string on your arm and tie it to your notebook, do whatever you have to do. If you have to write it in shaving foam on your vanity table mirror or write it in lipstick on your shaving mirror, do it. Send signals to yourself. You have to give your counselor a list of things you have thought of and would like to take up. You have to organize yourself. Is this easy, in terms of resisting patterns? I don't think so. All of us are pulled to drift into a session and say, "Make me well, counselor.'' Does that work very well? Nope. Can a session work lots, lots better if you plan it? Yes. I'm not just speculating. People have done enough of this that it's been proven to have good results.

I would like this workshop to become a center of infection for highly organized, completely responsible playing the role of client and playing the role of counselor. I would like you to infect every Co-Counselor that you know after you leave this workshop. Let your example and your little preachings that you throw in casually begin to spread this. I'll keep doing it; I did it all through England, not as much as I'm going to here and I'll do it at Las Cruces in a couple of weeks, and I'll do it in Philadelphia. But I would like this Community to be the focal point. After all, Santa Cruz has advantages that no other Community in the world has. Where is there a more relaxed, yet not quite decadent, style than in Santa Cruz? I love to come to Santa Cruz. I get a taste of elegant, carefree living without being corroded.

What's the client's responsibility? To be on time for a session or, if late, to apologize and offer to shorten the session. Something like that. To think about the counselor. To think about the counselor as client? No, that's a different business. If you're Co-Counseling, sure, you think about the counselor as client when you hear she is a client. But, when you are client, you think about your counselor in terms of what are the weaknesses and the difficulties of this *counselor*? This one has some kind of horror of sex that gets telegraphed in all kinds of ways and even though I'm just wild to get to my earliest sexual memories, I don't think I'd better do it with this one, not today. I'm going to take up my lofty goals for my life with this one, because he gets inspired by that and he'll be very enthusiastic and with me. I'll use the session effectively. I'll work on that earliest sexual memory with Fleetybelle. She never gets upset.

I'm trying to be a little humorous here, but the message is

serious. Plan how to use the counselor. Don't shove distress at him that's going to dismay him and give you another bad session, in which counseling didn't work.

Question: So you're saying to do that? Recognize what your counselor can handle well and go for that distress?

Harvey: Go for that. Make your sessions efficient. It will be good for you and it will be good for the counselor.

In your workbook are some suggestions. I think that each of you needs to keep a notebook, a very careful notebook from now on. One notebook as client and one as counselor. Keep all kinds of details. Maybe you can have two sections in the same notebook. I won't tell you how you should do it, exactly. You have to figure that out. But I think that you need one, because of the three pseudo-abilities of a pattern, that it can persist, it can confuse you, and it can make you forget. All of these pseudo-abilities can be combatted by the use of the written word, by clearly written out instructions and directions and information. I think you should keep these notebooks as part of your being in Co-Counseling.

They should be separate notebooks or separate sections. Don't confuse the two and say, "As the client blah-blah and as the counselor also blah-blah." Make them completely separate sections of a notebook, if not completely separate notebooks. Put some time in on them. The textbook that will teach you how to be a good counselor is the one you write yourself. You may quote what I've written or what anyone else has written. There's lots of good texts around, but the one you take to heart and put down because it is pertinent for *you*, that's the one that will do the job.

I have made some notes on these sheets in your workbook. The first page says, "My program as client," and I've left spaces under each heading. "Directions that have worked well for me." Now, what are the directions that have worked well for me? Well, I've got a whole history of ones that have worked well. The first one I remember is, "All is well." I don't think any of you are old enough in counseling to remember when I came up with that, but it served me (and others) well. "All is well." It led to the concept of the benign reality and then to various other breakthroughs. "All is well." It really is. The universe is progressing in just the way that it needs to progress. This lovely planet that I'm sitting on is turning at just the right speed. Sun rise, sun set. Tide in, tide out. All is well. I can look across there and see A— and know that A—'s mind is in contact with mine. What could be finer? If we ever get a chance to explore, A—'s mind and mine are going to have a ball together. All is well. Emerson came close to this in one of his poems. He said he was discouraged because a seashell that had looked so pretty on the beach didn't look so pretty on the mantel and he brought a bird home and it didn't sing, so, "Then I said, I covet truth, beauty is unripe childhood's cheat. I leave it behind with the dreams of my youth; but as I spoke, beneath my feet the ground pine curled its pretty wreath creeping over the moss and burrs. Around me stood the oaks and firs. Over me stretched the boundless sky, full of light and of deity. Again I saw, again I heard the rolling river, the morning bird. Beauty through all my senses stole. I yielded myself to the perfect whole." If you once start noticing goodness, what a lovely existence we have, what tremendous good fortune it is to have existed, to have been alive, to have been intelligent, to have been occasionally aware. Good fortune surrounds me.

So, if I'm preparing my client notebook, I write down, "All is well." It's the earliest one I can remember. What's the latest one? "I will care about myself first, not against the interests of other people, but in order that I can care about other people well, too. I will never again leave myself out of the picture." I've got a whole lot of others in between, when I write up my notebook.

So, all directions that have worked well for you, write them all down. Write these truths in block letters that are easy to read.

Heading, personal commitments: I have a personal commitment that I've worked on. I haven't been keeping it well, but the response to that is to keep it, not to be dismayed and give up on it. My commitment is to eat only one meal a day at bedtime. Haaard! Haaard! Haaard! But I'd better have it down there in black and white, or I'll start eating too much.

Commitments against my internalized oppressions: Here comes a whole battery. What are my commitments against internalized oppression? Well, the men's commitment. You heard me do it last night. You could tell it moved me, couldn't you? "I'm all man and I've never doubted it." It's great. I'm working-class. "I am a worker, proud to be a worker, and the future is in my hands." What others? Well, I don't have a commitment as a Native person yet. Maybe we ought to work one out. I haven't yet really practiced what I've preached, which is, "Whatever mixed heritage you have, claim every part of that heritage as all yours." I haven't done this. I haven't yet said, "I'm one hundred percent Penobscot." But I have said, "I'm a hundred percent Norwegian, a hundred percent French, a hundred percent Scottish, a hundred percent English, a hundred percent Irish." And I now claim I'm a hundred percent Penobscot. You and I ought to work out a good Native commitment when we can. All the places where you are. Can I use the women's commitment? Sure I can. "Never again settle for anything less than absolutely everything. Hah, hah, hah, hah." Does that hurt a man? No. Women have been forced to settle down here; men have been forced to settle here. That little difference because of the sexist oppression. The sky is there and that cracked blue plaster ceiling is not the sky. Can I as a man use the young people's commitment? Sure. Drop the word "young" off, or remember that I really think I'm fifteen years old inside. Either way it works. "Never again treat any person with anything less than complete respect." All of them are available. Do I need to have them written in my notebook? Yes, because some days I have trouble remembering my own name. The frontier commitments—the ones we've been working on. The only one we haven't taken a shot at is, "From now on I will inspire, lead, and organize all people to eliminate every form of humans harming humans."

Chronic patterns I am aware of: How can you figure out your own chronic patterns? Fairly easily. Look back at the end of the day at what you did that day that you wish you hadn't. There are your chronic patterns, pulsating, fluorescent. Write down what it was and then ask, "What would be the exact opposite of that?" You can come up with a contradiction. Ask your counselors, "What are my chronic patterns that I should be aware of?" They'll tell you.

Major incidents in my life: What happened in my life? I was born. My brother was killed. I lost my home. I had severe illnesses. I became a journeyman cowboy. I escaped to the university. I found Marxism and the international labor movement. I went through some fierce struggles. I found RC. RC survived. Many people started doing it. Many major incidents, a long life. Talking about any one of them with a good counselor, I'd discharge.

The things that my counselors have done that work well for me as a client: Thought about me, thought about me, thought about me. I can think of some other things, too.

Next, a direction to myself: I will try each suggested direction four times before I argue with it or decide that it is in error. Underline that one, all of you, because it is one weakness in your clienting that I find when I work with you, is that I come up with a brilliant direction, or at least a possibly brilliant one, and you say, "But I don't happen to feel that way." You rehearse your pattern that the direction is intended to contradict. You rehearse the pattern instead of using the direction.

Then again, "I will think about each counselor ahead of the session and plan to work only on material I think that particular counselor can handle." We already talked about that one.

I'll be on time for sessions because it's respectful of the counselor. I will act like a client only in the times that my counselor has agreed to be my counselor. I will express appreciation for each session, no matter how I am feeling at that time. If I'm feeling that was the lousiest session I ever had, I will nevertheless express appreciation, because I know that complaining doesn't work to improve counseling.

Songs that have brought discharge in the past: (Sings "I Love You Truly.") I remember when they first put Toselli's Serenade on our stands in the symphony orchestra I was playing in. I looked at it. I had three notes to play in the middle and I had to count 527 measures on either side. I thought, "Oh God, how awful" and the instruments that were playing took up the melody and then the melody just drifted into my soul, the sweetest melody I've ever heard. (Sings.)

Poems that have brought discharge in the past: That happens to be my specialty. I know about 3,000 poems. (Recites several.)

The three most satisfying validations I can ever remember receiving: I don't know, I haven't got them up there, but just trying to think of them I can feel some tears starting to come.

The concept that's more horrifying to me than any other: Now, these ones of mine aren't yours. You figure out your own notebook. The one that's the most horrifying to me? The idea of "evil intelligence." It was the greatest relief to me when I finally figured out, after counseling, that there could not be such a thing as evil intelligence, that there can only be a recorded pattern. The idea was with me all through my childhood, however, and it's still the most horrifying idea I can imagine.

The notion that angers me more than any other: The abuse or neglect of a helpless person, when somebody, just by taking a little trouble, could stop and help him as they go by. When I see a client in the Community who is just sitting trapped with their distress just sticking out begging for contradiction and all the Co-Counselors around them are treating them unawarely and paying no attention, I get filled with rage inside. I want to take some of the Co-Counselors' heads and just bang them together and make them look. Just a little bit of attention and caring could help this person have a good life. That angers me. This is my own notebook. It won't be yours.

I can ask my counselor to: (1) Stand guard for me while I rest. This is a recent discovery, extremely important, "standing guard."

(2) Say things to me that I need to hear. If the counselor can't be creative, at least he or she can be repetitive. Sometimes when I have badly needed to sleep and have been going way too long hours in this rushing life, I'll say, "Sit down beside me and tell me you love me, just that and say it over and over again." Sometimes they'll say, "I love you. I love you. What do you *really* need?" And I have to start over. I can go to sleep if somebody is committed to saying that. It means they're not going to say something that I have got to stay awake to guard myself against and I can go to sleep.

(3) Allow me to sleep if I'm tired.

(4) Remember that the session is completely confidential and confidentiality is not to be breached by talking about my material in his or her own sessions. This is a loathsome practice in the Communities: "Confidentiality, oh yes, of course, confidentiality, but I got so upset by what I heard in my last session I have to talk to somebody. Will you listen to me about it? Blah, blah, blah." It's a complete breach of confidentiality. All you need to say if you're upset is, "Something I heard upset me." You don't need to gossip. Anybody that's

going to counsel me, I'm going to have this clear.

The following are my best regular counselors. Fleetybelle, her strength is she's graceful. Her weakness is that her mind wanders. Georgie-porgie, his strength is that he really wants to do the right thing. He wants to. His weakness is that he doesn't know what the right thing is. Make a long list.

Then I have a last note: Decision can precede discharge and generally both living and discharge go better if it does. It's an important reminder to me as a client.

Now that's just what I was able to put together quickly, but you can put in the rest of your life working out a good client's notebook. Keep improving it. Check with others. Share your notebook with each other and come up with this guide to being a successful, rapidly re-emerging client. Put gold lettering on the cover.

Then my program as a counselor. Here's the second notebook.

Some notes—and again you can write better ones. This is just to give you some kind of notion.

My attention belongs completely on the client when I am the counselor. My thinking is about and for the client and not for myself. When I am counselor I have no distresses of my own. How would you like it if all your counselors repeated that five times before they came to the session?

Second paragraph: It is at least twenty times easier for me to think of good contradictions to the client's distresses, than it is for the client to do so. Write this in letters of fire. You have this enormous ability to be outside the distress, to be effective. If you don't use it, what are you pretending to be counselor for?

When I am a counselor, I am striving for complete excellence in the job I do, seeking to make each particular session the best session that ever occurred. That's what a "pro" does. In each game he plays, he tries to make it the best game he ever played. You try to make it the best session that anyone ever had.

Warm-up exercises: Giving up the ancient habit pattern is the first paragraph. The commitment against identifying with the distress is the second paragraph. No recording of past distress has any power at all.... This is another commitment, the third one, "I'll see to it that everything I am in contact with, including the session of my Co-Counselor, works well."

Then I've listed the basic notions: The job of the counselor is to (0) Review the counselor's goal as seeing to it that the client re-emerges decisively, remembering that the client is inherently a person of great intelligence, value, decisiveness, and power as well as needing assistance with emergence from distress, and, in particular, noticing and remembering where this particular client is capable, treasurable, and already functioning, or close to functioning, elegantly and well. (1) Pay enough attention to the client to see clearly what the distress is. (2) Think of all possible ways to contradict the distress. (3) Contradict the distress sufficiently. The client will always discharge.

Some other paragraphs: The client is always eager and almost always able to tell me or show me exactly what the distresses are.

Okay, do you get the picture? Keep these notebooks. Besides these exciting ideas, there are things that *you* plan. You plan your re-emergence as a client; you plan your counseling of your fellow re-emergians.

My Program As Client

Directions that have worked well for me:

Personal commitments:

Commitments against my internalized oppressions:

Frontier commitments:

Chronic patterns I am aware of:

Best contradictions to the above:

Major incidents in my life:

The things my counselors have done that worked the best for me:

I will try each suggested direction four times before I argue with it or decide that it is in error.

I will think about each counselor ahead of the session and plan to work only on material that I think the particular counselor can handle.

I will be on time for a session, be pleasant to the counselor, act like a client only in the times the counselor has agreed to be my counselor, and will express appreciation for each session no matter how I'm feeling at the time.

Songs that have brought discharge in the past:

Music that has brought discharge in the past:

Poems that have brought discharge in the past:

The three most satisfying validations I can ever remember receiving:

The concept that seems more horrifying to me than any other:

The notion that angers me more than any other:

I can ask my counselor to:
1) stand guard for me while I rest;
2) say things to me that I need to hear;
3) allow me to sleep if I am tired;
4) remember that the session is completely confidential, and confidentiality is not to be breached by talking about my material in his/her own sessions.

The following are my best regular counselors:

   1) _____
     strengths:
     weaknesses:

   2) _____
     strengths:
     weaknesses:

   3) _____
     strengths:
     weaknesses:

   4) _____
     strengths:
     weaknesses:

DECISION CAN PRECEDE DISCHARGE, AND GENERALLY BOTH LIVING AND DISCHARGE GO BETTER IF IT DOES.

My Program As Counselor

MY ATTENTION BELONGS COMPLETELY ON THE CLIENT WHEN I AM THE COUNSELOR. MY THINKING IS ABOUT AND FOR THE CLIENT, NOT MYSELF. WHEN I AM COUNSELOR, I HAVE NO DISTRESSES OF MY OWN.

IT IS AT LEAST 20 TIMES EASIER FOR ME TO SEE GOOD CONTRADICTIONS TO THE CLIENT'S DISTRESSES THAN IT IS FOR THE CLIENT TO DO SO.

WHEN I AM A COUNSELOR, I AM A "PRO" STRIVING FOR COMPLETE EXCELLENCE IN THE KIND OF JOB I DO, SEEKING TO MAKE EACH PARTICULAR SESSION THE BEST SESSION THAT EVER OCCURRED.

Warm-up Exercises:

It is logically possible and certainly desirable to end the ancient habit pattern of keeping attention on my own old distresses all the time (especially when I've agreed to be counselor) and so I now decide and will in the future decide repeatedly to keep my attention on interesting and profitable concerns such as present time and the skillfully-assisted re-emergence of my client.

No recording of past distress has any power of its own at all; therefore I now decide to deny past distress any credibility in the present or any influence or operation in my life and will repeat this decision until my life and my functioning as a counselor is completely free from the influence of past distress.

I will see to it that everything I am in contact with (including the session of my client) works well.

The job of counselor is to:

0) review the counselor's goal as seeing to it that the client re-emerges decisively, remembering that the client is inherently a person of great intelligence, value, decisiveness, and power as well as needing assistance with emergence from distress, and, in particular, noticing and remembering where this particular client is capable, treasurable, and already functioning, or close to functioning, elegantly and well;

1) pay enough attention to the client to see clearly what the distresses are;

2) think of all possible ways to contradict the distress;

3) contradict the distress sufficiently. The client will always discharge.

(The client is always eager and almost always able to tell me or show me exactly what the distresses are.)

The client is brilliantly intelligent, completely benign, has complete freedom of choice, and is completely powerful.

The client is also blindfolded, straight-jacketed, confused, enforced, and in agony from old distress recordings that I am easily able to help the client contradict and begin emerging from.

Key information and directions for my regular clients:

    Client 1: _____
        information:
        directions:

    Client 2: _____
        information:
        directions:

Client 3: _____
   information:
   directions:

Client 4: _____
   information:
   directions:

MY ONLY GOAL WHILE COUNSELOR IS THE RAPID, COMPLETE RE-EMERGENCE OF MY CLIENT.

I AM JUST THE INTELLIGENCE MY CLIENT HAS NEEDED TO THINK ABOUT HER OR HIM.

I AM ALWAYS A COMPLETE PRO, WHEN I AM IN THE ROLE OF COUNSELOR.

Keeping the Counselor and Client in Communication with Each Other

We have previously discussed the importance of the counselor keeping his or her attention on the client during a session and have developed theory and practice to enhance this (giving up the "ancient habit," commitments to put full attention on the client, etc.). There has been real improvement in this.

There are still areas for fine-tuning, however. I notice, in certain sessions and with certain clients, that the client has "gone off" by herself or himself and is wrestling with the distress pretty much alone and out of communication with me. I have been, in effect, left "standing by" only, providing safety but nothing else. Perhaps I had earlier helped the client get started repeating a commitment and had been in contact and communication with the client while doing it, but now the client is repeating the commitment by herself or himself, accepting no more participation by me as the counselor than that of being watchman.

I became uneasy about the slowness with which a particular client seemed to be re-emerging. There were tears and shaking to some extent, but also a great deal of "suffering" in the tone of voice and facial expression of the client. When I required the client to keep her eyes open and look *at me* and talk *to me* about the distress there was a dramatic change. Rambling on and on about the gory details of her distress and "suffering" with her eyes closed gave way to laughter. Yawns came very quickly behind the laughter.

Appeared in **Present Time** No. 69, October 1987.

Trying to think about this and to draw some useful conclusions, I've decided (and this perhaps should have been obvious all along) that one requirement of a *good* session is that the client is in communication *with the counselor* and not handling the distress in isolation; that the good sessions, the decisive sessions, that we've had in the past, have been where this condition has been met.

I suggest that you try watching this and see if it makes a difference.

An Initial Marriage Counseling Interview by a Re-evaluation Counselor

—Inge Snipes, in conversations with Harvey Jackins
revised March 22, 1988

(This type of interview, with slight modifications, works well for any pair or group of people in a relationship that has become restimulative and distressing. Married couples with a troubled relationship are a prototype for such difficulties, and the interview structure is here presented for such a couple.)

The counselor asks an agreement by each spouse to abide by three rules:

First, that each spouse agree to speak only to the counselor during the interview and not to the other spouse directly.

Second, that each spouse do his or her best to listen without offense to what the other one says; that each try not to hold anything said against the other person; in other words, that each resist being restimulated as far as possible.

Third, that each spouse make a firm commitment not to discuss out of the interview anything the other spouse says during the interview, neither with each other, nor with any other person, except the counselor. The interview is a privileged conversation and a confidential one for both partners, and is not to be shared with anyone else, nor referred to with each other. Failure to follow this procedure has been found to lead to intense restimulation. The counselor does not proceed with the interview until each has agreed to this last condition.

The counselor then turns his or her attention to and ques-

Appeared in **The RC Teacher** No. 22, 1988.

tions the partner who appears most reluctant to take part in the interview. This is usually both reassuring and disarming to her or him. It results in greater cooperation and openness if the reluctant one is given the counselor's full attention and allowed to speak first.

(If it is a second marriage, ask a few questions about the previous marriage. The roots of the present difficulty may lie there, and this may become apparent as it is talked about.)

The counselor directs a series of questions to the first spouse, explaining that the other spouse will get her (or his) turn later. (The other partner should refrain from commenting on what the first says until that time.)

Ask, "How long did you know (spouse) before you were married?"

Then, "Before you got married, what did you like about her (or him)?" Persist with this, and ask further questions, if necessary, such as "Did you think she was pretty? intelligent? friendly?," etc. until positive attitudes from this earlier period have been expressed.

With this perspective of desirable qualities firmly established, then ask, "If you had had a magic wand (or some other light wording) at that time and could have made some little changes in (your prospective spouse) in order to make her or him perfect, what changes would you have made?" Be sure the answer is in terms of the changes that would have been wished for *before* the marriage and not in view of subsequent events.

Next ask, "How long was it a good marriage from your point of view?"; then "Was sex good for you in the beginning?" The second question may or may not be important, but a couple asking for marriage counseling generally expects to be asked that question, and once the tension about its being asked is gone they can relax about this.

After dealing with this, ask, "What happened when the relationship began to go bad?"

After this is answered, bring the questioning up to the present situation by asking, "What do you like about her or him now?" If there is little or no positive response, say, "Take a fresh look at her or him *now*." Further questions might be, "Is she still pretty? Is he handsome? Is he still a good cook?," etc.

With these answered, ask, "If you had a magic wand and could change some things about her or him now, what would you change?" or "What bothers you about her or him now?"

This is the crucial part of the interview. The answers to these questions reveal the structure of the patterns which have become entangled in the relationship and which need to be discharged. If necessary, take notes on these responses.

Then turn to the other spouse and ask the same questions.

Next, give each spouse a chance to comment on the remarks made by the other, keeping in mind throughout that both parties should continue to address their comments *to the counselor* and not to each other.

In the course of the interview, discharge may occur from either partner. It should be listened to attentively and encouraged. This will help the counselor to spot those patterns which are causing the difficulties in the relationship. It is these patterns in particular which are becoming entangled and which must be worked on to ease the relationship.

Having given the couple a full chance for expression, the counselor might then restate the point of view of Re-evaluation Counseling regarding marriage problems: Both spouses are basically good people. They have acquired rigid patterns of behaving, thinking, and feeling which can become entangled and result in poor relationships. With counseling, these patterns can be eliminated and the relationship improved.

The counselor can point out that theoretically, at least, both partners still love each other, even though it may not feel that way. People never stop loving those they once loved. The love can become hidden by feelings of distress which can be cleared away.

Neither partner can simply walk out of the present relationship without taking along into other relationships the patterns which are spoiling the present relationship. Until they are at least on friendly terms with each other, they will carry their distress with them wherever they go. They need to get free of their distress feelings and they will *then* be able to decide rationally whether the marriage should be continued or terminated.

The counselor should make clear that this decision must be theirs, not the counselor's. When they have discharged some of the tense feelings about each other, they will be in a better position to make the right decision.

Finally, the counselor should make a firm recommendation to both partners regarding next steps. The counselor might recommend one-way counseling at Personal Counselors, Inc. for one or both. She or he might suggest that they join a class or classes. In any case, the counseling directions which contradict the patterns which came to light in the course of the interview should be communicated to the couple and to their counselors or Co-Counselors.

The counselor doing the interview might try these directions out with the couple then and there, to sharpen them and find out in which form a particular direction works best.

If the couple has severely tangled patterns, they should be cautioned against attempting to Co-Counsel with each other to start with.

The couple is, at parting, reassured, individually and as a couple, that they are good people and that problems can be solved. If they have not yet decided to accept individual or class help, they are reassured that the counselor will be glad to hear from them.

The above sample will be useful only if used flexibly. It is not a set of rules; it is a possible sample approach. The counselor's caring for the couple will determine the usefulness of the interview more than any set of procedures.

Liberation

It's Time For Men To Organize

We've covered a lot of topics but so far we haven't discussed the biggest weakness in our men's work. This is organization.

The 1985 World Conference challenged every experienced Co-Counselor to build a world-class community around herself or himself as an individual. Each of you would become the center of your own world-class community. This is not just pie-in-the-sky fantasy; it was a sober estimate of what's possible for experienced Co-Counselors. (We say "experienced Co-Counselors" because, in general, it does take a little shake-down time to get the whole picture of what we're about and what the possibilities are. We have a lot of Co-Counselors who have now been around years and years, and quite a few who've been around less years but have caught on quickly.)

The idea behind this was to release individual initiative. Our estimate was that the group activities of the best organizations we know, the nuclear freeze, CND, Greenpeace, the Green parties, are still operating in rigid, ineffective ways. Even the Re-evaluation Counseling Communities, wherever the habit is still of thinking as groups or operating as groups, simply are not moving well enough to give us any kind of a guarantee against the total destruction of all complex life by the collapsing society and its nuclear warheads. We have a clear picture of the capability of individual initiative, however, and we judged that if we can release enough of it, decisive actions will be taken.

From the Men's Leadership Conference in Connecticut, USA, October 24, 1987. Appeared in **Present Time** No. 72, July 1988.

BUILD YOUR OWN WORLD-CLASS COMMUNITY

So it is proposed that you, as an individual, build a world-class community around yourself. It is not proposed that you and your cronies mill around and hope that you will grow into a world community, but that you as an individual do it. So far this has been taken seriously by a handful of individuals who are gaining world-class influence.

I mention three: D— is undoubtedly already the most influential woman leader the world has ever known. Just her following inside of RC is more support than any previous woman leader has ever had, and she has a lot of influence outside RC. G— is watched by several million people through her television spots for parents. She told us in July that people who come up to her on the street to say "I've seen you on television," frequently add "It's the funniest thing but my children drag me to the TV whenever you appear and say, 'That's the way to do it, Mom.'" A— is being sought out all over the Pacific, operating on her original brilliance and her commitment to decide first, act second, and discharge as she goes.

Can you build a world-class community? Is it possible? Is it feasible? Yes. That was already plain in 1985. One individual had built a world- class community. It had taken him thirty-five years if you count from the first beginning or fifteen years if you count from the time that RC left Seattle, but it had been done. Does it have to take that long for you or anybody else? No. Almost every possible mistake has already been made and well-publicized. The road to do it is staked and blazed. Is each one of you competent to do it? If I could do it you certainly can. If our theory is any good at all you're at least as smart as I am. You have to be. You also have enormous advantages that I didn't have. You're much younger and in better health and better looking. There are absolutely no excuses available to you. As I've indicated, a few dozen people have taken the challenge seriously and their influence is rapidly spreading world-wide.

Do you have enough theory available? Yes. Do you read and re-read RC literature regularly? If you don't, acquire the habit. Quite a number of people are getting the habit. I'm beginning to understand why religious people practice their prayers and liturgy daily. Unless I read some RC literature every day my thinking becomes cloudy. Our literature is so anti-pattern that it has to be thought about repeatedly. Exposure to these ideas has to be repeated.

We're setting up complete lending libraries of all the literature in print in many new places in the world. We set them up wherever there is a small group and an individual is willing to take the responsibility to keep the literature organized and up-to-date. It's having good effects.

The group in Bombay has used such a library well. One of the group, Ramakrishna Iyer, wrote he'd found a way to handle the quick question, "What is RC?" It is often asked of him just as his elevator door is about to close, or he is about to board a bus. He's learned to answer, "Listening well to begin with, and later taking over the world." He says that, without fail, whoever he answers this way seeks him out later and wants to know more.

The possibilities for wide use of the literature are there. We need more translations, of course, but we have the most fundamental literature in quite a few languages already. We have **The Human Situation** in German, finally. It looks like we're going to get a lot of help in translating everything into Chinese which will make a big difference. We will probably need to spend some money to get much of the literature translated into Russian because if we're going to go in there officially we want the literature all ready to go.

So, if you want to feel really safe, you must build a world-class community around yourself. You've heard in the introductions estimates of how many people look to you individually for leadership. Some said three, some said three hundred, and many numbers in between. This is already a profound change from two to three years ago. A while ago hardly anyone in RC thought of themselves as being a leader. The notion of everyone taking leadership has not been pushed hard enough or long enough but the idea is permeating. Many RCers and certainly most RCers on the level that come to a conference like this now think of themselves as being a leader. They take it for granted that leadership is part of living. They're finding rich rewards from being leaders (as we report in **Present Time** and the other journals as fast as we can).

YOUR RE-EMERGENCE IS ACCELERATED

Your individual re-emergence is enormously accelerated by taking leadership. Leadership moves you forward and the more clearly you take leadership, the faster you move forward.

We have a general perspective laid out. We know that the world-class community you're going to build around yourself is going to have you in contact with my community for a while. We've got a rich accumulation of knowledge and experience and literature and good ideas and procedures for keeping our theory correct and for keeping it growing and fresh here. Nobody has to resign from my community to build their own world community. In general there's going to be some overlapping. The ones of you who have gotten started building, know that your world community already overlaps with mine to a considerable extent and there's no conflict. Everybody's much happier to have two or even two thousand leaders they can depend on than to just have one. It just works much better. There's no conflict. In a few cases you may have to build this RC portion of your community away from mine. This may be the case in certain of the eastern countries. We'll have to see what our experience is when we start dealing with the Minister of Education in the USSR. Whether our communities continue to overlap or not, you're going to need a portion of your community to meet the same kind of standards that we try to maintain in the present RC Community where there is a commitment to rigorous, consistent theory and a commitment to continuous review and updating of the theory. Every one of our policies is a draft policy which we continue to review and improve in the light of experience. Every attitude we decide on is a tentative attitude to be plunged ahead on but also to be reviewed periodically. Every good decisive session leaves us with a better idea of how to lead. The idea of growth in policy, that our policies are continually to be advanced and updated, is almost unique to the RC Community. Most innovative organizations of the past made a breakthrough to one good idea, grew because of it and stayed with that as a rigid policy except for periodic upheavals a hundred years apart or so.

The current question for most of us is, how do I go about building my world community rapidly? We men are part of the existing Community. Getting started becomes a crucial question for men because our organizational work has been weak. We have been backward about organization in our men's work as compared to the women and compared to certain other sections of the Community.

The original proposal said "full permission granted to build a world community." You have full permission. You will win people to those important ideas. You have to state these ideas as your own. You have to do this because, in general, people don't want to hear you quote anybody else. If you tell people, "A group of us have some ideas I think you'll like," nobody wants to join the group. They've been conned into cults and churches before and they've been ripped off in many ways. They don't want to hear that "a fellow in Seattle had some good ideas." They have no interest in second-hand quotes from a fellow in Seattle, but they'll be delighted if you as a person they know have some good ideas. You have to offer the theory as your own. Of course if it isn't your own, you have no business offering it to anybody. If it isn't what you've realized you always thought anyway, you shouldn't be peddling it.

So you offer it as your own and if you're someone they know, people will be delighted to hear it. Sometimes RCers get hung up on "but I won't be giving proper credit." In academia you always have to "cite your source." Well, for us that's nonsense. It's your own thinking. You don't need to cite a source. Sometimes the question comes, "But if I give them some literature they'll find out you wrote it." My response is, "Take full credit for it. You have my absolute permission to claim any idea I ever wrote as your own." (I picked your brains to get these ideas anyway. That's what I do at workshops.) If your friends say "You stole Jackins' idea and claimed it was your own thinking," you have my full permission to tell them "Jackins stole it from me." If the question comes to me I'll back you up. I'll say, "I stole it from him. I plagiarized it from him." Go ahead, put out the key ideas as your own thinking.

PRECISE INSTRUCTIONS

"How do I build my world-class community?" The original announcement said "precise instructions included" and I now repeat the precise instructions.

You have to give up something to start with. You have to give up your life-long habit (which you share with every other one of the five billion people alive on the surface of the earth today) of trying to get someone to listen to you all the time. Everybody in the world does this. Some few of them have an inhibiting pattern that they can't open their mouth but inside they're straining to be listened to even if they're not talking all the time. Everybody in the world acquired this ancient habit pattern of trying to get somebody to listen to them all the time. You have to give it up. By decision. By repeated decision. You will not try to claim other people's attention for yourself.

You will not try to claim other people's attention for yourself with one exception. That exception is if the other person knows how to counsel and has agreed to be your counselor at that time. That's the only exception. Some RCers have objected, "You know I'm two hundred miles away from the nearest Co-Counselor. I'll never get counseled." Well of course there are people living all around her and it's time she went to them and trained some of them to listen to each other. Also, of course, many an RCer in a crisis has discovered that you can create a counselor quickly. Something has just befallen, she's slipped into restimulation. She goes up to a stranger on the street and says "Excuse me sir, would you listen to me for ten minutes please? I just had a crisis, I need badly to be listened to." And the stranger has said, "Well, I'll try." And the RCer has said, "You don't need to say anything. Just listen and if I start to cry put your arms 'round me and hold me." And the stranger has said, "I'll try." The RCer had a good ten-minute session and cried and said, "Thank you, sir; that helped me a great deal to be listened to. I appreciate it very much," and gone on her way with the crisis half resolved and the stranger has gone down the street thinking, "Life is more interesting some days than others."

Notice, the two conditions were met. The stranger knew how to counsel (he had thirty seconds of instruction on how to be a counselor which is all that was necessary). And the stranger had agreed to be counselor. That way it would work. People had been telling me how I must have made up this ridiculous situation. Then Pat Barry in the July **Present Time** wrote that she did just this in the Washington, DC airport. After bidding farewell to a friend who flew to Europe she was feeling sad and went into the lunch room where there were three people sitting alone. Two women were reading. One man was alone. She went to him and told him that she needed to be listened to, she cried for a while, thanked him and he went off. They were good friends by the time he left. If these two conditions are met, that the person knows how to counsel and has agreed to be your counselor at that time, that's the only exception. Otherwise, you do not try to get people to pay attention to you, you do not try to get people to pay attention to you, you do not try to get people to pay attention to you, even though it's a life-long chronic pattern to try and do it. It's an ancient habit pattern which you share with everybody in the world.

Our experience indicates that to resist the pull of a pattern is possible but very difficult. It is much better to not just resist the pattern but to replace the patterned activity with a contrary activity. So, you replace the patterned activity of trying to get other people to pay attention to you with the activity of paying attention to other people when you are with them. (The only exception being when the other person knows how to counsel and has agreed to be your counselor. Otherwise you pay attention to them whenever you are with them.)

You don't become a compulsive counselor. You don't say "What's the worst thing that ever happened to you? Come on. Tell me," except on rare occasions; but you do pay attention to each person in a way that enhances the person's survival. You're validating. You're interested. You're bright-eyed. You're cheerful. You look at them as if you like them. You offer useful information. You show them the way to the toilet. You do whatever is helpful. Your attention is on them, enhancing their operation, enhancing their survival.

Now, is this possible? Yes. I do it, except for the times when I forget and slip into trying to claim someone else's attention.

Is it workable? Yes. It works very well. Is it satisfying? Yes. It's enormously satisfying to play this role because you become effective and you know you're effective.

ENORMOUSLY POPULAR

If you will do this for three weeks consistently you will become the person you always dreamed of being. People will turn to you in droves. You will become the most popular person in the community where you live. People will seek you out on any pretext. They'll come to you and ask your advice. They will drop by your house on the chance that you may be out front raking leaves.

Remember the big high school or middle school or gymnasium where there were five thousand students but three of them always got elected to any office they ran for, just because everyone liked them so much? You would have liked to hate them but you couldn't quite because they were too nice. They just accidentally did a little of this.

If you do this consistently for three weeks you will have become the person you always dreamed of being. Everyone will want to be with you. Everyone will seek you out. That's nice. That's rewarding. This is exactly all you have to do, pay attention to the person, enhancing their operation by your attentions.

There are about twenty people in the whole RC Community who somewhat accidentally have been managing to function like this. They did this before the theory became this clear. They have been functioning like this for a few years. I notice when one of these persons moves to a new locality they get an RC class going within two weeks even if the language is new to them. I receive a phone call, "Rush twenty **Manuals,** I have a class starting next Tuesday." I ask, "How in the world did you get a class started so soon?" "Oh, no problem." "Where did you get your students?" "Oh, they volunteered. I just talked to some people I work with. Yesterday at lunch I said I was going to start a class and five people asked if they could be in it without asking what it was about." There is a small bunch of people who already function like that. Wherever they land the Community grows.

You can do this by sheer determination.

How much attention you pay to a person at one time is up to your judgment. You will not become a compulsive counselor that everyone can come up to and fall apart on. People will stream toward you.

Some people will turn to you with their heaviest material but you don't have to handle it unless you want to. You handle just as much as you desire to handle and if a stranger comes up and says, "I just don't think I can go on." You just say, "I'm sure you can go on. Aren't the autumn leaves beautiful?", and turn and go your way. If your friend, with whom the friendship is important, says "Have you got fifteen minutes? I feel awful this morning." You can say: "You don't look that bad. I'm sorry you feel so bad but that's a beautiful blouse you're wearing. I don't have fifteen minutes. I've got to go." For the real clammy-fingered ones that clutch at you hard remember that everyone has been thoroughly trained to respect one need. Everyone has been toilet-trained. So when you can't get rid of them any other way you can say, "I've got to go to the toilet or the loo, or the john or the wachamacallit." Everyone has been trained to respectfully say, "GO!" Open the toilet door a crack and if they are still waiting outside, close it, lock it and climb out the back window.

Pay as much attention as you want to. I usually think in terms of a spectrum of paying attention. If my daughter or sons or Gill Turner call for help I will drop everything and come. I made a total commitment to them and it's been smart. It's paid off. The way Gill has moved ahead inspires me every time I think of it. I would leave this conference if I got a wire that said she needed me right now.

There's another man who lives in Newcastle-Upon-Tyne that I use as the other end point of the spectrum. An old gardener was pulling off yesterday's roses in front of a university building when I stopped and appreciated him on my way to a class at a workshop there. It took about three seconds, I told him how much we appreciated his roses. Every morning after that he was out there waiting for another appreciation.

STAY IN CHARGE

You do what you have time for.

You are in charge of your time. Always your attention is on the other person.

People will stream toward you to the extent that you do this. Quite a few of the people here already have sizeable influence based in part on this. People will come to you.

They'll need some theory. They'll need to know things. They'll need to have some literature to read. You don't tell them, "Read this. It'll be good for you." You don't tell them, "You'll be interested in this." I have a whole room full of books that people have given me telling me they know I'll like them. It's almost impossible for me to open them. I've read maybe two. But you can use a little sense, and say "I'm puzzled about this book **The Human Side of Human Beings**. I don't know whether to take it seriously or not. Could you look at a couple of pages of it? And tell me what you think?" No one can resist having their opinion asked. It is absolutely irresistible to be asked for advice about something. They'll read two pages and then they'll read two more pages. Pretty quick they'll say, "It's hard to believe, but it's kind of interesting. Can I borrow it for a while?" Use the literature, give them information, organize them.

Now we're men leaders as well as RC leaders. Let's stress that fact. We're going to give up our minority status in RC. Our numbers are already pretty good. This has been a shift in the last few years. There are lots more men in RC now. I now hear complaints from various sources such as "I don't know how to keep women in my classes. I've got eighteen men and only two women were tough enough to come into that atmosphere." This is like music to my ears. Actually in the early days of RC we always had a majority of men in Seattle classes. A majority of the professional clients were women but the men were always a majority in classes and the majority of both men and women were working-class in those days.

ORGANIZATIONAL FORMS

You've got to organize. The organizational forms we've evolved in RC are very effective in RC and in the wide world. The content of these forms is what makes them effective, not their names. The names are useful for communicating among ourselves and the names in general aren't a block to people using them. "Support groups" for example certainly began in RC and the name began in RC, but I'll wager there's a thousand organizations in the United States organizing support groups at this point that never heard of RC. They call them support groups because the content spread under that name. The names are not necessarily blocks.

What are the organizational forms that we've evolved?

THE SESSION

Probably the one we will use most if we make this commitment to always pay attention to other people is the session. We have many variations of the session already. We have short mini-sessions and longer mini-sessions. We have telephone sessions and we have one-way sessions and we have intensive sessions and we have sessions by mail.

The content of the session, the basic content, is two or more people paying attention to one person. Whenever that content is achieved it works fine. Much of your time with other people will be spent in this form following your commitment to put your attention on other people and pay attention to them. What you do with your attention may vary but it is still a session even if you just compliment the person on the way her hair curls and go on your way. It doesn't have to take a long time or it can take a very long time. I once stayed with a man who cried violently for fourteen hours. He wasn't even a client. He just came in for an interview and looked up and saw I was really paying attention and exploded. I was curious as to how long he could cry. He didn't do anything for fourteen hours except violent, violent crying. He never became a client. He left quite relieved and satisfied. I learned a lot from him. Sessions can assume a great variety of forms and intensities but the content is always two or more people paying attention to one person. A great deal of your time will be spent using this form with other persons.

THE CLASS

Another organizational form I'll call the class. The content of a class is the communication of RC to another person or persons. By "RC" I mean any of the precious information about humans and reality that we've dug out from under the great mass of occlusions and misinformation and lies and confusions that ignorance and patterns and society have heaped together. By "RC" I mean such precious knowledge as that almost every human being is enormously intelligent; that human beings are inherently good; that almost everything wrong with any human being is a result of a distress pattern being left by experiences of hurt; that there is a crucial difference between the person and the pattern. I mean all this desperately important information that we've dug out in our thirty-seven years of floundering progress and have gotten together into pamphlets, books, journals, and tapes. Any communication of this is a "class."

We have dozens of kinds of classes, already. With heavily oppressed people, for example, the meet-every-Thursday-night-class, which has become so standard with white-collar middle-class RCers, doesn't work. Their lives are too difficult and disrupted to come out the same evening every week. They can't do it; but if you plan for an all-day Saturday class once a month and take appropriate steps to encourage them they will attend and learn well. Once-a-month classes for four, six, or eight hours work much better in the United States with working-class people, with black people, with Native people. If the oppressions are heavy it's too hard to fit into the schedules you've been using with lawyers, doctors, college professors, and students.

Classes can take all kinds of forms but every contact you have with a person can include some element of a class. It's a class if you go up to the desperate mother in the supermarket who's about to slap her baby because her screaming is embarrassing her and just say, "May I hold her while you shop? I've heard it's good for babies to cry." You will have transmitted a crucial piece of information in a way that can be heard.

A second form is the class, the transmitting of crucial RC information in a way that people can hear it.

175

THE SUPPORT GROUP

What's another form? The support group. The support group has spread widely around the United States to many places and populations that never heard of RC. What's the content of the support group? Each person in a group having a turn of being listened to without interruption. Does a support group necessarily include a lot of discharge? Not necessarily. Just being paid attention to is quite marvelous. In an RC support group the leader will usually also try to counsel, will try to help members discharge in their turns because that's what everybody wants and is ready for and will understand. But the general support group outside of RC will often operate with little discharge besides laughter and talking.

The general rule for any RCer is to organize a support group whenever with two or more other people who are not preoccupied with some other activity. If you are with two or more other people, organize a support group. See that each person has a turn being listened to without interruption. If you're at the bus stop with others you can say, "Have you noticed the autumn leaves?" One person says, "Yes, fall weather always reminds me of what happened one fall in Vermont...." A second person says, "Autumns are short in Alaska, where I grew up." Then you say, "Well, the bus is coming, but I want to say that I feel uplifted whenever I see the fall colors. It reminds me of Bliss Carman's poem—

There is something in the autumn that is native to my blood.
Touch of manner, hint of mood,
And my heart is all in rhyme
With the yellows and the purples and the crimsons keeping
    time.
The scarlet of the maples can shake me like a cry
Of bugles going by,
And my lonely spirit thrills
To see the frosty asters like a smoke upon the hills.
Ah, here's the bus."

One nice thing about a support group is that you always take a turn even if you're leading. It pays off in carpools on the way to work. "Have any dreams last night, Margaret?" "Yeah, as a matter of fact I dreamed—" "I know what she dreamed about!" "Shut up, Tony, I'm listening to Margaret." Then, later, "All right, Tony, what was your dream?" "I didn't have any dreams, but I wish I knew where I could buy a good used car." So he talks about what he needs to. You take your turn, too.

Whenever you are with two or more people and not engaged in other necessary activity, organize a support group. When you are out on the town socializing with your friends, organize a support group. That's what people go out hoping will happen but they don't know how to get it to happen. So, they usually setttle for alcohol or sex and go home feeling frustrated. Organize a support group. This is what everyone wants, a chance to be listened to without interruption.

THE WYGELIAN LEADERS' GROUP

Other organizational forms? The Wygelian leaders' group. It cuts out all the time-wasting nonsense that had seemed so necessary whenever leaders got together. It eliminates "agreeing on a unified plan," or "appointing someone to check up on everybody to see that they carry it out," or coming together again to see how far we got and blame each other for what we didn't do. All these things that used to go on in leaders' meetings were completely useless. One great advantage of the Wygelian leaders' meeting is the things we don't do anymore. We do do the important, useful things.

We afford every leader a chance to report on what she has been doing with the attention of fellow leaders on what she's saying. You do need the attention and communication of your fellow leaders occasionally to lead well. One of the good biographies of Picasso said that in his later years he no longer attended the shows of his paintings. The people who lived with him would go to the shows and they would come home and be eager to tell him that the crowds were ecstatic and every painting was sold and what people had said and what the reviews in the newspaper had said and so on. He would listen them out but then always ask, "What did the artists say?" This is what mattered, what his fellow artists, his peers thought. There is a real need for leaders to know what their fellow leaders think. The first point on the Wygelian leaders' agenda is to report on what you've been doing as a leader of your kind of Wygelians in the hearing of your fellow leaders.

The second point of the agenda is for each person to be listened to in his or her estimate of the current situation, to share information. What's the situation facing the people we're leading? "I think this. I've seen this. I've heard this. I've found this book. I've found this magazine article I'll pass around." We need to share information. The first Wygelian leaders' groups in Seattle would start off with enormous discrepancies in knowledge levels, in what people knew. After they had met a few times they were all in possession of everyone's knowledge. It had a great effect on their leadership.

The third point on the agenda is to set goals for your leadership in the hearing of your peer leaders. "What do you propose to do as a leader in this next period?" This is important. You think much better about what you're doing, you think much better about what you are proposing to do, if you can do it like this. Each leader has a turn doing this.

On the fourth point, the Consultant (who has acted as chairperson until now) becomes a counselor. Each person has at least a demonstration session in response to the Consultant's question, "What's getting in the way of your leadership that a little counseling might help?" There is a demonstration session and possibly an arrangement for someone else to keep going counseling this individual later in the same way.

You can't always take all the time you'd like to. In the early Wygelian leaders' groups in Seattle where we started we would often have seven-hour meetings, six hours of it on point four. That really paid off in rapid development of leaders, but you can't always invest so much time. You do as much as you can.

That's the Wygelian leaders' group organizational form. It's a crucially important form of organization, invented in RC. We backed into it. We learned to do it while trying to solve certain problems. After we'd done it a few times we realized we'd made a major breakthrough in the relationship of leadership. It's so effective in part because of what we don't do any more in old patterned ways. One thing we don't do is meet regularly. No regular meetings. We meet only when there is something to meet about.

THE TOPIC GROUP

The topic group is a rational discussion group. These occur in great numbers at RC workshops and gatherings but can take place in any circumstance where groups of people are present. The topic is proposed by an individual who is interested in having such a discussion take place. This individual becomes the Convenor of the topic group. He or she announces the topic and the time and place of the meeting and when the group meets, presides until a chairperson and a reporter (preferably two reporters) are chosen. The Convenor may or may not fill one or more of these roles.

The chairperson sees that a rational discussion takes place. The basic guidelines are that the discussion is kept to the issues around the topic, not veering to the personalities or problems of the people present; that no one speaks twice before everyone has spoken once; that no one speaks four times before everyone has spoken twice; that no agreement is necessary between the topic goup members; that each person is listened to with respect and without interruption, no matter how strongly the person is disagreed with.

The oral reporter prepares a report to the larger group of whatever seemed significant in the discussion. Experience has usually been that a four-minute limit on the length of the report is about right. The written reporter prepares a report for publication, in RC for **Present Time** or the other RC journals, in the wide world for the press (letters to the editor, etc.) or for radio or TV stations.

THE THINK-AND-LISTEN

What other forms? I'll mention the think-and-listen. We haven't used it much. It was invented at an early workshop in Santa Barbara. The topic group has often been miscalled a think-and-listen. The topic group is not a think-and-listen.

The pure think-and-listen has never occurred outside of RC. We need to use it more. In the think-and-listen we divide into groups of about four people. The time is divided equally. Each person is simply listened to with everyone else committed to make no response except aware attention. Group members don't make faces of delight at a good idea or frown at something they don't understand. They simply listen. Each person has the others' promise that they will never speak to her or anybody else about what the speaker said in her turn. If any listeners want to refer later at any time or to anyone about what the speaker said, they are pledged to act as if it were their own idea, and not to attribute it to the speaker. People who have experienced being in a think-and-listen are amazed at how liberating it is to talk freely, perhaps shakily at first, but with increasing confidence, of one's own loftiest ideas. Until one experiences this, one will have had no idea what a burden it has been on one's thinking to be on guard against other people's reactions or responses. It will seem like a crushing load hanging over one that one had never noticed before. We need to use the think-and-listen form more to really free up our thinking.

Question: How is this different from a support group?

Well, in the support group you're paid attention to without interruption, but people later refer freely to what you said, being "inspired" by it or disagreeing with it, or otherwise responding to it. The same can happen in the topic group. In the think-and-listen group there is no response beyond that of attention. Not then, not later, not ever. You have this "crystal chalice" of attention where you can finally think without having to worry about what people's reactions are going to be. Until you experience it you will not have known what an enormous lift that gives to one's thinking.

BEGIN WITH SUPPORT GROUPS

How are we men going to organize? We're going to organize support groups. Support groups are a natural channel of entry into RC. People can feel the benefits of being paid attention to in support groups, even before they've heard any theory. As they feel the benefits they will become curious and want to know more. It's a natural introduction to RC. We've experimented with having this be the place where people start RC, and the results are good. You will have to provide some leadership, have to avoid recruiting people or patterns that you personally aren't ready to handle, but you will find it good to rapidly organize men's support groups.

In the first place, we need to organize support groups for the men already in RC. Our men have to some extent been wandering around like second-class citizens in the women-dominated Community to date. Now we've begun to move. The reports here show how many men's support groups we have or are encouraging, but I would guess that at least the majority and probably closer to three-fourths of the men in RC are not yet participating in men's support groups. There's no reason why you, in particular, should not organize a men's support group so that the men could get going. If you've already got one going, organize another one. A support group should never be static. One feature of the agenda should always be, "Do you have anyone you want to invite to our next meeting?" When the group gets to be eight members, divide into two groups of four, ask your most aware member to be an assistant leader, and have him take off four men into another room and run it as a separate group so people can have longer turns. Later, have a private talk with the assistant leader, making his four a separate group and recruiting additional men. The support groups should divide and divide and divide. They should be like busy amoebas that divide themselves every few weeks.

You'll have to produce new leadership. You'll see the necessity of it. You'll encourage people to become leaders. Always tell them they can refer back to you, do some counseling of them over the phone, be encouraging. All people want to be leaders. I emphasize this—everyone needs to be expected to become a leader. Everyone needs to be expected to become a top leader. (Harvey to an individual) Did we ever meet before this workshop? *(Man) About six years ago in Holland.* (Harvey) I don't remember; but I now expect you to become a world-class leader and I don't want any lack of such expectations from me to slow your progress.

As we become more aware of the tremendous mass of internalized invalidation pounding on us all the time such as "men are beasts, we have strong backs and weak minds, we don't know how to love and are interested only in sex" and all such garbage that has been dumped on us, it becomes plain that unless we have high expectations of each other and actively express them, we're passively invalidating each other. Does this make sense? It has got to be some part of our routine attitudes to expect the ultimate from each other.

ORGANIZE LEADERS' GROUPS

Organize support groups that grow and divide and grow and divide and produce new leaders. As soon as you have two groups bring the leaders together in a Wygelian leaders' group. Don't meet regularly, but only when there's something to meet about. Wygelian leaders' groups do not meet regularly, they only meet when someone or some issue needs a meeting. When you have two RC men's support groups started, you call the leaders together in a Wygelian leaders' group and you also invite all the other men in RC that are leaders. One is an executive with an insurance company, one is a head sorter of trash at the dump. He's a leader, bring him in. Bring any man who is leading, in men's work or otherwise, into a men's leadership group. As soon as it gets too big, you will have to divide it, probably by function. We haven't solved this division of leadership groups yet but we know how to solve it. Your Wygelian leaders' group mustn't get too large either.

With support groups, people won't have long enough turns

if it gets over eight. If you're over eight you should divide into two groups of four, meeting in different rooms or even different corners of the same room, so that each man gets a long enough turn.

Organize support groups that divide and divide and spawn leaders groups. Set up a City-wide Men's Coordinator. Have men's workshops, have a one-day workshop or have a half-day if that's all you feel up to leading, but have a men's workshop.

MEN'S PANELS

At general workshops insist on a men's panel. Many of you have seen these at other workshops. Set up a panel of men who each tell what it's been like to be a male, what it was like as a baby, what it was like as a toddler, what it was like in early school years, what it was like in later school years, what it was like in middle school, what it was like in college (if he got there), or the factory (if he went into that), what it was like in graduate school, and what it was like out in the wide world at whatever age he got there, what it's like now to be a male. Hear the details of this enormous oppression that has been pounded into us. Conducting these panels I've often asked each person as he tells these awful things that went on in his life, "Where did you go for comfort?" The most common response is something like "Comfort? Oh, I had a dog for about three months once before it was run over. I used to hold onto him." Or, "There was a record that I'd go into my room and play over and over and over." Or, "I got to visit my grandmother once a year and she liked me." Women sit and listen with saucer eyes. They have had no idea what miserable lives we men have led, what's been done to us. Well, we know. The women say, "Why haven't men talked about it? Surely men talk to each other, don't they? Women do." No. Tell them. We have been trained never, never to complain, that it's unmanly. If a guy has had both legs cut off in an accident and his wife has run away with the butcher and his house burned down and his friend goes to see him in the hospital, the friend says, "How's it going, Joe? I hear you're feeling tough." Joe says, "Yeah, it got a little hairy there for a while, but I think I'll make it." That's men's lives.

Get the lid off. Tell each other how tough it's been. Touch each other. Say "Okay, okay, you're probably going to die but put your cheek against mine." Let's get together and do a good job on each other. Women haven't listened to us well. They've been terrified of us. When women hear that the men are beginning to resurge and take leadership their immediate fearful response is "Oh, my God, we can't lead anymore." This is just old fears. Their leadership is not threatened by us. We want them to continue to lead and share leadership with us as we begin to lead.

Diane and I are leading a campaign in the women's conferences that are currently taking place against the "plateau" that the women's movement in RC has hit and stuck on. Women in RC have been celebrating "We have achieved so much. My life is free. We've got leadership. We're women, women, women." They've slipped into ignoring the fact that, still, when one man comes into the room they stop talking. They are still cowed and intimidated. They have a terror of men. We've been trained to be violent to them and it's not our fault, but they are scared to death. So they haven't dared listen to us. When we started with men's liberation the general feeling among otherwise quite brave women leaders was "Oh, my God, if they've been oppressed, their liberation will mean they'll be back stomping on us." There's a little basis for that fear. If we're careless our resurgence is going to lead us into patterns again. It's not liberation for us to come home and holler "Get the goddamn dinner on the table, woman." We can't afford to do that. We have to take women into freedom with us. We've got to do our share of listening to the baby crying or we won't get anywhere. We can't go where we want to go and be oppressive at the same time. Our old oppressive behavior is just like a ball and chain on our legs. But we're manly enough to change that. Fairness has always been an important part of being a man.

CITY-WIDE COORDINATORS

So, organize in every city (or if it's a rural region, in every region). In every city see that a City-wide Coordinator for men gets chosen. This is primarily Charlie's job, but don't just leave it to Charlie. Charlie has had some blocks on organization. You don't have the same blocks so you don't have any excuse. Go ahead, do organizational work and hand it to him on a platter when he comes around. See that a City-wide Coordinator for men is chosen who can go into any Area. He needs to reach an agreement with the ARPs that "I'm free to go into your Area and organize men's support groups and men's leadership groups."

Often in a city you'll get one support group in the city to start with. But keep on. Have as a goal a series of men's support groups in each Area in a city. New York City has about seven Areas now, Boston has a lot of them, and Seattle's got a few of them. Try to move toward a massive men's organization in each Area. You'll have to build the Area, too. You'll have to take leadership of women as well as men. You'll have to see that young people get the support they need. But see to it that there is a City-wide Coordinator for men in every city and every Area and Region. There'll also be City-wide Coordinators for women set up, City-wide Coordinators for young people, and so on.

Let's see that we have City-wide Coordinators for men everywhere who are able to take initiative. Our big problem everywhere is releasing initiative. Everybody that you get to take on a leadership job, pat them on the back and tell them to go, go, go. If you think they're doing something dangerous or incorrect, check with them on it, otherwise just release initiative. We men have got to get organized, take over responsible leadership of the whole Community. I think we know how to do it well, or at least we can learn.

Most of the leadership roles in RC are filled by women at this point. This is fine. We don't need a title to lead. We have some very fine leaders who lead "from behind" all the time. What you do is to see that every leader functions well. Become at least unofficial leaders wherever you are. You don't have to have a title. Do a nice, sneaky job. You'll be surprised at how much satisfaction you get.

LETTERS TO LEADERS

We've got to get organized. Charlie will be getting out a letter to every local leader at least every four months, hopefully every two months for a while to catch up. We've got an arrangement now that the computer's finally working well enough in Seattle. Charlie will send in a draft letter. It will get edited quickly and Charlie will okay it over the phone. He will send us his list of local leaders and we'll combine it with our list of accumulated local leaders. A mailing will go out and Charlie will get back two copies of the updated local leaders' lists, which he keeps corrected and up-to-date on additions and changes he hears about. This he sends back to us with his next letter. We've got it streamlined enough in Seattle to do some of this. It's a lot of work, but the staff in Seattle works hard and gets this kind of letter out in two or three days. It will make a big difference.

You'll be setting up support groups everywhere. You'll be City-wide Coordinators. Let Charlie know and let me know when a City-wide Coordinator is chosen. If I hear of one I'll tell Charlie and if Charlie hears of one he'll tell me. We need to have parallel knowledge with Charlie and in Seattle.

Basically, let's get organized.

The Realistic Way
to Eliminate Racism

(This workshop was for white leaders of anti-racism work. The International Liberation Reference Person for black persons, for people of Chinese heritage, and for Puerto Ricans—Barbara Love, Tommy Woon, and Emma Ramos-Diaz—were present as an advisory panel.)

I'm going to talk a little this morning about the situation in our work of combatting white racism. I don't have my thoughts highly organized yet. I'm just going to talk.

It became clear last night that we have respect for the theory that we've evolved so far for dealing with oppressions, and in particular, racism. Our intentions are admirable and we've made lots of effort. Compared to the racist atmosphere around us in the United States we are relatively non-racist. It is also plain, however, that we're dissatisfied. Many of us feel that, in terms of performance, we must be pounding on the wrong target. We suspect that there's a door open somewhere that we haven't seen yet. Something is missing. I am beginning to be able to think about what that is.

I'm fairly successful at establishing close relationships with members of oppressed groups other than my own. I've told some of you that I've long thought that spending time doing "three-step techniques" is a clumsy process. Conducting anti-racism workshops where everyone is "thrilled" at what they heard, but where the people conducting the workshops don't have people of color among their intimates, or their circle of

From the Eliminating Racism Workshop in New York City, New York, USA, November 6-9, 1987. Appeared in **Present Time** No. 72, July 1988.

close friends, or among their workmates, or in their Areas or Regions, misses the point completely. My own contradiction to my racism is to make up my mind to love a person of color whenever I can get in contact with him or her. It seems to short-circuit all the embarrassed prancing around on pointed toes that most "liberal" whites do around people of color.

I don't think you can really love a person, really be close to him or her, and be oppressive at the same time. I don't mean the chintzy, embarrassed "love" — "my, my, how admirable your culture is. I must read a book about it sometime." I mean really love the person.

START CHANGING INSIDE RC

I don't want to break anyone's rice bowl. Those of you who have been making a living or a share of your living out of leading anti-racism workshops, go ahead and do it outside of RC. It can at least raise some glimmer of hope in otherwise seemingly hopeless situations. It allows the communication of some basic theory about oppression. If school boards and other organizations are willing to pay you, keep doing it. (I've done all kinds of work to earn a living.) I'm not saying you should quit, but it seems to me that you should in your own mind be completely unsatisfied with how you've been doing it. Unless your RC Area is non-racist (someone objected to the term "integrated"), meaning that there are at least the proportion of people of color in your RC Area that there are in the wide-world community around it, I don't think you have a great deal to tell other people. Unless your RC class is non-racist to the same extent, unless your friends include many people of color, I don't think you're an expert at combatting racism. Go ahead and lead wide-world workshops if it means your livelihood, but I think we need to make a sharp break with our tolerance of that inside RC.

We have a general rule in RC that leaders are not to go abroad and do workshops unless their home base is in excellent condition. That rule hasn't always been kept, but it's a good rule. It applies to work against racism.

Whites who claim to be expert at combatting racism should really have to show, as credentials, the fact that they have intimates and close friends of people of color, a non-racist group of casual friends, a proportionately representative constituency. If we call a group whose numbers of people of color are at least as high a proportion as that of the general population a non-racist group, then we need non-racist classes, non-racist leaders' groups, non-racist Organized Areas, non-racist Regions. Go ahead and lead workshops but shift your goal. We're all good, we've all done the best we could, we all had the best of intentions. I don't want you to take what I say as scolding. I do want you to hear what I'm trying to say.

There's an article in the October **Present Time** called "Some Improvements in Workshop Demonstrations" (page 30). It's from Eileen Hayes. "We have some keen insights coming out of the workshop this past weekend. The sizeable Third-World presence at the workshop was a powerful contradiction to my internalized oppression. I could devote my sessions to topics of my predetermined choice rather than to have my attention drawn to the restimulation of an 'all-white' workshop."

There was a sizeable percentage of people of color at that workshop. In the demonstrations, I went after new people as well as established leaders. Pretty much every person of color was in a demonstration. The tone was fine. There were no mysteries. By the time the demonstrations were done, every person of color there was clearly a person, not an exotic mystery. X— was particularly delightful because he was so pleased that RC actually worked for him, instead of being a bunch of theory. He was shaking hard but filled with delight that counseling was working for him.

THE RACISM IS A PATTERN

It seems to me our enemy is always patterns. Our enemy is the pile of hurts to which our intelligence has been vulnerable, that have accumulated on us. The one that happened to us accidentally is our enemy. The distress pattern that was put on by contagion is our enemy (the one our parents imposed on us because they'd been treated that way as children, or the one the teacher put on us in school because she'd been treated that way in class). The patterns that have been put on us by the society are very much our enemy. There are a whole bunch of distresses that come from the oppressive society. These oppressions are our enemy. One of them is racism.

Racism exists in most places of the world. In the U.S., of course, it is a dominant part of the society. It is so dominant that much of it carries on all the time, without our being aware of it. We don't question it. It's pounded into us so early, and so reinforced over and over again, that we live in a racist fog. This is true of the victims of the oppression as well. They live in an internalized cloud of racism.

YOUR PERSONAL ENEMY

I think the first thing to say as first-person-singular is that my racism is my enemy. It is spoiling my life. It is not only something that I owe help to people of color in winning freedom from. White racism is spoiling my life as a white person. I've got to get rid of it and help other whites get rid of theirs. One result will be that people of color's lives won't be so hard. It will have that effect, but I don't think that effect is going to motivate us whites enough. In our confusion and self-centeredness, we usually think, "me, me, me." I think we whites need to realize that the racism that we carry is demeaning our lives all the time. Every time I break through my white isolation, every time that Barbara and I hang out together and love each other passionately and deeply, I realize how good this is compared to how I spend my life mostly. Every time Tommy and I break through and have some real communication, or Emma and I, it's a much better life for me.

I have a lot of closeness with a lot of people of color, and it's a source of richness in my life. The fact that I can go into an Arab culture and be accepted and be at home, or that people in India ask me to come back, is one of the things I am proudest of. The way I transcend these racist barriers that have been put upon me has some generality to it. I love the person. Of course I have to go against some personal patterns of fear of rejection in order to reach for Barbara the way I want to. Of course the moment I saw Barbara I wanted to be her full-time lover forever. As far as I know, everyone feels like that when they first see her. I had to go against some of my fears, but she is a very smart woman, and she encouraged me a little bit.

I would like to have you say and mean something like, "I am tired. I am impatient. I will no longer tolerate the limited life racism has forced on me. I will no longer put up with it. I will no longer cooperate with the culture around me which segregates and segregates and segregates."

YOU CAN ACT ALONE, IF NECESSARY

I have learned some things.

Over and over again I have come to do a workshop, and there's one black person there, or two black people out of 102. I used to internally curse the white organizers for their foolish unawareness, but that didn't do any good, so I tried other things. I learned something here at Appel Farm with D——. When she showed up she was the only black person, and in my head I thought, "Oh, damn this stupid Community that would let her in for a situation like this." Then I thought, "Rather than curse the difficulty, maybe I'd better do something positive," so I went after her. She was shy, but I hugged her and kissed her neck and I loved her. She never came into the room when I didn't drop everything and hug her. She was so busy discharging with me that she was insulated from the other, uptight attitudes. After a while, she started seeking me out in the free times, and we walked around arm in arm. I discovered that I, by myself, could provide enough safety for her, regardless of the frozen white attitudes around us.

I did something similar at La Sherpa, with a black man, who was the only black at a big workshop. In his introduction, I asked, "What are you thinking?" and he said, "God, look at them!" I said, "You mean the roomful of white faces out there?" He said, "Yeah." It took a little firm support, but he was able to discharge. I stuck with him, and he had a long, long session. The next day I asked him how it was going. He said, "A little better. Maybe I can stand it." With help he had another long session. At the end of the workshop he said, "This is the best workshop I've ever dreamed of being at. I decided to discharge my internalized racism. There wasn't another black around to hear and be upset by the things I had to say." One aware, committedly anti-racist person can be enough to make it safe for a person of color in a workshop.

This workshop is deliberately all white. We only invited the panel of leaders of color in order to guide us whites. Most of our workshops are automatically racist because the proportion of people of color is not representative of the general population. A person of color in the U.S. culture is continually abused by the attitudes of the white people around him or her. People of color continually feel this pressure regardless of how much they are used to it or toughened against it. They are continually abused by the unaware white racism around them. That racism could be in a vicious form. Or it could be simply your unawareness. It could be your acting afraid. Any distress you have about a person of color, whether you're terrified of them or embarrassed because you don't know what to do, is racism. Any distress at all you have about a non-white person, any distress that is called up by the fact that they're non-white, is racist. It operates as racism, it makes their lives difficult. The person of color should not have to put up with that.

Your tolerance of it as a white, your failure to change it, completely and effectively, is racism. It is spoiling your life every second. It's spoiling mine. Just incidentally, it's also an unjust burden on the non-white person.

It's a pattern. The pattern is your enemy. What do you do with patterns? You contradict them. You don't go along with them. In your life, in your city, no matter what remote part of a white suburb you live in, there are people of color within reasonable distance. You must actively go and become a friend and ally to those people of color. No matter how many miles you have to travel on a creaky bus or whatever. No matter how few opportunities you have because "there aren't any of them living in our neighborhood" (which is usually not true).

I remember years ago, when I asked about inviting Chicanos into RC in Santa Barbara. The local leaders all assured me that I'd have to go eighty miles out to the hop fields to find Chicanos. I stayed in Santa Barbara the next two nights at a motel and ate at local restaurants. Every cook, every busboy, every motel maid, and every other holder of a low-paying job in the town of Santa Barbara was Chicano. They were completely invisible to the white RCers who had agreed that "white racism was a problem we should do something about."

I propose that we whites actively contradict this chronic white racism. I propose that wherever there is a person of color, we actively go to make contact with that person; that we work on establishing a relationship with that person.

That person of color is not necessarily going to be eager, or welcoming, or even well-behaved.That person may have unattractive patterns. That person is going to be, statistically, just like the rest of the population, only with an extra layer of racist oppression in addition to all the other distresses. If you are a white woman and you go to make friends with this black man, you had best remember that he's probably been conditioned, like other males, to think he can't have your friendship without trying to offer you sex. Like any other male, he's been conditioned to think that necessarily when you say no, you really mean yes. That's like any other male. The fact that he's black doesn't change the male conditioning. So, as a woman, you're going to have to handle him as you'd handle any male with that conditioning. That doesn't mean you don't make a friend of him. Remember how we worked it out how every woman could have one hundred warm, close male friends? She's got to like herself as a woman. She's got to let him know she's interested in him as a friend. She's got to let him know she won't reject him, even as she rejects his patterns. If she has to split a man's head with a baseball bat to reject his patterns, she leans over his bleeding body to say, "I still want you as a friend." You have to do this with any man. The fact that it's a black man doesn't change that at all. The fact that he's black and you don't try to make a friend of him is racism. Do your best. You may have to put him on hold like you do lots of other men. Tell him, "Come back when you can hear what I'm saying, but I want you for a friend." You will no longer buy into racism in its ever-present form which is, "They are not part of my associates." The separation.

Hunt up people of color. Most of you don't have to do too much hunting. You get on the subway every day and you're surrounded by five thousand people of color. Some of you to some degree will have to discharge these excuses.

Whenever you are with a group of people and some of them are people of color, what are you going to do? You're going to put your attention on the people of color. That's a priority.

Because racism is the least consistently challenged of all patterns we deal with in this racist culture.

If the whites in the group get grumpy about it, say, "Come on. I want to hear her story." "Fleetybelle, this is Fluvia. Fluvia's just moved here from Mississippi and is a fascinating person. Fluvia, Fleetybelle is my uptight friend that I've almost given up on!"

Be consistent in that you model that the attention goes to the person of color, as a deliberate tool against the racism. "Will I have time for my 'real' friends, my white friends?" I don't know. If they insist on being racist and not joining you in making friends with people of color, you just may have to give them up temporarily. (Until they see how much fun you're having.)

I think ending this isolation from people of color must become a major preoccupation in our lives. Our theory has come a long way and I'm very proud of that theory. We have a good theory, a good perspective, everybody agrees. Our practice of it hasn't really started except for little nibbles here and there. At this workshop we heard from at most five people who have some start at having normal, close relations with the persons of color in their environments. The rest of us have been still hesitating and pretending.

What gets in our way? What stops us? What's the block, outside of the habit and model and drift of racism flowing on forever in our culture? Let's look at some of the patterns.

Embarrassment: "I don't know how to talk to a black person. I don't know what the Asians are interested in. Heh! Heh!" Fear: "I've heard things are violent in the ghetto. I know how badly persons of color have been treated by whites, and I am a

white, and therefore it would not surprise me at all if they are
dreaming of ways to cut my throat and leave me in my own
blood in partial revenge. That scares me. Heh! Heh!" Resent-
ments are there. "They're getting all the good jobs. Affirmative
action is unfair. The Supreme Court said so last week." Mono-
logues like this are playing on, inside the white patterns.
Embarrassment, fear, resentment. They don't have to be reasonable. These distresses will discharge if contradicted. Can
we counsel each other on these distresses? I think so. I think the
main reason we haven't is that we've been too embarrassed and
self-conscious as counselors and clients to reveal them.

(To C—) You're as liberal as anyone I know. Should we try
a little counseling to see if we can dig something up? We
haven't talked for years, so it's a fair challenge. Say, "Hi, I'm
terrified of people of color."

C—: *(laughter) That's what I have to say. I'm terrified.*
(tears) That's a good phrase.

HJ: Use it. Don't just agree that it's a great direction.

C—: *I'm terrified of people of color.*

HJ: Again. Just stick with it and give us your thoughts in
between. Commit yourself to saying it, not discussing it.

C—: *I'm terrified of people of color.*

HJ: Thought.

C—: *I haven't got one yet.*

HJ: Okay. Phrase.

C—: *I'm terrified of people of color.*

HJ: (To the audience) Now, does the fact that she hasn't
thought of a profoundly significant phrase yet mean this session isn't working? I think we often tend to distract ourselves
with words. We don't appreciate that she's shaking and sweat-
ing and crying a little bit and laughing. Discharge is on its way.
Don't look for a profound conclusion so we can quit counseling
on it and put it away. This is what happens to many, many
sessions. (To C—:) I'm terrified of people of color.

C—: I'm terrified of people of color.

HJ: And I want to tell you all about it.

C—: I did have a thought about that one. In a class we were teaching last year, one time Barbara didn't come and it exploded. It was terrifying.

HJ: Thank you. It puts it out where we can see it. "Without Barbara here to protect me, they'll make mincemeat out of me."

C—: (laughter) Right.

HJ: They'll take on all my liberal patterns.

C—: I'm terrified of people of color.

HJ: I know. Even if I'd picked you at random, I would have been sure.

C—: Well, the thought there is that I'm pretty much terrified of everybody.

HJ: RIGHT! But if it's toward people of color it's racism.

C—: Right.

HJ: I'm terrified of people of color, she said cheerfully.

C—: I'm terrified of people of color. Why do I get a feeling sort of like yuk?

HJ: That's your new phrase, that sound.

C—: Yuk.

HJ: (to the audience) Watch for your client's spontaneous emissions. Especially the first one. Don't look for a carefully phrased sentence. Look for the first sound and have them stick with that one. That'll bring the discharge. The sound. Look right at Barbara and make the sound.

C—: (tears while making the sound) I think of counseling Patsy and Willie, that's scary.

HJ: Yeah. Patsy'd scare anybody. But she's black and you can't afford to stay scared of her.

C—: No. I'm doing a very good job.

HJ: I believe you.

C—: She even told me so.

HJ: Look right at Barbara and make the sound.

C—: Yuk. I just think of how I back off as soon as the going gets hard.

HJ: You're making pretty sounds, make that original sound.

C—: Yuk. (tears, trembling)

HJ: What's the thought?

C—: I was just thinking about growing up in Brooklyn, New York. It's scary. The whole thing is scary, everything. Everything people say, standing here.

HJ: Pick a spot and just say "Yuk" when you look at Barbara.

C—: (sound, crying)

HJ: Okay. You're on the track. Let's put a check on it.

Who's here from Vermont? Let's see if we can get a little embarrassment. What's your name?

K—: K—.

HJ: "I don't really have any close black friends, heh! heh!" That's your phrase. Use it.

K—: I don't really have any close black friends, heh! heh! It's true. I don't really have any close black friends. What comes up is—

HJ: You left off the part, "heh! heh!"

K—: (laughs) (tries the "heh! heh!" Harvey corrects her.)

HJ: I guessed at embarrassment and we got fear instead, which is all right. Stick right with it.

K—: I don't really have any close black friends. I grew up in Brooklyn.

HJ: I got Brooklyn instead of Vermont.

Question from audience: You've asked people specific things. What if people are living in a Native community? Do you always assume that it's a black person that they are not close to?

HJ: No, but if you're going to deal with racism in the United States, you must deal with the black issue. All the other forms of racism are extremely bad. I've sometimes thought that the racism toward Filipinos is possibly a little more vicious, maybe. But you've got a big colonized nation of black people in the U.S. This is where the main historic roots of U.S. racism lie.

I want to get some embarrassment now. K—, do you have any close black friends?

K—: I'm good at being embarrassed. (laughter) I don't really have any close black friends, heh! heh!

HJ: I think all you have to do is say it. You don't have to say it in any funny way. Just say it in your most sincere, Scandinavian way.

K—: (cries) I don't really have any close black friends.

HJ: "I've never been sure they wanted me for a friend."

K—: I'm not quite sure that that's exactly it, but I can't think of what it is.

HJ: As client, try a phrase before you discuss it.

K—: I've never been sure they wanted me for a friend.

HJ: "I've never been sure they wanted me as a friend." Say it wistfully. It ties in with your general desperate isolation. But the part of it that is turned on people of color is racism. "I've never been sure that they wanted me as a friend."

K—: (repeats phrase)

HJ: What are you thinking? Yeah?

K—: I'm still feeling that I like the original one better.

HJ: Okay, do that one.

K—: I don't have any close black friends. (cries)

HJ: Let's put a check here.

Question from audience: Is that grief about white racism?

HJ: Sure. All of us whites have a deep sense of loss because our lives are very empty compared to what they could be.

Whites suffer enormously from racism. (And then they are told that they have advantages because of it.)

If, from now on, in practice, we see that any person of color that comes into our ken gets our attention, becomes someone for whom we are an ally, and, if possible, becomes a close friend, and assume this as a priority, I think we will begin to do some decent work. (Instead of coasting on our good intentions.) I think this is going to force a lot of discharge off us whites.

Unless we do this, I think all the other stuff that we've comforted ourselves with is largely window dressing.

If white RCers are effectively combatting racism, then RCers should be spotted immediately in the general milieu by the fact that they have excellent relationships with people of color around them and are always seeking them out. It should be as characteristic of an RCer as being sensible and rational in discussions.

I've heard stories of people who have gone to conferences (on nuclear physics or on the new super-conductors at higher temperatures or things like that). They say, "Something was going a little awry in the program and this person across the room got up and made some very sensible proposals. He sounded so good, I drifted over there, stood by him, and said, softly, out of the side of my mouth, 'RC?' and he said, out of the side of his mouth, 'Yeah.'"

That's nice; but I think the appearance of being a white who obviously loves and is at ease with people of color and is always seeking them out should be an observable characteristic of white RCers. I think this will force all kinds of discharge off of us, to our great benefit, and it will have repercussions far beyond that.

As you seek to make friends with people of color, some will have been caught in all kinds of addictions and self-destructive and mutually-destructive behavior. There is going to be a certain substantial amount of suspicion, contempt, hatred of you, and even eagerness to do violence to you. It has to be. It has to be.

Being RCers, we're likely to be in the habit of going to look for "nice" people, of course, like we always have. (This has given us a disproportion of timid people in our Communities.) What are you going to do if you run into an un-timid, un-"nice" person of color? Are you going to say, "Whoop; I got hold of the wrong one. We'd never want this one in the Community"? Well, you may have to do that if the particular one is heavily into addictions and has fifty-nine warrants out for him. It's going to be too hard to integrate that one into the Community; but you have to find that out, not assume that because the person doesn't treat you "nice."

One responsibility you must assume is that of counseling the person of color well on his or her distresses about whites. This is necessary for them to be able to function well in the RC Communities. You whites are the logical counselors for them on these distresses.

Barbara, will you try working with me on what I've suggested? I've done a dozen of these demonstrations, and it's often worked just marvelously. Barbara's so thoughtful and responsible, and our relationship is already so great it seems a shame to ask her to do this, but I'm going to pick on her because racism in this country means white racism against blacks, first and foremost, historically and in every other way. The other forms are not unimportant, but they are not the heart of it.

B—: *Can I have two minutes for something else?*
HJ: Sure.

B—: It's about what you just said. Maybe I'm too thoughtful and too sensible. I have three thoughts. I don't have a strident voice any more. I gave up struggling. I'm somewhere else. The thought is, maybe I'm not the one to be doing this job I've got, the job of International Liberation Reference Person for black people. Maybe it needs somebody with more antagonism, because I'm not there any more. I once was there, but I'm not any more. If that's what the job calls for, then we're going to have to start looking for someone else.

HJ: You never lost a single ability you ever had, Barbara.

B—: Well, what it seems to me like (and then I'm going to stop this and do what you want me to do), what it seems like, what I gave up was not an ability. I gave up a piece of distress.

HJ: Good. I agree. You're smarter than you once were, but I don't think you're free of the distress.

B—: Okay. Let's try.

HJ: Don't look sideways if you will. Look me right in the eye and let the blows land on my upper arm with the words, "You arrogant white bastard."

B—: (pounds his upper arm with her fist) You arrogant white bastard. You arrogant white bastard!

HJ: May I help you with your tone of voice?

B—: Yeah.

HJ: You arrogant white BASTARD. (snort, growl)

B—: (laughs) Do it first right? You arrogant white bastard.

HJ: Again.

B—: You...bastard. (Repeats)

HJ: Shorten it to "white!"

B—: White! White! White! (repeatedly)

HJ: What do you think?

B—: Well, I can take off another layer of clothes. I'm warm. You know the real Barbara's in there somewhere.

HJ: You've trained yourself carefully not to rehearse distresses, but you discharge them wonderfully.

B—: It's in there somewhere. White! White! White!

HJ: Look into my eyes. Blaze at me.

B—: White. White.

HJ: Don't just repeat it; it has to have a meaning. "I hate your crummy guts and I'm going to get even with you for what you've done to my people!"

B—: Let me see if I can think of things that have been done to my people.

HJ: You heard Elizabeth's grandfather died. You remember Mr. _____.

B—: Yeah.

HJ: The body and the tree when they went to church.

B—: Yeah. I remember those stories.

HJ: Here I am, white as hell.

B—: I have all those stories, about the awful things that happened and all the people who tried in my family. There have been lots of awful, awful things that happened, and there have also been lots of white people who have tried. I have both stories. My grandfather would have died except a white man called the doctor and said, "You goddamn son of a bitch, you gotta treat him and you gotta treat him now." And he did and my grandfather lived. Stories. (crying throughout) My other grandfather died cause the whites killed him. Both stories. They killed him because he did everything. He came to the hospital and they gave him something and killed him. I know all the stories.

HJ: I invite you to get rid of some of your rage because I love you. Not because it's fair or balanced or anything of this sort. Just for a few minutes see if you dare to rage.

B—: Oh, I know what we can do. Remember that dream I had? With that little man? Well, part of the story that I might not have said is that that little man was white.

HJ: Get him.

B—: Yeah. I could go for that. The last I saw of it, he was lying on the ground with a broken back. But maybe I can get him back.

HJ: Make the ends of his spine grate against each other.

B—: I can do that. (Angry sounds)

HJ: You're doing fine. Just keep going.

B—: Just let me connect with the thought. Let me keep thinking about my grandfather. (tears) You know my grandfather. You bastards, you got in his way! You got in his way! You got in his way! I told you. He was a lawyer. He was a judge. You know what he would have done if you hadn't gotten in his way. You goddamn bastards. You got in his way. My life would have been different if you hadn't gotten in his way.

HJ: You're carrying the white evil one over to the edge of the canyon and you're going to drop him a thousand feet.

B—: (crying) You got in his way.

HJ: People should look after their own.

B—: He did so much. I think about what he might have done if you hadn't gotten in his way! He did so much. But the racism died him down. It didn't die him down, it just slowed him down. And it killed him, killed him. You killed my granddaddy. You killed him. You killed him. (over and over)

HJ: Can we put a check there?

The central point of this demonstration is not helping her get this distress off. This is real important, but the central point right now for you whites to see clearly is that it isn't going to hurt you a bit to listen to the full rage of people of color. The second person that did this with me was S—, the reporter. She "didn't want to do it" and she "knew better than that," and so on, but finally agreed to trust me. She took about eight whangs at me, and when I said; "What are you thinking?" she said, "I am amazed at how good this feels."

After that she went to work. She really went to work. She did a lot of discharging looking at a white and raging, and it was quite important. She obviously discharged this stuff at a much greater speed, doing it directly to a white who didn't run, who didn't get upset back. It was a good demonstration, and we were cooperating well. Barbara and I have an affectionate relationship, but S— didn't wind up affectionate with me, so that is not a universal result. However, there are a whole bunch of things that would have been good for her to do in the Community, which she was very reluctant to do. In part I think it was because it is a white Community, and in part I think because I as a white man had asked her to do them. She didn't make any announcement of a change of heart, but she went ahead and took on these jobs afterwards. When I hear from her these days, it's obvious that we have a clear communication channel. She may not love me yet, but she respects me and trusts me enough to go ahead. So listening to people of color rage like this is no big deal. I wish we could do many demonstrations of it, but at least you got a little glimpse of the possibilities. The fact that you whites are going to get all kinds of resentment thrown at you occasionally, because people of color are not free of it, not free of hurts, is no real obstacle to what you're after, which is to eliminate racism from your life. There's not any excuse for you not doing your job.

Another "block" that you're going to hit is that sometimes the person of color "doesn't want" a relationship with you. You may have to listen to quite a bit of how much they don't want it. "Get out of my yard and don't ever bother me again." "Stay out of my part of town." Just be logical about it. If you were a person of color living under racism all the time, think what an advantage it would be to have a decent white ally. Of course the person of color wants a white ally. Of course it's of great advantage to him or her! He or she may not be able to say so, certainly even think it, let alone act like it until much of the accumulated grief, fear, and anger from being a victim of racism is discharged out of the way, but, given the oppression, alliance with you has to be very desirable, if it's a real alliance and not phony. It has to be a great assistance to living. Louis

Armstrong, in his autobiography, told how when he came North and started to have some successes, he knew he had to have a white ally for safety. So he found a white man who had some prestige and clout, and worked out a deal with him where he would be his "Ally." He needed a white ally who would come to his support. He didn't care what he paid. He knew the advantage of it. We're not proposing anything like that, but it may help you get a glimpse of the reality hidden under your fear that the person of color doesn't want you for a friend.

Of course, you can make a huge difference. If one has been a person of color, to have one or more dependable white allies (leaving aside any partial advantages) gives one a different picture of the world. If you can see a white person really acting like a human being, that is entirely different than the picture you've gotten most days of your life, up till now. It gives one a little hope. Remember when you first heard that patterns weren't people, how your heart lifted up? This is parallel to that.

I think we need to set a practical goal that if you are an RCer, and you have any chance of making contact with a person of color in this racist society, you do it. We're not setting up programs here for India or China or anything like that. We're talking about the United States, and to the extent it fits, to Canada, The Netherlands, and England. They're not too different. (England seems like they're trying to copy the racism of the U.S. these days.) I propose that in these situations, to be an RCer is to give priority of attention to any person of color when you are with them, is to seek them out in your community, is to make close friends of them, is to be an ally to them. This is not to get them into RC, not necessarily to help them to build black RC or Asian RC or Latino RC, but to clean our lives of racism. This is so we don't hate ourselves in the strong undercurrent of our feelings so much of every day and every night for living in a restricted world and tolerating it, for living in an unfair, unjust, destructive world and tolerating it.

I get a huge satisfaction from being able to make contact quickly over the barriers of any oppression. I've been motivated to do it because I took on this job. Somebody has to go first, somebody has to try to model for the RC Community. I go ahead and try overcoming these barriers, and when it works, my confidence gets higher and higher. It's very, very satisfying. I think your building close relationships with people of color will be thoroughly rewarding in just that way. We need to keep it very clear that we're not doing this to make life easier for people of color, we're not doing it to prove we're hotshot RCers, we're doing it because our lives are stained and corroded every day that we don't. Something like that. To reassure your timidity, I say that in the nature of things you can count as a fact that all persons of color would like a white ally no matter how much distress they have to work through before they can even say it or trust you even this much. All my experience says exactly that if you make the right moves, the response will be overwhelming.

I hope this will be a revolution in RC. That we'll quit doing the posturing and the euphemisms and making a professional career out of anti-racism and going through motions like that, and just get down to the basic acts. There are enough RCers that if this many white RCers, or even a quarter of them (because not all white RCers are in the habit of leaping to the front line positions quickly) made a sharp break with this in the next six months, I think the situation in the U.S. would change dramatically. This is the groundwork which has been missing. We haven't had enough whites doing this. We have enough white RCers that even if other whites didn't follow us in any substantial numbers, this groundwork would make possible the building of all the coalitions that have been so hard to get started. There will be enough whites who can be trusted, who can negotiate between the great groups of people who need to be setting up coalitions right now against atomic war, against the crushing depression that's going to make some of us hungry if we don't get our act together real fast. Does that make sense?

Question: Are you saying that the primary strategic thrust of our living and working needs to be the building of these relationships with people of color, rather than working with other whites on eliminating racism among whites; that that means expanding the influence that what we're doing can have?

HJ: Well, as I said, those of you who are making a living or part of a living or "gaining prestige" from doing these "white racism" workshops you've been doing, fine. It won't hurt anything. The things you speak of can be important side effects, but I think the thrust has to be that our lives change, individually. You, E—, must start reaching for and making large numbers of close relationships with people of color. (Not treasuring the few you've got and thinking "I'm not as bad as some people.") I think this is where the blow must be struck. If we get distracted to the side activities, we'll get into maneuvering, and going through motions, and living out our embarrassments, and letting our fears operate in these side areas, instead of going to the persons of color and paying attention to them.

Our first tool in building a world community (remember?) is to give up the habit of trying to get other people's attention. In order to do that, we commit ourselves to paying attention to other people whenever we are with them. Now we're saying, knock the racism aside and seek out and pay attention to people of color. They will become a substantial part of our Community.

Whites in large numbers are enormously eager to be in a relationship where they can humanly relate to people of color. Under their distress, even the most blatant racists hate the fact that they are separated, segregated, terrified, and all that. I'm guessing out loud that the key point is a close relationship with the person of color. If you achieve that, it will enhance your world community, enhance the success of coalitions, it will enhance the anti-racism work that you do for the Portland school board. Take the whites this, instead of what you have been teaching them, which has been very ennobling, and got them excited, and made them want more workshops, but hasn't really changed their lives at all.

E—: What was specifically in my mind was doing a workshop or two with other whites in RC on this. How would you see that going?

HJ: I don't know. If it's a substitute for you going out and reaching people of color—

E—: No. In addition to.

HJ: Okay. I'd do the other first, before I did a workshop. It's so easy to find something "satisfying" and not so difficult to do, as a substitute for what needs to be done.

E—: Would you address the question of how whites feel about other whites' attitudes about racism?

HJ: I think we need to do that.

Question: I've read that some people believe that whites are equally as much hurt as the target groups are by the effects of racism. Do you believe they are hurt to that degree, or should that be stressed one way or the other?

HJ: Well, I don't think you can measure it or equalize it or compare it, because the hurts are different. The statement that racism is equally hard on the whites and the people of color is confusing. When someone is beating someone up, both people's humanness is suffering, but it surely makes a difference which end of the stick you're on. To attempt to assign any comparison or equality is misleading and a waste of time. But we pay a heavy price for tolerating racism as whites, there's no question about that. The obvious harm done by racism to the oppressed group is ghastly. The harm done to the oppressor group, to the agents-of-oppression group, is hidden from us quite a bit. When we would do the three-step technique (which in practice turns out to be the two-step technique, doing the second step well is where you get all the discharge), we got a picture of the tremendous hurt that was imposed on the small child when they gave up and succumbed to the racist or other oppressive roles. The broken-hearted sobs went on for a long time at that point. Yet that person often had no previous awareness of feeling that it was bothering them at all, except for a sense of guilt. Racism does huge damage to the people in the oppressor roles.

Q—: I'm confused about something. I understand that if you have only a few people of color in your class, it would be all right to focus your attention on them and counsel them. Is it beneficial to have them work on what's been difficult about being a person of color in a class of whites?

HJ: Sure. That's also very precious knowledge for the whites.

Q—: I know it's good for whites, but is it good for the people of color?

HJ: Sure. They've been waiting all their lives for whites to listen to them about this.

Q—: I assume as a principle that there are unique aspects to each oppression, which need to be learned about and understood. Would you agree that there are also some commonalities in reaching across any barrier?

HJ: Yes.

Q—: How do you see racism in a key role in terms of what we need to be putting emphasis on? In the light of other major oppressions, all the other oppressions, but I'm thinking in particular of sexism, oppression of the disabled, oppression of the elderly. Why is racism an area of key emphasis?

HJ: Good question. Remember that all oppressions are rooted in classism, the economic exploitation of the working classes. All the rest of the oppressions have been invented and perpetuated in order to divide the working people from each other. Every oppression is extremely important. No oppression is so small as not to deserve the full attention and support of everybody to eliminate it. Every oppression is part of the overall nastiness of the oppressive society which is spoiling people's lives. Patterns created the first oppressive societies, created slave societies, but the organization which accompanied the slave society handled the environment better, let more children live to maturity, allowed populations to grow larger. Actually, we now see that we could have had the organization without the oppression, but no advanced brothers or sisters from other planets arrived in their flying saucers to tell us so at that point. So we blundered into the class society rigidity, starting with slave societies.

Every oppression is important, especially if it's the one that's oppressing you. We have tried, in RC, to advance notch by notch. We've tried to advance toward general responsibility, estimating with some reassurance that our complex central nervous systems inherently gave us vast awareness and intelligence, but also complete freedom of decision and complete power, and therefore complete responsibility. There is nothing beyond our reach or possibility to handle. Therefore we assume responsibility for ending all oppressions.

We are able to have this meeting against racism this weekend in part because we have done at least a fair job at combatting sexism. We're not satisfied. We've got that battle to the point where many RC women have gotten caught on a "plateau" of being "self-satisfied" with their liberation, until a man walks into the room and they start talking in small voices. We're making a battle on that at the West Coast Women's Conference and the one in Boston in December and the one that will be in England in July next year, to get women moving off this false plateau of "aren't we free and liberated" while still settling for great gobs of oppression that they are "comfortable with" and "used to."

Owning-class people are oppressed. We're currently challenging them on the patterns they're "comfortable" with, the arrogance, the condescension, the always taking over, the assuming that what's good for them is good for everybody.

We're having this workshop on racism because we have been and are in real danger of going on putting out lots of effort with not very much result. A lot of people intuited something was wrong. Emma and Judy have been calling for this workshop for a long time. A lot of us have been concerned. I have tried here to bring this to a general awareness. I'm very confident of what I'm saying. We were settling for working on the wrong issues. We were trying, but we need a better policy.

Every oppression is the most important oppression. You can say that classism is the most important because it is the source of all the rest, it's the reason for all the rest of them being invented. You can say that the oppression of young people is the most important one because it's the one that trains everybody to submit to all the rest. In this society, in this U.S., racism is one of the most evil characteristics of the society. It has deep roots and a long tradition. We should be moving out of it faster than we have been. We need these policies and clearer programs.

Emma: All the other kinds of oppression that you mentioned affect people of color the same as they do white people. The issue of peace in the world is something we have to solve together. We have to work together to eliminate sexism and adultism, and all of the other oppressions. Eliminating racism means uniting our forces. That's why I think it is such a key issue and that's why I wanted this workshop.

HJ: Our policy has not been correct enough.

Q—: I've heard quite a number of times that the other oppressions were invented to divide the working class. It's obvious how it actually works that way, but "invented" seems like it was the initiative of a single person.

HJ: The process is hard to describe, since our usual language doesn't allow for the existence of patterns. We're continually having to borrow ordinary words and phrases, and redefine them. A pattern doesn't "invent" anything, since it's completely rigid. There must have been intelligence involved, but it must have been enslaved by the pattern at that point. It's easy to imagine that, once, a war leader kept some war captives and thought, "If I scare them enough, they'll herd the sheep for me, and I won't have to do it myself." You can see that it might have seemed to him like a better and more kindly thing to do than killing them.

That was the "invention" of exploitation, the "invention" of class society. I don't pretend the word fits, but we don't have any better words in most languages. When we translate RC literature from English to other languages, I always hear this complaint, "We don't have words that mean this in our language. Only in America do you have words that mean this." I have to explain that in the United States we don't have them either. We borrowed them and redefined them.

Q—: I wasn't so much picking on the words. I was wonder-

ing how you think sexism would develop as a capitalistic function.

HJ: It developed as a slave function, and then just persisted through feudalism and into capitalism. Once the slaveowner had some war captives working for him, and his wealth was piling up, it was inevitable that he'd think if a few more people were doing this it would be neat. In a male-dominated society, women and children were right there to be enslaved. They may have been equal before, but not now that exploitation had developed. Once the greed patterns are installed, the exploiter looks for anybody else who can be exploited. Then you set the men slaves against the women slaves, to keep them busy fighting each other, instead of the slaveowner.

Q—: First clarify for me, are you saying the policy that you are putting forward now is a policy of white people going after and making friends with people of color as the way, or one way, to end racism?

HJ: To end their own racism. To enrich their lives.

We'll still have to have lots of detailed policies. We'll push every group of people of color, to develop Chinese RC, black RC, Puerto Rican RC, and we'll throw support to them; but to push for this policy for whites becomes crucial. We need work on the internalized racism within every group. We need better counselors who are white, to help them work on that. It's much easier to help on internalized oppression from outside the oppression, than it is for the person in the middle of it. So we will have lots of facets of struggle, but this is a key one, that we whites no longer tolerate our isolation from non-whites. At this moment, I excitedly think that is the key link in the chain.

Q—: I want to ask Emma, Barbara, and Tommy, what do you all think about this position?

Emma: I agree with it totally. When you are living your life a certain way, it really helps to take a look at the perspective of that place and move from that place.

Barbara: I always advocated this in my work, in my workshops, that people do it for their own lives. In my class at the University, I make it an assignment. It's a required assignment. Yes, I think it's a useful policy.

Tommy: Ditto.

The Oppressions of
Women and Men

Our work on liberation from various oppressions has gone well. Work on the liberation of women from their nearly universal relegation to second-class status in human affairs has begun to be accompanied by work for the liberation of men. Work against both of these oppressions has in practice, however, led to confusions about the relationship between these liberation struggles and to a certain weakening of the momentum of women's liberation.

The battle of women and their allies against sexist oppression has been the most widespread and the most hopeful of people's struggles in the last decades. This vicious oppression of over half of the people of the world had perpetuated itself without effective challenge for thousands of years. It was called into question and much of its foundations eroded in a remarkably short period of time, speaking historically. The main structure of the oppression still stands, its cruelty and viciousness still operate, but it is a sick, wounded monster. It can never recover its domination of human populations in the ways it dominated them for so long.

The oppression of men must be as ancient as the oppression of women, but its very existence has, until recently, been largely obscured by the assignment to men of the roles of oppressors of women, and the conditioning of men to accept and play out these roles. The shortening of men's lives by the special conditioning against discharge, the saddling of men with over-fatigue and over-responsibility, and their cannon-fodder military role in war time—have been clearly identified as the key features of their oppression.

Appeared in **Present Time** No. 77, October 1989.

These two oppressions have to be equally ancient. Neither of them could have arisen until class societies had become established. The fundamental oppression in class societies is economic, the robbery of the majority producing class by the minority ruling class of much of the value produced by the majority. All other oppressions, including the oppression of women and the oppression of men, arose as a means of dividing the economically oppressed against each other and keeping them from uniting against the economic oppression. Certainly there were greed patterns operating in pre-society cultures, but there was no advantage to be gained by people operating in such greed patterns from the oppression of either women or men until economic exploitation had entered the picture.

Similarly, individual cruelty arises only from distress patterns. Such patterns certainly existed pre-society, but there was no motivation of profit to support and perpetuate such mistreatment patterns until economic exploitation could take place.

Separate gender roles can arise from economic necessity, from the restrictions of child-bearing or from accidental cultural developments. However, these separate gender roles do not involve oppression until economic exploitation can begin to operate.

Since class societies have existed somewhere for several thousand years, this will mean that the oppression of women and the oppression of men have been operating for thousands of years, effectively unchallenged in the one case and effectively unrecognized in the other.

As the twentieth century draws to a close, it is plain that women are everywhere oppressed. They are everywhere held to a kind of second-class citizenship involving economic, educational, and cultural deprivation and, often, sexual degradations. Men also are oppressed.

Real progress has been made toward both women's liberation and men's liberation in the current world around us. Real progress has been made toward women's liberation and men's liberation within the Re-evaluation Counseling Communities. The policies and techniques of RC have made a substantial contribution to the effectiveness of both liberation movements in the wide world.

Past progress is not by any means sufficient, however. This is a dynamic universe in which continual progress is necessary. Although rates of progress will vary at different periods, holding back on ongoing progress will quickly lead to stagnation, mistakes, and defeat. If thinking is not taking place in any struggle, if progress is not being currently made, then mistaken ideas will easily gain currency and "get by." Under such conditions, out-of-date ideas will tend to be accepted unthinkingly because of their association with past progress or with previously effective leaders.

I have recently heard the oppression of men described in an RC group as "the other side of sexism." In a similar discussion I heard someone say, "Men are oppressed by sexism, too," without anyone taking exception to the statements. I have seen women leaders draw back from their own liberation plans and postpone their own activities because "it's now time for men to work on their oppression," as if only one liberation could receive attention and support at a given time. Women speak of themselves as "liberated" who still automatically lower their voices and change the topic of conversation among themselves, when a man or men enter the room.

I think it is time for clarification of our work in these two liberation movements and for updating of our policies and plans.

First of all, if "sexism" is the accepted label for women's oppression (and it is), then the oppression of men is not part of "sexism." The oppression of men is a completely distinct oppression. Certainly men are disadvantaged by, and suffer from, their participation in the oppression of women ("sexism"), but this participation and the negative effects upon men do not meet the criteria for an oppression. The oppression of men is very real and drastic, but it consists of exactly the factors that we have defined above—denial of recovery from distress through the active discouragement of discharge, enforced over-responsibility, enforced over-fatigue, and male lives being made hostage to military whim. Men are no more oppressed by participating in the oppression of women ("sexism") than parents are oppressed by participating in the oppression of children.

The most liberated of women have achieved only a fraction of what complete liberation will bring them. The women's movements inside and outside of RC, with their present relative inactivity and lack of long-range perspective, are settling for the tiniest portion of what full liberation will bring. Men's liberation should in no way excuse any hold-up or delay on the progress of women's liberation, but instead should bring millions of powerful allies to the support of the women's movement.

Men's liberation activists cannot accept any "separatist" position such as that it is "now the men's turn to be liberated." The two liberation movements must fully support each other's most far-reaching programs for either one of them to achieve what is within their grasp. It is part of men's reclaiming of their power that they become powerful fighters for women's rights, powerful full partners in the struggle for equality and respect for everyone, powerful champions of the oppressed of every variety. Men have rich traditions from the past of being such champions and will be thrilled to be challenged to be successful on these fronts again.

I call on all men's and women's liberation leaders to at once form powerful, public alliances, to inspire and support the development of more advanced liberation policies by each other. There is a valuable clarity which each movement can offer the other through being outside the other's oppression. I propose that men and women become expert, devoted counselors of the other gender in each case, using their excellent and clear view of each other's internalized oppression.

Draft Policy for Artists' Liberation

1. The essence of being human is the ability to be creative; to create new responses to new situations; to construct new, significant complexities where they did not exist before; to take charge of the environment and move it farther along the upward trend.

2. It is true that spontaneous processes within the universe also move in this direction, but the human artist, being possessed of human intelligence, is able to move more directly and more rapidly. The artist can greatly enhance the already inherent tendency within the universe toward meaning, toward complexity, toward independence, toward freedom. The artist is, in this sense, a prototype of a human being.

3. The artist is also a prototype of the working-class person in that society takes the value of the work produced by the artist (which may be extremely valuable) and returns to the artist only a small portion of the value produced.

4. In another sense the oppression of the artist is much like the oppression of parents in that the production of human beings and the production of new ideas and new concepts are the most important achievements of human beings in the society. Yet the work for either parent or artist is decreed by the society to be unpaid or almost totally unpaid.

5. Artists are oppressed for being artists in addition to whatever oppressions they may suffer because of their race, their class, their gender, their sexual preference, their physi-

Appeared in **Creativity** No. 2, 1988.

cal state, their age. Artists suffer a great deal from this oppression. Their work is belittled by certain systematically perpetuated attitudes of the society. Artists are invalidated as non-producers, as drop-outs, as lazy triflers. Their lives are made very difficult economically. They are frequently forced to work at another job in order to support their own production of art, in much the same way as parents must find other careers in order to support the production of children. They are forced to compete for crumbs. It is made very, very difficult for them to offer their art for the appreciation of the public. A horde of exploiters surrounds the art business, living well off the value produced by the artist while allowing very little of this value to be shared by the artist himself or herself.

6. This oppression becomes internalized in two main ways. One is that most artists fight terrible feelings of self-invalidation. They often are made to doubt that their work is significant and must persist in creating, burdened by heavy feelings of discouragement and hopelessness. A critical review can not only damage the public's appreciation of their art but also their own self-esteem. Artists are also pushed by the internalized oppression to be critical and disparaging of each other. Artists usually have to compete for very scanty opportunities to sell their art. They are often pushed to work in isolation for fear that the creativity which they have achieved will be plagiarized. They can feel very envious of other artists' successes, which may saturate the scanty market which might otherwise have existed for their own work.

7. A complete end to the oppression of artists will require the elimination of the oppressive society. Until then the motivation of profit as the overall driving force in the society will tend to exclude rational motivations and rational opportunities for artists, and re-inforce every oppression. For their own survival artists will tend to become wide-world-changers. Artists tend intuitively to associate themselves with the forces of progress. Artists can be very effective in inspiring people

for successful struggle to replace the oppressive society with a non-exploitative one. History is full of brilliant examples of artists putting their art at the service of the people, at the service of social change.

8. Artists need to fight for their own liberation as artists as well as the liberation of society, and this can not be postponed until the change-over to a rational society. The struggle for the liberation of artists needs to be conducted every day in every way.

9. Artists need a clear policy as a necessary precondition for the great changes in the society. They need unity among themselves. They need to win allies for themselves, just as every other liberation group needs to. Artists need to establish their organizations on as narrow a basis as the society has divided them. Undoubtedly leaders' groups and support groups need to be organized separately for dancers, for painters, for musicians, for actors, for writers, for performers of every kind. Once organized in their homogeneities they need to establish unity and mutual support between the different kinds of artists and their allies in an overall front for the advancement of art and of artists.

10. Artists need to achieve unity in order to make their economic force effective. Artists *do* have economic power, just as does any group of important working-class people, in that it is their work that furnishes the value which is the income of the entire establishment. If artists do unite they can require far better recognition and remuneration and working conditions than they have been granted by the oppressive art establishment and society so far.

11. Collective dealing with gallery owners or collectors, for example, can secure better terms. (The actors unions have improved conditions considerably, even with the most limited policies.) Artists can join in cooperative endeavors to provide their own showcases for their work. Artists can, with a cor-

rect policy, enlist art students and amateur artists as allies and supporters for the work of the serious and professional artists, instead of treating them as threatening competition.

12. There can be no such thing as "too much" art. Undoubtedly in a rational society everyone will be creative. Everyone will produce art in some way. There will always be people, however, who, through choice and dedication, take their creativity much farther, who will be recognized as "artists" for their special contributions.

13. Some city governments in the U.S. have, in the last few years, allotted a certain percentage of their construction funds for the purchase of art. One percent of a building's construction cost is set aside for art, for example. Even this tiny concession has multiplied many-fold the avenues open for the artists of the city to market their works.

14. Everyone's life should be enhanced by art. People will intuitively support this idea if the artists themselves will take leadership and show the possibility of unity and correct policy.

15. The principle obstacles to creativity by any artist are exactly the distress recordings which have accumulated upon the individual artist from past mistreatment. RC has a fundamental role to play in allowing the creativity of the artist to come free from these inhibiting patterns.

16. Artists occasionally express fear, as they begin Co-Counseling, that their creativity is tied up with their distresses and they will lose it if they lose their distress. This is just the echo of slander from the oppressive society that "all artists have to be a little irrational or they won't be creative." Nothing from reality bears this out. It is true that many meaningful artists have suffered from heavy distress, but they created *in spite of* the distress and not *because* of it. The record of the many artists in RC is that their creativity is greatly enhanced by their re-emergence. There is nothing they could do while distressed that they can't do better with the distress discharged.

17. RC offers to the artist a rational view of the world, a theory which not only explains oppression and liberation but empowers individuals to do something about it. It also offers tools for the recovery of one's mastery of the environment, of taking power and of creating more and more wonderful and exciting works.

18. In organizing among artists RCers will need to face the division of artists from each other by the society and organize support groups on the basis of finer and finer distinctions. For example, actors and actresses may begin meeting in support groups with mimes, but eventually there will need to be a mime support group (as well as a support group for musical comedy performers and one for Shakespearean actors).

19. Unity between all these different groups of artists can be established through leaders' groups (Wygelian type) which meet from time to time as meetings are needed. Artists in the wide world are eager for this kind of support. The isolation which many artists endure is a galling hardship to them. The organization of artists in these simple forms that meet their real needs, i.e. support groups for discharge, classes to improve their Co-Counseling, and leaders' groups for planning policies and actions, will meet enthusiastic participation everywhere.

Preliminary Report to the 1988 Young People's Leaders' Conference

—Gill Turner and Harvey Jackins

Young people are oppressed.

The oppression of young people plays a vital role in maintaining our oppressive society. The oppression is profound and effective in reducing our power and trust in our own thinking to the point that we can fit into, be abused by, and support the non-human society which, as adults, we must function within and maintain. Particularly as young people, we are trained to be silent in the face of other oppressions.

We are living at an exciting time. We now recognize the existence of the oppression of young people, its severity, and its universal nature. We are becoming clear about the ways the oppression is installed. These include systematic invalidation, denial of any voice or respectful attention, physical abuse, lack of information, misinformation, denial of any power, economic dependency, lack of rights, lack of high expectations, and combinations of all of the above.

The manners in which the installed patterns of oppression are maintained include repetition of all the methods of installation, intense rehearsal of the internalized oppression by the young people at each other, and the installation of inhibitions on discharge.

We understand how the oppression is maintained by the continuing activity and attitudes of the agents of young people's oppression—adults, parents, teachers, schools, religions, police, "mental health" systems, armed forces, and others.

Appeared in **Present Time** No. 70, January 1988.

Adults who care deeply for young people have sometimes been confused by the myth that oppressive attitudes toward us ("discipline," "training for adult life," "guiding us well") are actually of benefit to us. This has always been false and has served to perpetuate the oppression.

The inhibition on discharge has had a major role in preventing us from recovering from our initial hurts and in maintaining the oppression. We now see the devastating effect of the internalized oppression, of invalidating ourselves and each other constantly. We are now ready to organize specifically for the ending of the oppression.

Why do human adults participate in the oppression of young people? Because the same patterns were installed on the adults themselves when they were young. Now when they are adults they are being restimulated and pulled into the opposite role in these patterns by the presence of young people.

There is no rational reason, or necessity, for the oppression of young people. All humans deserve complete respect from all other humans. Differences in age, physical size, information, skills, or experience between people are interesting variations. Without underlying patterns, already installed by oppression of the previous generation, these would be no excuse for mistreatment or disrespect of any kind.

In the world as a whole, the oppression of young people plays the crucial role in keeping the entire world population powerless. Until the oppression is imposed, young people have a wide world view, expect the best, have high aspirations, see the entire picture as a whole. One role of the oppression against young people is to narrow their view, to make them feel powerless, and to limit their concerns only to their narrowest survival of themselves and of their groups— to "lose the big picture." This prepares the whole world population to be powerless in the face of the oppressions. If the human race as a whole is to be liberated, then the oppression of young people must be ended to interrupt this process.

THE CHARACTERISTICS OF THE OPPRESSION OF YOUNG PEOPLE

The fundamental characteristic of the oppression of young people is the lack of respect toward them. This is manifested in many ways: physical abuse, the institutionalized oppressions of schools, lack of legal rights, lack of political voice, denial of information, misinformation, and the lack of any economic base.

Economically, as younger young people, we have no economic independence at all. As we begin to earn, we are massively exploited in terms of our wages and the conditions we work under. The lowest paid, most dangerous, and most boring jobs are·imposed upon us. We are told that we must be grateful for this because we are "receiving training." Our work is never appreciated as the valuable work that it is. In any work situation, young people tend to be at the bottom of the situation as a sort of "sub-working-class." We are the most intensely exploited, the least appreciated, and the most disorganized. Even when some protections have been won for young people in work situations, these operate in a patronizing and condescending manner. This enforces the notion that we are powerless and must be taken care of by someone else rather than encouraging us to be responsible ourselves for insisting on decent treatment.

WHAT IS THE CURRENT SITUATION?

At present young people constitute approximately one half of the world's population. Potentially, with clear program and unity, we are in a position to change the world completely within a very few years if we do not allow the present oppressive situation to continue. All young people want liberation, yearn for liberation, and if given an opportunity, will participate in it. Young people are of great variety and of many fresh ideas and are ready to move quickly and decisively in ways that adults have great trouble in moving.

Young people are not without allies. There are significant forces within the adult population that are deeply concerned about what is happening to young people in the present collapsing society. Even where their present attitudes are patronizing and condescending, these allies can be reached and their attitudes can be clarified. They have power, influence, and money, and they can be decisive allies for us.

The oppression of young people is completely wrong and abhorrent. It is a complete falsehood that oppressive attitudes toward us are for our own benefit, that they represent "caring" for us, or "educating" or "disciplining" or "supporting" us, or that they "prepare us well for adult life"—these are myths. There is nothing about the oppression of young people that is pro-human. It is always destructive to young people and to the adult agents who perpetrate it.

A world-wide young people's liberation movement is crucially needed in the interests of the entire world population and the interests of the whole world's survival. If it wasn't for the conditioning by the oppression for us to be silent, we would all be in a continual vocal outrage and would not tolerate for an instant the current anti-human tendencies and destructive actions in the world.

There needs to be an organized, coordinated liberation *movement*. Young people standing individually against the oppression will not be effective enough because of the depth, persistence, and severity of the conditioning of young people's oppression throughout the entire world population. The individual young person alone, daring to speak out for liberation, to rebel against the oppression, is in such a vulnerable position against the various agencies of oppression, that he or she can be intimidated or even destroyed by the legal system, by the violence that is always available. It is absolutely necessary that young people act in concert. While it is useful for the individual to speak up, individual rebellion is not enough.

WITHIN THE RC COMMUNITY

Within the RC Community, there is support for the principle of young people's liberation, and although patterns may interfere with effective, enthusiastic support and encouragement, there is agreement that there should be an effective young people's liberation within RC.

There is now a network of young people who understand the theory of RC and the theory of liberation and understand the necessity of a young people's liberation movement. Within the Re-evaluation Counseling Community there are a substantial number of young people who, through using Re-evaluation Counseling, have regained their ability to lead, to trust and share their thinking. The quality of young people's leadership and our numbers have increased. We have learned a lot in our discussions with each other about the nature of the oppression and we have learned a lot about how to assist each other to discharge the hurts from the oppression and the internalized oppression.

As young people and young leaders in RC have become older and have become young adults, they have in the main remained clear on the nature of young people's oppression and the importance of young people's liberation. We have at least the beginnings of mutual support between young adults and young people in RC, seeing the transition to young adulthood as an opportunity for being better allies, rather than as separation from, the young people's movement. We are learning to use the information, skills, and experience of the young adults while the young people themselves remain in the leadership role and are completely in charge of young people's liberation. This needs more clarification. Learning to do this more and more effectively will be an ongoing process.

SOME WIDE-WORLD TRADITIONS

We are not the first liberation movement of young people. Movements consisting primarily of young people have played an important part in achieving improvements in society. In the present liberation struggles of the world young people twelve to eighteen are often the majority of the freedom fighters. Within other organizations, for example, churches, political groups, etc., young people have been able to move toward liberation, despite the limitations and oppressive attitudes enforced by the adult organizations. Young people have been able to achieve some independence of thinking and communication and cooperation with one another.

The possibility of a real young people's liberation movement probably could not have arisen without the concepts of Re-evaluation Counseling. It is the opportunity to discharge, to free our own thinking, to get outside these patterns, that has made it possible for at least some young people to begin thinking independently and rationally in this area—to begin to draw up the guidelines for what will be a real young people's liberation movement.

The young people's liberation movement must *belong* to the young people—it cannot be sponsored or guided by outside forces.

While we do have good ideas and we are very clear about the things that we want to change and the policies we will follow, we do not as yet have any clear idea about what a wide world young people's liberation movement would be like. We do not have such a movement or even the beginnings of it. Even in the most progressive movements in the parts of the world where young people are the vanguard of the liberation fighters, it is still not for young people; it is an extension of the adult movement, fighting for the adults' cause.

Let us speculate for a moment about what the characteristics of such a movement might be. It needs to be available to and representative of *all* young people. Its primary program needs to be the liberation of young people *for* young people, not within any other context. It needs to be for all ages of young people, with mutual respect between all ages. It needs to have adult allies but also be very clear that the adult allies do not determine policy, that adult allies only support the policies of the young people as determined by the young people themselves. The liberation movement must be so organized that it is open to and representatively led by working-class and other additionally oppressed groups within young people as a whole, rather than to be dominated by middle-class young people due to their greater freedom to participate.

It must be structured and function in such a way that every young person's thinking is heard and not dominated by those who, because of training or class position, are able to be more eloquent or more widely-informed. It needs to be independent of adult organizations in everything except the support which the adult organizations offer, and which the adult organizations offer without any strings in terms of determining policies or practices.

As young people, we need a dependable base of support. In the past, we have had to rely on parents, family, individual adult friends and existing organizations of the oppressive society, and this has been a major limiting factor in our liberation. As our actions to combat the oppression cause conflict within these supportive relationships, we need to provide reliable support for each other, and our liberation movement must have a clear way of operating so that the support of other young people is immediately available to each one of us. Due to the severity of the oppression, this may need to have some of the characteristics of a "secret" society, of a private fellowship or sisterhood. Young people need a dependable base of support. Having had to rely on parents, family, and existing organizations of the oppressive society has been a major inhibition because young people's liberation will certainly, and does, come in conflict with the patterns that infest all these relationships. We must have a clear way for our liberation movement to operate so that the support of other young people is immediately available to the young people in it. We must be able to rely on each other and not permit the isolation which has dominated our lives to continue.

Eliminating the oppression of young people is a *big* job. There are many things to change, overt and subtle forms of the oppression to identify, clarify and abolish; institutionalized oppression to dismantle along with many oppressive attitudes accepted for centuries. We must not underestimate the extent of the oppression and its ability to disillusion young people and limit their thinking and power, in addition to the practical, legal, financial and political hurdles that young people must overcome. However, we have huge resources to hand: the young people of the world, our numbers, our commitment to liberation, our diversity, and our ability to respond and act quickly.

WHERE CAN WE START?

We start with the resources and the numbers and the individuals that are available to us. We here at this conference will be a somewhat representative small sample of the great numbers of young people who can be quickly contacted by the ideas of Re-evaluation Counseling through a structure of support groups, classes, young people's leaders groups, and a communication network. This can be based on **Young and Powerful** and regular letters from the international leadership to the local leadership, and a system for emergency use of phone resources. We can furnish the unity and contact which will enable us to work through to the finer points of organization in growing numbers.

The depth of despair of most young people about their real freedom needs to be faced. We must find the way to gather and use the resources and communicate the contradiction to this despair that is immediately available. We have at least enough resources for the exciting job at hand, a job central and essential for human liberation as a whole.

An Introduction to
Middle-Class Liberation

All class societies which have existed among humans so far—the slave-owner/slave societies, the feudal lord/serf societies, and the owning-class/working-class societies which presently dominate the world—all have consisted primarily of two classes—the oppressing class which exploits the majority of the population economically, and the oppressed class which is exploited.

In every one of these societies, the invention, development, and enforcement of auxiliary oppressions has taken place in order to divide the majority of the economically oppressed against each other and keep them from successfully uniting and rebelling against the economic exploitation.

Some of the auxiliary oppressions that have been invented and perpetuated are the oppression of one gender by another (usually the oppression of women by men), the oppression of young people by older people, the oppression of many groups of people "racially" on any basis on which they can be distinguished from the rest of the population (often, but not always, skin color), and oppressions based on language, features, size, culture, diet, sexual preference, disability, age, etc.

A PARTICULAR KIND OF OPPRESSION

In each society so far a very important form of division which needs our attention, analysis, and a liberation program has been the division of a part of the working classes on the basis of the functions or roles assigned to them in the economy

Appeared in **Present Time** No. 73, October 1988.

and culture. Some members of the working classes have always been rewarded, bribed, educated, conditioned, or enforced to play the role of the agents of the owning class in carrying out the functions involving management, culture, education, religion, and military leadership.

These functions are necessary for the economy and the culture to operate, and are part of productive work, but the intent, the education, the conditioning, and the enforcement are to make them operate on behalf of the oppression and against the interests of the oppressed, so that these individuals are under heavy conditioning and training to regard their interests as being the same as those of the oppressing class and counter to the interests of the other working classes.

IN PAST SOCIETIES

Under slave-owner/slave societies certain people were allowed to remain free if they would play these roles, or were given privileged positions as slaves, or were promised freedom for their children. In the ancient Roman slave society people were rewarded with citizenship, "Roman citizenship," if they would play these roles well on the behalf of the actual rulers.

Under feudalism, people who carried out the will of the barons and the highest Church hierarchy were given livelihoods as priests and bishops and nuns and monks, as overseers, knights, guildmasters, etc.

LARGER AND LARGER NUMBERS

Under the current owning-class/working-class societies, a huge variety of specially trained, specially educated, specially rewarded working people have been trained and conditioned to be managers on many different levels, professionals, clergy, military officers, or even small subsidiary entrepreneurs or franchise-owners who will take much greater responsibility for the intensive exploitation of a small group of workers in order to feed sub-assemblies or partially produced products into the larger enterprises of the economic system.

Since we are very clear now that members of the owning class are also victimized by the system, and do not deserve the blame of the rest of us or their own feelings of guilt since they, too, have been forced by the system into playing their oppressive roles, it is certainly ridiculous that the guilt which is universal in the current middle classes should be supported or enhanced, or that any of the rest of us in the other divisions of the working classes should rehearse our resentment against the people in these middle-class sections. They have been victimized, bribed, and enforced in a special way, but they share the same oppression basically which the working classes do, and their freedom to be fully human and fully productive lies in the same direction as it does for all the rest of us, which is in a free society without classes where people who work are also the ones who own the means of production.

The middle classes are simply sections of the working classes. The conditioning which has separated them from the rest of the workers and kept up the hostility and resentment on the one side, the guilt and condescension on the other, are simply patterns that need to be discharged. The interests of all of us are in common.

TWO CONTRADICTORY IDEOLOGIES

The effects of the conditioning upon individuals in the middle classes have gone roughly in two directions:

1) The internalization of the conditioning, leading to their acceptance of the notion that they are "special," that their interests are identical with that of the owning classes, that they are "better than" the other working people, and that they must fight to defend and perpetuate the exploitive system, and

2) Widespread rebellion against all this conditioning, enhanced by the relatively freer access of middle-class people to correct information, knowledge, and reality. This has led large numbers of middle-class people to become leaders of reform,

rebellion, and revolutionary movements, and to assume leadership and guidance of movements of the rest of the working class.

The pull in these two directions is responsible for much of the widespread feeling of "confusion" that is almost typical of the distress of middle-class people.

We in RC have been slow to recognize the actual state of affairs for middle-class people, and while we have correctly concentrated on developing the role of the overwhelming majority of the working class (the people who know they are working class) and have even responded to the needs of the owning-class individuals in RC by developing some clarity about their role, we have been very slow to recognize the relatively great importance of middle-class individuals in the movement for re-emergence and the movement for liberation of all people from all oppressions.

At this point, it is essential that we help to initiate, clarify, and organize a vast movement of middle-class people based on the following special characteristics:

1) Middle-class people are actually a section of the working class subject to enormous pressure and conditioning to feel, think, and act as if they were not;

2) Middle-class people are natural allies of all the other working classes, and should be respected, sought out, and welcomed by the working-class movement in general;

3) Ideological clarity must be sought, fought for, and attained for middle-class people in RC and in the wide world movements. Middle-class people must be welcomed as sections of the working class, but the ideology which has been enforced on them, that their interests are the same as those of the owning classes, or that they are smarter than, more dependable than, or superior in any way to the rest of the working class, shall be rejected;

4) Middle-class people shall be helped to establish a movement distinct from the blue-collar, pink-collar, farm, computational, etc. sections of the working class.

5) Middle-class people will be welcomed as members of a division of the working class, but are expected to build, organize, and clarify the ideology of their own movement, and to join the rest of the working classes in their own strength and clarity, rather than simply try to identify with blue-collar, manual, labor, or other working people.

Overall, of course, all the working classes will be united, but not by ignoring the differences in our backgrounds.

All human beings, including the owning classes, are sought as allies and fellow fighters in preventing nuclear holocaust, in establishing a new, rational society, and preserving and enhancing our earth as an elegant home for all living things, a home in which human beings play the role of elder brothers and sisters and caretakers to all other forms of life.

Draft Liberation Policy for Owning-Class People

We propose:

—That it be the policy of owning-class people in RC to welcome into participation in RC and in the RC Community all the members of the owning class who will accept and implement the one-point program of using RC to recover their occluded intelligence and helping others to do the same.

—That we make the RC Community a place where the humanity of owning-class people is understood, accepted, and insisted upon.

—That we insist that class differences, both in the functioning of the society and in the patterns accumulated, are rooted in distress and in the operation of the oppressive societies, and that no person in any class shall ever be blamed or reproached for their position in their class. We welcome the expressed attitude of the working class that we owning-class people are their children who have been taken away from them and conditioned to think we were different, and they welcome us back to the fellowship of all productive humans. We welcome this attitude and we agree with it.

—That we welcome and take joy in the successful re-emergence which owning-class people have attained through their Co-Counseling with each other and with other members of the RC Community. That we especially note our gains in freeing ourselves from isolation, guilt, fear, confusion, ignorance about the real nature of the economic system, and the distress that

Appeared in **Present Time** No. 73, October 1988.

says we have no personal worth but that our worth is determined by our material possessions or our money.

—That we remind each other that other features of the distress that has been imposed upon us as members of the owning class are not so easy to become aware of or to contradict from our association with each other. That these distresses that we call on each other to take notice of, and assist each other to emerge from (and ask help from the working class and other RCers) include: a kind of self-centeredness, the illusion that "what's good for me" (in the narrow sense) is necessarily good for everyone else, arrogance, condescension, assuming we should "take over" in all situations, ungenerousness, irresponsibility to the welfare of others, and a kind of "bargaining" to get the most out of RC we possibly can while contributing as little as possible, or only contributing on a comfortable level.

—That we keep in awareness that the actual power in these owning-class/working-class societies is wielded by the society itself, and that the number of owning-class individuals who can even create the illusion of making important decisions is rapidly shrinking. Most of us may appear to enjoy, or may have the illusion of enjoying, comfort, luxury, and security, but any feeling of "power" or of "independence" within the confines of our class position is purely an illusion for most of us. We are manipulated and dictated to as thoroughly as the poorest members of the working class or the most impoverished declassed individual.

—That we remind each other that our conditioning has set us against each other in vicious competition, and that intelligent cooperation between us can not only free us of this distress but will actually return to us some measure of the real human power that has been taken away from us. (To regain it all will require a new society.)

—That we remind each other constantly that we are completely human and ordinary in every respect, that we as individuals, just as all other RCers, are challenged to build world-class communities around us and to lead, inspire, and organize all people to eliminate every form of humans harming humans.

—That leading, in our case, usually take the form of being a superb support person for helping working-class individuals assume public leadership and freeing them from their internalized invalidations and low self-confidence patterns through our nurturing and counseling them.

—That we suggest to each other that we use every special privilege and the benefit of every privilege that we've ever received, or still receive, to eliminate all special privileges from society.

—That we owning-class RCers discharge and re-evaluate towards a goal of resigning from the owning class, with all deliberate speed and at our own pace, in the way that will most effectively bring real power to all people and real human lives for us.

—That we owning-class RCers plan to intelligently free ourselves from the structures of unearned income and unearned capital, and apply these resources with great intelligence and effectiveness to the liberation of all humans.

—A small minority of the owning class is Jewish. A small minority of Jews are owning-class. Along with members of all other classes, we will eliminate the special oppression of anti-Semitism from the society, and expose and reject the anti-Semitic propaganda that seeks to identify Jews as responsible for the oppressive role of the owning class. That we act similarly toward the special oppressions of any other minority group members of the owning class.

HOW IS THE OWNING CLASS OPPRESSED?

Owning-class people are oppressed because their real power has been denied to them, the same as the members of all the other classes. They have been subordinated to the power of the dead, rigid society, and made to operate for the basic motive of that society, which is the robbery of the majority of the people by a minority for the pseudo-benefit of the minority.

Owning-class people are oppressed because they are subjected to organized, intensively vicious oppression or conditioning in their childhoods in order to prepare them for the exploitive, inhumane role they are expected to play as adults.

The owning class is oppressed because the role they are forced to play or cooperate with imposes on them a huge extra burden of guilt and confusion. Being human, they feel they are responsible for the societal roles which have been forced upon them.

The owning class is oppressed in that they are isolated from the main bulk of humanity to an extra degree. Isolation is a problem for all people in this society, but it is systematically enforced upon the owning class. This is a grievous oppression. It denies them most of the benefits which the wonderful gift of being alive and being intelligent should include.

In the final stages of the owning-class/working-class society, the owning class is oppressed by being largely relegated to meaningless roles. In the beginnings of this society, the functions of management and initiative allowed owning-class people to retain in some part a sense of meaningful purpose. This has largely been wiped away by hired management and the intense concentration of power and wealth in very, very few hands.

The owning class is oppressed by being forced into a position of being the object of intense resentment, hatred, and sometimes, the patterned desire for revenge.

The owning class is oppressed by being largely forced to lead lives of pretense.

Sorting Out One's Own Culture

Each culture is composed, on the one hand, of useful knowledge, information, lore, and practices. On the other hand, each culture contains many distress patterns.

In becoming aware of and moving to end their particular oppression, the members of every oppressed group will tend at first to have difficulty in appreciating and validating their own culture, since it has consistently been invalidated and demeaned by the dominant culture which has been oppressing it, and the members of that oppressed culture will have tended to internalize that attitude.

As a first step, it is probably useful to take the viewpoint that the *entire* culture is all right. It *is* certainly, overall, as valuable, rational, human, defensible, and enjoyable as the culture which has been oppressing it.

As we begin to regain confidence in who we are and begin to take pride in the culture we have been raised in, sorting out and identifying the oppressive and irrational aspects of our own culture also becomes important. Rejecting these irrationalities will free us to target and discharge our own individual patterns where they have been tied into the cultural patterns.

Frequently, an irrationality in a particular culture will turn out to be a fossilized relic of much earlier oppressions. We find traces in some current cultures of ancient slave civilizations, of medieval feudal civilizations, or of early, pre-industrial capitalism. Discovering these and targetting them for re-

Appeared in **Present Time** No. 69, October 1987.

evaluation can be very liberating in our individual lives as well as giving us a much more accurate view of reality.

Rachel Noble and others have written about the harsh invalidation of black children by black parents in the U.S. This "educating" of children, begun in slavery days as a device for preserving the lives of children by conditioning them to be submissive enough to avoid the worst cruelties of the slave-owners, continues to the present as a devastatingly harmful pattern in the U.S. black culture.

Mothers training their daughters to take a "woman's place," the Jewish culture emphasizing "never forget the horrors of the Holocaust" rather than "organize and unite to see that such things never again happen to anybody" are familiar examples.

In my youth, we were all urged to the assumption that "hard work never hurt anybody." Physical fatigue and over-loading of one's body was presented as something to be accepted patiently or complacently. (It still is in many parts of the world.) That may have seemed to make sense in a time when hard physical labor appeared to be necessary for the production of enough value that people could have well-nourished, well-furnished lives. It did considerable damage, however. Parts of my physique have been permanently damaged by over-work, lifting too-heavy weights and over-exhaustion. In a time like the present, when heavy or routine work can be handled with appropriate tools, using electrical or other energy sources, or even by sturdily-built robots, the glorification of overwork serves no purpose at all and should be rejected. The young people of today deserve to have strong muscles from exercise, not from exhausting, back-breaking labor over too many hours.

Sorting out one's own culture can be confusing. Many of our individual distress recordings are tied into irrational portions of our cultures. It will help if we can find some applicable guidelines (aside from our individual feelings) for determining whether a particular aspect of our culture is rational and helpful or nonsensical and debilitating.

I find it helpful (and recommend that you try) to take a look at other cultures, and notice your intuitive responses. Which quotation or scrap of poetry or strain of music makes your heart "leap up"?

Is it not an early insight into the benign reality when the psalmist says, "The Lord is my shepherd, I shall not want...surely goodness and mercy shall follow me all the days of my life..."? Is it not a marvelous early insight into the importance of decision when Lao Tse tells us that "a journey of ten thousand li begins with a single step"? An early twentieth century U.S. worker is quoted down the decades, saying, "It takes longer if you don't get started."

Do you not feel immediate marvelous communication with Hillel when you read his words of nearly two thousand years ago, as he asks, "If I am not for myself, then who will be? If I am only for myself, then what am I? If not now, when?"

I tend to feel that if I hear another mind speaking to my mind in that other culture, that portion of that culture is rational. I can understand immediately that Robert Burns is reassuring and advocating patience when he says that "many a mickle makes a muckle." The same Scottish poet is reminding me that rigidity is a test for nonsense when he writes, "My son, these maxims make a rule and lump them all thegither, the rigid righteous is a fool, the rigid wise anither...."

This is not conclusive. Perhaps I have some patterns which thrill to patterned nonsense from another culture (or from my own). Perhaps it isn't always a contradiction to distress that gives me a sensation of "meaningfulness."

However, I can always share my response with individuals

from other, different, cultures, encourage discussion, listen to each person on how the particular cultural aspect appeals to each of them (without argument or interjection on my part). After such discussion I should be able to more clearly approach rational appreciation of what is great in all cultures, and amused tolerant rejection of the patterns in them, whether these patterns are coming from long ago or from the present.

With this practice in looking at other cultures than my own, I should be better prepared to "turn the periscope back on myself" and examine my own culture or cultures.

If I look at the culture that surrounds me, it seems easy to decide that boozing, beer-drinking, tobacco, coffee, cola, chocolate, or the use of sugar as a main food instead of a condiment are irrational. But what about trying to be "in style" in clothing, what about driving to work instead of using bus, train, or subway? Staying up late watching TV? Overeating? Under-exercising? Not bothering to organize politically? Thinking about our own distresses when we are supposed to be counselors? Not really listening to our children? Deafening popular music? Procrastinating on rest? Procrastinating on vital work? Procrastinating on needed sessions?

Are these part of my culture? Are they irrational? Are they changeable?

(1) When have you heard "another mind speaking to your own mind" from another culture? From your own?

(2) What parts of your culture do you suspect are irrational?

Comments and Questions
at the First International Mental Health System Survivors' Workshop

Sunday Morning

Question: What do we do at an RC workshop or in a class when someone is too disruptive for our current resources? My suggestion would be, have the person get the best, appropriate help needed, and be sure the person feels welcome to return.

Harvey: Well, I don't have much more to say than that. The "flip out" at workshops phenomenon I interpret, after trying many other theories on it, as an unaware decision to try to force enough attention to get out all the person's distress right now, under the illusion that there's that much attention available because people are acting so well.

Once that mistaken decision is taken, the person gets lost in the distress that they dove into, and with the resource not available, the situation spirals down. I have learned, I think, that to pay *attention* to the person under these circumstances simply reinforces the mistake. I have learned, I think, that to get the person in contact with present-time reality, *not* being paid attention to is the immediate emergency measure. Where I've succeeded in just grabbing the person, sending them back to town, and making them promise that they would go back to *work* on a job that required their attention, the pull-out has been the quickest. Not all jobs are equally demanding of attention—a good mechanical, dishwashing, or gardening job, or running a lathe or something is the best.

Appeared in **Recovery and Re-emergence** No. 4, 1988.

Also, there's generally a sprinkling of psychiatrists around who have gotten into RC, and used it for themselves and are committed against drugs and shock and lobotomy. They can sometimes, for pay, or as a donation of gratitude to the Community, work with such a person patiently and remotely, in the way that fits this particular circumstance.

X—: I still don't understand what you're talking about—what circumstance?

Harvey: Where somebody splatters their distress all over a workshop.

X—: What does that mean?

Harvey: Goes into completely irrational behavior and dramatizing and the more attention you pay to them, the more they do it. On a couple of occasions since I decided this was a correct policy, I have had to fight other RCers at the workshop. I've gotten a commitment from the person acting irrationally. I've said go to *sleep,* and if you can't sleep, just *lay* there. Then I find that crews of people have been organized to sneak in to listen to the person, and they're very disappointed in me that I don't understand RC. (laughter) They feel that what the person needs is attention.

Y—: I'd like to share that I've done that same kind of thing with friends in the mental patients' liberation movement, and exactly what you're saying is the exact thing that worked.

Harvey: Yes, they need to get their gardening fingers into soil or run and chase a rabbit, or something like that that pulls their attention out, because the basic decision to extort attention is irrational. Now, should people be blamed for it? No. God, they've been waiting all their lives. To make a miscalculation is the simplest thing. I sometimes get furious with them after the twentieth time, but that doesn't mean that I *should.*

To go back to where I was answering, when we have such a psychiatrist, we get the person to them, and generally it takes only a little while. If they go into a hospital, if we've got an RC doctor around, we try to get that doctor to be their physician, so the doctor can protect them from the usual mistreatment. People come out of it, and some of them come out of it and resume leadership. We've got some very fine leaders right now who have done this sort of thing, so it isn't a permanent habit that they get into. Some of them have come back and joined the Community and have been "pills," but no greater proportion, on the average, than anybody else. The only distinctive thing that there seems to be about this kind of occurrence is that in the apparent presence of so many goodies, of an apparent warehouse full of attention, the mistaken decision is made to try to feast on it, and it doesn't work.

Z—: Yesterday you were talking about people taking on withdrawal from medication at a workshop. It's unpredictable in terms of how they're going to respond.

Harvey: They are often extremely uncomfortable and discharging wildly. Most of withdrawal is discharge, if there's any attention available. It's usually so tough simply because you get locked away and don't get paid attention to. That isn't the same phenomenon. For somebody to discharge voluminously and need lots of attention, that's one situation. We know how to handle that, if we can drop other things and give them attention.

Question: The derogatory term "shrink" seems inappropriate and offensive from this group of aware, loving people. Any comment from you?

Harvey: I guess my offhand response is that I thought it was a very neat, humorous invention to deal with an authority figure and cut him down to size a little bit. But if it is derogatory, then it shouldn't be used. The vicious malpractice carried on by psychiatrists is one thing; the psychiatrist is something else. The person should not be maligned or put down. They use the term proudly but perhaps defensively themselves. I don't know...I'd have to think about that a lot more.

Comment: There's a psychiatrist who wrote a book called **Shrink**. *Maybe he was just trying to sell copies.*

Harvey: I'll tell a little anecdote. There's a friend of mine, J—, whose patterns are difficult for me, who's a longshoreman on the waterfront. He's part of the crew that ties up and unties the big vessels when they come into the docks. I've never been able to work with him successfully, but he won't leave me alone, either. He says he hates my guts and writes me hateful letters, etc., but he won't go away.

He's acquired a considerable practice among distressed people that seek him out, and he works with them night and day and has many successes with them. But he says he despises me because I haven't been able to help *him*.

At a time when our relationship was a little more workable than it is now, he had told some people that he worked with that he was doing counseling. He's French. He was a commando for the French in Indo China. He can kill with one finger, and he's terribly afraid to use his strength for that reason. Word had got passed around, distorted, that he was "mentally ill." There's a system of seniority under the union agreement with the longshoreman's union where he would have become crew chief at a certain point, and when it came that time, they passed him over. When he asked why, the company told him that the word out was that he was "emotionally unstable" and they couldn't trust him in such a position of responsibility.

He was very upset, and he came and told me about it. I asked him to go and talk to the business agent of the longshoreman's union, which is a pretty good union. He did. I told him to tell the man he could call me. So the vice-president of the union called me and asked me what was this, and I explained. He said, "Is he *nuts*?" And I said, "Well, I wouldn't guarantee he is *completely* free from nuttiness, but no more than for you or me or the average person." Then he said, "Oh, well then, what's this business?" I said, "Well, he's studying to be a counselor." (Actually, he couldn't stand to stay in class, but he read all the literature.) I said, "to help *other* people." He said, "Oh, he's being penalized for trying to help *other* people, is he? Well, we'll see about *that*."

Meanwhile, my friend J— was being heckled *unmercifully* by another member of his crew who'd got the word. He said, "Ah, J—, you go crazy today, huh? I think I gotta stay away from you, J—." And J—, because he feels that if he ever lets loose of his temper, there'll be dead bodies all around, was suffering acutely from all of this. The crew member rode him, and rode him, and rode him, and J— would come tell me about it; the man was just unmerciful in his heckling.

Then the union acted. At the shape-up, the company officials came out, called everybody into a meeting, and explained that they had acted on false information. They publicly apologized to J— and gave him his crew chiefdom, which was fairly satisfying. J— said that the next night, after he'd driven his car down on to the dock and was waiting for a ship to come in, the man who had ridden him so unmercifully came up, opened the door, got in and sat down. He said, "Well, J—, as long as you're the head shrink on the waterfront (laughter), I'd like to tell you something. My life hasn't always been easy" and burst into heavy sobbing.

B—: Harvey, could I add a piece of information?

Harvey: Sure.

B—: A lot of the stigma that we ourselves have experienced as victims of the mental health system attaches to the psychi-

atric profession. It is the least respected among doctors of any of the medical professions.

Harvey: With good reason. (laughter)

B—: A lot of psychiatrists do some of the things they do to prove *how medical they are, that they can use drugs, too, that they can use surgery, too, that they really are scientific. I think this stigmatization of mental health workers adds to the whole cycle of further oppression of the victims of the system who are labeled "patients." Psychiatrists are not an esteemed profession within the medical profession.*

Harvey: No, but I think for good reason, that there's a deep sense that they *don't* know what they're doing. And I wouldn't want to disturb that. (laughter) I wouldn't want to put respect on top of that. Respect for the individual, yes; for the profession, no.

X—: There really are some excellent psychiatrists. Thomas Szasz has done some brilliant thinking. He's shown that it is an important field. Cooper, and a few others, are also doing some fine things.

Harvey: But they are rebels against the profession.

Y—: They almost got kicked out of APA meetings.

X—: Just forming *a profession, perhaps.*

Harvey: Well, they hope to. But they're not in the *tradition* of psychiatry.

B—: I think the point is that we know that further stigmatizing any group doesn't make them more rational, and that our attempting to further stigmatize people who feel a stigma will not make them treat our fellow people who have gone through what we've gone through, better than the way we were treated.

We don't want to give them respect for what they've done to us or other people, but that stigma is not the way of making them more rational.

Harvey: Okay, how about this? Supposing we agree to attack psychiatry but not psychiatrists?

B—: That makes sense.

Question: It is not clear to me what the difference is between maintaining the balance of attention and what you were talking about this morning about making the decision not to be weighed down by distress and to focus our attention outward.

Harvey: What we were seeking for when we said "the balance of attention," when we used that phrase, is the same thing that we're seeking when we say "contradict the distress" or when we say "take your attention *away* from past distresses." What we're seeking is a situation in which the distress turns to discharge.

All of them were and are understandable descriptions of it. But the "balance of attention" phrase is not as helpful practically as the newer formulations because it implied, or seems to imply to me, that sometimes you have to put more attention on the distress. We were led to that by the phenomenon of occlusion. But I think the reality is that the attention has always been in the distress, *locked* in it, and holding the distress up to awareness is quite a different process. So I think that in practice the words "contradicting the distress" imply a better picture of what needs to be done.

In my opinion, at least at this point, the distress *always* has more than enough attention on it, whether we're aware of it, or whether it's occluded; that our efforts need to be directed completely the other way to *attain* what we called a balance of attention. I don't intend to use the phrase "balance of attention" much anymore except in answering questions like this, because I think people understand and act much better on the notion of "contradicting sufficiently" or "pulling attention away from."

Question: What relationship makes sense between survivors and family members of survivors? Does it make sense to make distinctions sometimes? Should there be separate support groups or not? And what about "mental health" workers?

Harvey: I assume this means in RC. Yes, separate, separate, separate, separate. The basic process of attaining unity, the big insight that RC achieved about attaining unity, is exactly this: separate first, unify later. Let me spell it out, and try to remember it and tell it to each other.

The insight is that our yearning for immediate unity is undependable, *but* should not be acted upon. It isn't workable. We've always had this yearning, and in the last millennium, it's been tried repeatedly; it does not work. The divisions caused by distress are too deep to be handled that way. The groups that merge into one loving mass never really merge; they cover themselves with pretense, or, at best, they achieve some kind of an accomodation.

First the different groups need to separate, with expert help and leadership available to them; they need to meet in as small divisions as possible.

To set up Third World groups separate from whites allowed us to make some gain. Then we learned to set up black groups. Later, at a workshop we organized a U.S. black group, a West Indies black group, and an African black group. In these separate groups, with expert help, people work out excellent programs. Then they come together, report to each other, and work out the common parts of their programs easily.

This doesn't mean they can't use an expert from outside. A

good RC leader can be helpful to whatever brand of Wygelians she meets with. Help from an outside person is fine, but each group needs to be separate.

Later temporary mergers, or coalitions, can take place. At Liberation I and II, the Africans, West Indians, and U.S. blacks got together after a day. On the next day, they were negotiating with the Latinos who had meanwhile fused with the Cubanos, the Chicanos, and the Puerto Ricans into a Latino/a group.

At present, the key organizational move in RC is the Wygelian leaders' groups. All my experience would say that the effective leader, the Regional Reference Person or whoever is going to do the job of being the organizer and consultant for these groups, should call them together in the smallest divisions available. Even if you've only got one of each, meet separately with the plumber at a plumbers' leaders' meeting; meet separately with the machinists at a machinists' leaders' meeting. It will take time. It took eight months of meeting with the first working-class group in Seattle before they ever did a thing except come back for more counseling, but *eventually* it works; the process is workabɩe.

Then, if the machinists and the ironworkers and the plumbers get together separately at first, they can later work out a coalition. Later still they will meet with the hospital workers and the office workers and the psychiatrists in a workable way.

This is basic. First the divisions. First the safety of *whatever* division you need. Working-class groups that at first brought together people presently working in blue-collar jobs, and people who are now social workers and professors but have a sentimental alliance with their past—were ghastly. The present blue-collar workers felt completely unsafe and would have left completely except the theory was too good.

The basic principle is separation first for safety and working out a program, then unity on a coalition, of equal basis, where the individual positions are taken into account and the joint positions are negotiated. Negotiations are similar to those that work between a man and a woman. Each should prepare their programs separately and then negotiate with each other on what they now agree on, what they will work to agree on, and what is forever banned.

SUNDAY NIGHT

Harvey: In thinking it over, it seemed to me that I had not communicated what the general thinking of the RC leadership is in this field. Maybe I had better try.

Much of this comes out of the work at Personal Counselors in the early years of RC, when most of what we learned was from working with one-way clients for a long period of time. There was a period of something over two years when I sought out and took as many "deeply distressed" people as I could, to find out, if possible, if there *were* two kinds of people in the world, which the prevailing opinion then was, and still is, to a great extent. I tried to find out whether there were the "sane" and the "insane."

I worked with these people under very difficult conditions and without adequate resource, but persisted long enough to settle the question very completely in my own mind. Based on that experience and the continuing one-way work, and interactions with many people both in the "mental health" system and those challenging it, I'd like to say what *my* opinion is at the present time.

First of all, there is only *one* kind of human. Second—and this will be rambling a little bit—the term "mental health" is a completely fraudulent and misleading term. It has nothing to do with "health." We need another term completely. I suggest "behavioral function," or something like that. In the "mental health" professionals' draft policy, I make the point that we have no definition of what is "mental health"; particularly in RC, we reject any definition of what is correct functioning; we see no limits to the functioning of human beings. This doesn't mean that we can't tell *mis*functioning, and I try to define in that policy what misfunction means.

The whole notion that there is such a thing as "mental health" which can be defined, is simply a spinoff of the basic attempts of the oppressive society to define roles for all people for the purposes of oppression. This makes no sense at all. We cannot define mental well-functioning because it's a continually burgeoning, ever-more creative process. We don't think that there are any limits to the excellent functioning of people. We'll continually function better and better and better.

But there is such a thing as misfunctioning. It is a problem that needs to be dealt with, but the term "mental health" misleads completely. It has nothing to do with "health" in the usual form.

There are misfunctions that arise from physical reasons. Certain dietary deficiencies, very basic ones, can make our central nervous system misfunction. That *practically* never happens. Almost always, if it does, it's an indirect result of some other part of our physical plant misfunctioning, from a dietary deficiency. But it *can* happen. The cases usually adduced as examples of this were almost certainly frauds or wild guesses. They had very little or nothing to do with the reality of it.

There are behavioral misfunctions arising from physical damage. Certainly the results of lobotomies are tremendous misfunctions. The destruction of a large part of the central nervous system leaves the person with just a faint, flickering part of their ability to be human. And it's amazing what *gallant* attempts these people make to function with the shreds left to them. In the period of which I spoke, I sought out work with victims of lobotomy and leucotomy to see for myself what the actual situation was. I found that they did respond to counseling, but very, very slightly, and with tremendous slowness, and were unable themselves to ever report any improvement. However, in both the cases that I worked with at length, they had not been able to find jobs before, and they both got jobs and held them after that. I comforted myself a little bit with that. In terms of their enjoyment of life, it was difficult to indicate anything. The equipment with which they could re-evaluate had been destroyed by surgery.

Mechanical damage to the central nervous system does cause misfunction, behavioral misfunction. The mechanical damage can be caused by injury, it can be caused by destruction of tissue by syphilitic lesions, for example. To what extent electric shock does it is not yet determined, and I'm not very anxious to find out. I think we need to hold out a hopeful future for all its victims in that regard.

And it is done by cancer. There was only one client I ever had who did not respond to counseling in the predictable way. She discharged every session she came in, improved during the session, felt better at the end of it. She came back the next week having lost ground. I was beside myself, because it was apparent she had lost ground. She'd been under the care of a psychiatrist for a long time. Her husband was reluctant to have her have a physical exam because he felt sure the psychiatrist must have given her one. Finally I got her husband to take her to a good clinic and they discovered a brain tumor which was spreading rapidly. She died two weeks later. She could re-evaluate slightly, but there was too much misfunction caused by the destruction of the tissue by the cancer to allow for more re-evaluation.

So there are such things. We don't pretend mystically that the mind exists apart from the central nervous system, or anything like that. It's a function of the central nervous system. If the central nervous system is damaged, misfunction can occur.

But having said that, as a footnote, *almost* all behavioral misfunctioning is the result of the acquiring of distress patterns from incidents of hurt of one kind or another. Almost *entirely* the situation is the result of the familiar phenomenon of distress patterns, distress recordings. This is one of the central discoveries of RC, and a discovery which makes all other theories completely obsolete which do not deal with it. Once the explanation of the distress recording and the discharge and re-evaluation process are out in the light, then it doesn't matter how well-intentioned or humanistic Dr. Freud or others are, or what historical credit should be given to them; all theories that do not include this are completely obsolete at this point, and ridiculously so. The distress recording is the central undiscovered factor that explains *everything,* if applied intelligently, and it leads to useful work. Current theories that do not include this are ridiculous, in the historical sense that they are completely out-of-date.

Besides what has been called "mental illness" for reasons of non-conformity (like political protests), what has been called "mental illness" is a kind of misfunction. With the tiny exceptions noted that actually are based in physical destruction of the central nervous system, it arises out of distress patterns. It would not be upsetting in most cases in a culture that was not already wound up in terror about this issue. There *are* cultures which have been explored in which the different behavior is regarded with respect. I don't know whether that helped a lot, or not. It did not lead to the *vicious* kind of destruction that we see going on today in this culture. There were cultures in which it was treated with even greater fear than ours, where the person who misfunctioned, in certain ways at least, was simply wiped out.

If the entire society, the entire population, were not so deeply wound up in misinformation and distress and in the coils of the operations of oppression, it's quite obvious that almost every, if not every, indication of so-called "mental illness" is exactly a very intelligent person holding out a distress pattern as a way of asking for help. In a population where intelligence was functioning, responding to that with resource and attention would accomplish very quickly, not only the alleviation, but the disappearance of the misfunction. Almost every misfunction would be correctly interpreted as the holding out of a distress, asking for help with it.

Probably the great bulk of the "symptomatic behavior" for which people get caught in this destructive setup, is simply discharge itself. What are the "symptoms" of a "nervous breakdown"? Crying, shaking, laughing wildly, "weird" yawns rolling off, over and over. Discharge, the healing process itself, has been identified as misfunction. Now, *we* know *one* thing; we know better than that. Also, we have learned in RC that any dramatization is a call for help. We tell people at our workshops that if a person comes up and says, "I don't like you, and I'm going to knock your block off," that if you keep your head and think, you'll be able to recognize that the person is *really* saying, "I have a problem here, a pattern that leads me to go around threatening people. It creates all kinds of difficulties; I wish I could tell you about it in mild language, but I can't, so here's a sample." (laughter) This is the *real* meaning. Any dramatization, including the ones you feel most justified in being upset about, *is* a cry for help.

Now I'm not saying here that you turn to the mugger or the rapist and say, "I understand you're just asking for help." (laughter) Call for a cop. There are all kinds of ways of handling the differently threatening situations.

Even if it's not clearly discharge that's regarded as the misfunction, which is *completely* wrong, we know that the rehearsal of a distress is in itself a call for help. Understood, all those situations that have led people into these *enormously* repetitively destructive courses of action, could have been *completely* avoided. Now, does that help the person in the wide world, at this moment? You see, you don't need a psychiatrist, you don't need drugs, you don't need a doctor, you don't need an institution, you just need people to pay attention to you lovingly. That's valuable information, but you know what the person asks you. "Where the hell do you find people to pay attention to you lovingly?" (laughter) That's a good question.

Almost all the questions asked to me at workshops are asked in the role of client, "How can I cope?" Sometimes they say, "How could *someone* cope with this kind of condition?" Very thinly veiled; it means, "How can I cope with this problem?" And the only *real* answer I can give to people is, "Get yourself a good counselor. A good counselor would have you discharging on that very quickly." Of course they ask me the question, "Where can I get a good counselor?" Sometimes I say, "Well, if you're well-heeled, come to Seattle. Give us plenty of time ahead of time to arrange an intensive for you, if you've got lots of money to spend." But almost always the person says, "Geez, I can't afford those prices," and I agree with her/him.

So I have to give another answer, which is what I give repeatedly: "You have to train counselors. You have to master the theory and train your Co-Counselor, and do it carefully." I'm offering this nice, rational solution, you see. "You should improve your environment." I say this to the person who feels they're sitting on the nose of an express train with the brakes locked and it's heading for the edge of the abyss. Okay. But I don't know any better answers; and certainly other answers offered as a substitute are going the wrong way—those of the "mental health" system being expressions of a most destructive edge of the oppressive society, operating in order to force people to conform.

Now, should we be of poor cheer because of this? I don't think so. Here our point of view comes in. It's true that things are bad. My God, look at what the people in this room have endured, and how big the problem is, and how slender our resources, and how oppressive the societies are, and how many guns and atom bombs they have, and so on, and so on. But look at it the other way. Compared to any previous times, this time is filled with hope. This is the best time there ever was. We have connections, we have knowledge, we're in the process of making things work, we have allies outside, we're *enormously* fortunate to be living here, to have a chance to be a "mental health" system survivors' champion, to play a great role in overthrowing one of the nastiest expressions of a nasty society, to have a chance to play hero. What does anybody want out of life, outside of living forever, which we're working on? You want to have a meaningful life, a good life. What an opportunity we have!

In terms of the chemicals, my personal opinion, but a thought-out-one, is that all drugs used, all mood-altering drugs—including lithium, as a sample of a lot of things that are rationalized with the same excuses—are simply destructive. The human organism needs fresh air, good water, food, exercise, rest, and almost anything else you put into your physical plant is going to cause difficulties. Despite all the native home-remedies, all the herbal things that "must be good because they're natural," people get well only because their bodies recover. I'm not saying you shouldn't use antibiotics. Antibiotics are poisons, but they poison the bacteria more than they poison you. If you judge the dose right, that's a great help. There are other helpful things like that. You cut your finger and you paint it with mercurochrome. Well, mercurochrome kills about three million of your cells. But in the process, it kills off the bacteria so the infection won't get started, and the cells replenish themselves very quickly.

So you can be smart about it. Not everything we do is *absolutely* "upward trendy" because we evolved to live in a world of enormous, complex conflict. But anything that interferes with our essential us, such as our central nervous system's operation, is destructive. I don't think there's any question about it. Can you survive lots of it? Yes, we're very sturdy. We can recover from months after months of drugs. Is it going to be some extra work? Yup.

I thought J— made an important point in his talk at the "mental health" professionals' workshop. Somebody had said (I've heard the same arguments here), "But you *have* to use drugs because it's a better alternative. We don't have the resources; therefore, we *have* to use drugs." J— was very patient and dear with them. He said, "I understand how you feel about it. There are certainly some things you have to do. But do remember that the drugs you gave me to 'make it easier' for me represent many extra hours of counseling I have to do to get the results off...."

You got all the drugs, and you'll recover from them, but you've got lots of discharging to do, lots of yawns, because they're all poisons. It's true that some have "weirder" effects than others, but they're all poisons. And what do you want to alter your mood for? Basically, the answer is, so you won't discharge. It's just about that simple. A drug is to interfere with your discharge. Now it's true that you can't discharge unless you've got enough support to contradict it out there, and it's true that we haven't totally solved that problem. So we don't run up to a psychiatrist and say, "You murderer, you, you poisoner of people, RC will take care of it," when we haven't got the slightest notion of how we're going to give them enough RC resource.

We don't have the alternatives yet, but that doesn't mean we buy into a wrong position simply because we haven't brought order out of this terrible mess that we've inherited; it doesn't mean that we don't know what a correct policy is.

Basically, the "flippiest" that any of us ever acted needed only some time and some reassurance, and we would have found the way to discharge, and we would have been *just fine,* long, long ago, had we not been hacked to pieces by the operation of the so-called "mental health" system, which destroys people, does not recover people. I think we have to be flat about that.

Discussion of the "Mental Health" System Survivors' Policy Statement

Discussion of point no. 24 (See First "Mental Health" Policy Statement, **Recovery and Re-emergence** No. 3)

*S—: I agree with everything that's been said there, but I think somewhere here we need to address the fact that some people's behavior is violent. We need to acknowledge it. Maybe we need whole new ways of protecting either the perpetrator or the victim of violence. As someone who's been locked up, it's hard for me to say that this is something that sometimes is needed. But, we need to find an **elegant** way to do it. I think this particular paragraph more than any other in the entire statement is going to create anxiety in people that are scared by "crazies" to begin with. We're advocating that people run around discharging.*

Harvey: There's obviously disagreement, but we just want impressions here, not conclusions.

Una Parker: Legal rights vary from one country to another, sometimes from state to state in this country.

Dewey Bandy: This applies to drugs as well as the violence issue. With violence, if a psychiatrist rapes somebody, that's seen in a different context. There's a need to protect people against violence, but it can't be focused exclusively on one particular group, such as believing that the "crazy" "mental patient" is going to kill you while allowing psychiatrists to be free to do psychosurgery. We have to address violence in a context that doesn't single us out. I don't think "mental pa-

Excerpts from the discussion of the first draft of the "Mental Health" System Survivors' Liberation Policy Statement at the first International "Mental Health" System Survivors' Workshop, May, 1983. This article appeared in **Recovery and Re-emergence** No. 4, 1988.

tients" or ex-"mental patients" should go around killing people, but neither should psychiatrists or generals, or police officers or other agents of social control. And that's where the real violence comes from, not the stray "lunatic" that axes somebody up with a hatchet. That's a real danger.

Harvey: Only mass murder is encouraged. (laughter)

Dewey: Well, I guess if you're going to go for it, go all the way (laughter). One thing about drugs: the way the statistics on drugs are kept, side effects are underrepresented because of the nature of the oppression. Many "patients" know that if they're in a hospital and they're drugged and they report the side effects, it will be seen as an indication of their "insanity." Of course the "solution" will be to increase the drugs. Also, there are large numbers of "mental patients" dying from the effects of psychotropic drugs and these are not recorded in systematic ways in which we can get a clear glimpse of the situation. If there's one person who claims to be helped by drugs, there is also in New York, for example, an institution where 62 people died from the effects of drugs and they're just now investigating it. The point is, it's real crucial that we (1) point out that the way statistics are gathered on "mental patients," the way the problems and issues are developed, are by the rules of empirical logic, invalid. (2) On the violence, it's crucial that we point out that we're not defending violence by any sector of society. However, we must show where the real violence is so that there's not a standard of making sure that "mental patients" don't go out and kill somebody while we do nothing about surgeons cutting people's brains out.

A—: It's not true that inmates don't have legal rights. They are frequently ignored and they're ridden roughshod over, but they do have legal rights.

Harvey: Both are true. There are places where they have none. It varies all over the place.

A—: Sometimes the best thing you can do is get a potential inmate a lawyer.

Harvey: Very good point.

M—: We might use that term institutionalized violence— you're talking about that kind of violence, the lobotomies and so on.

Jamie Alexander: In dealing with the whole question of violence, it might be helpful if we go back to what you were talking about in that film clip where the rapists were talking. The key part of it is to acknowledge that anyone who is acting violently has gotten that pattern from someone else acting that way with them.

B—: I'd like to make the point that the molestation of "patients," including by their psychiatrists, happens very often, often theoretically with consent, when people are in distress.

Harvey: Going on—there's more on this?

Jamie: About the use of the term "misfunctioning," I think it's a very important part of our policy that we've called what's going on "misfunctioning," not "illness," and I think it would be a mistake to totally throw out the word "misfunctioning." If we don't face that in our policy and deal with it, "mental health" workers and other people are going to be able to point to our policy and say, "You're ignoring the reality and you're not really providing us with any answer or any solution."

Dewey: There's a stereotype that some "mentally ill" president is going to push the button, or the Ku Klux Klan are "mentally ill" and that's where racism is coming from, or the threat of nuclear war is from the "lunatic" who will creep into the White House and punch the button that launches all the missiles. Part of the stereotyping is that when there's a

social oppression, it's blamed on "sickness": racism is
"sick," people who are anti-Semitic are "sick," Hitler was
"sick," the Nazis were "sick," when in fact they would
probably be diagnosed as mentally "normal" people by most
psychiatrists.

Later on in discussion:

Harvey: There's a little information I think would be
helpful. In the early years of RC, every year three or four
young psychiatrists became enchanted with it and decided to
make it their life work (before they got bemused and went off
on something else). They were mostly working in hospitals,
and they would want to use it in the wards. I would discuss
this with them and encourage them to do it. We had several
experiences of the psychiatrist teaching very simple RC on the
ward, setting up a class, using his authority to get the drugs
stopped, and people would attend the class and learn to Co-
Counsel. What was especially noteworthy was that they did
excellent Co-Counseling as long as they worked with each
other. They Co-Counseled well; they had permission to go
off and cry from the authority of the psychiatrist, and in
general the people got out of the institutions very rapidly.
They discharged enough to figure out how to fool the Boards
at the very least. Because they improved quickly and left, this
tended to make the classes quite unstable.

It's the same thing in prison classes: you lose all your
leaders right away because they discharge enough to figure
out how to con the parole board and get out.

What spoiled these classes in the wards, over and over
again, was the young psychiatrist became so fascinated with
what *they* were doing, that he had to get in and counsel with
them, and as soon as he did that, the peerness disappeared.
They all turned helpless on him and it quit working. But as
long as he followed what he'd offered to do, and just taught
the people and let them Co-Counsel with each other, there

was no lack of ability at all; everybody had good sessions. Comments on this last one?

Comment: The sentence that I would like to add is: "mental health" workers allow for discharge and not use the client's discharge as a reason to increase their medication or use other methods that would prohibit discharge.

Harvey: At Northern State Hospital in Washington, if you cried you got shock. The patients used to set up warning networks to try to let somebody cry, and word would be passed along when staff approached to stop the crying and dry up quick. In order to protect them from shock, this was necessary, a marvelous underground movement.

Programs and Policies for Labour Unions in Britain

Working-Class Caucus
Leicester Teachers' and Leaders' Workshop
August 5-9, 1987

This meeting is proposed to be a founding group for a movement for intelligent labour unions in Britain. I choose the word "intelligent" carefully. It hasn't got rigid connotations attached to it yet as far as I know. I propose we simply constitute ourselves a group that draws up a program. I'll advance some ideas to start with that may not fit because I don't really know the detailed situation in this country.

The proposal is that we build an intelligent labour union movement in Britain. We propose that the existing unions where they are intelligent be celebrated, where they are not quite intelligent they be improved, where they're notably unintelligent they be vastly improved, and that new unions be organized on an intelligent basis.

Let's think of the features that will characterize an intelligent union. I would say that it will be democratic. That may not be a big problem over here, but it is in my country where the Mafia rules many unions on behalf of the employers. An intelligent union will be democratic. The union meetings will be a pleasure to attend. The union meetings will provide for some discussion by everybody by breaking up into small groups (you don't have to call them topic groups) for discussion that will be reported back to the whole meeting. There will be two or three times in every union meeting for people to

Appeared in **Present Time** No. 70, January 1988.

take turns in pairs or dyads to exchange what they have heard and what they think about it.

Every union local will have a committee to think about and look after the organization of workers adjacent to the ones in the local (not necessarily into *that* local). Every union local will have a functioning committee working on the organization of all the workers in their town or locality into unions, not necessarily into the local doing the organizing, but into appropriate unions or new unions. The organization of the unorganized will be a continuing program of every union local branch. Every branch will have an active, functioning committee, which reports regularly, that takes responsibility for the organization of all the unorganized workers in the locality into unions, not necessarily into the existing ones. We don't want to get into the "competition for the new members" sort of thing.

The unity of *all* working people will be the program of every union on a branch level, on a district level, on a national level. Internationalism, that workers of all countries be united, will be part of the program of every intelligent union. Each union will establish close connections with workers and unions of other countries as much as possible. Each intelligent union will be seeking the international organization of working people in a great and unified movement. That hasn't been really attempted since the First International that started out in London over a hundred years ago. Later attempts were distorted by other considerations.

What else would be the characteristics of an intelligent union? Will it be proper to say that the union will seek to enhance the well-being and the self-confidence of every union member? It will take concern for the safety and healthfulness of working conditions. That's already common, but it's not universal. It will look after the safety of working conditions. It will seek to promote the general health and general welfare of its members. It will seek and watch over an adequate health insurance program.

I think an intelligent union will recognize that leaders function better if they are kindly corrected when they make mistakes but are not attacked for them. We don't want to put our leaders beyond correction. An intelligent union will surely work out a program for dealing with unemployment and training schemes that purport to be employment but are not.

What else would be in the program of an intelligent union? How about special attention to the interests of its women members, including child care? A firm stand against any racism or discrimination and a welcome into the union to members of all races? A continuing program to develop rational policies toward new and improved technologies?

Within the broad organization of a union we have opportunities for specialized organization. How about a permanent committee in each branch taking the initiative for planning for a better society in the future? Or another one on eliminating negative or divisive attitudes toward ourselves? Should every intelligent union have a program of seeing to it that the Labour Party advocates progressive policies and seeks to educate the public to support them rather than attempting to win elections by conciliating existing prejudices?

Does it make sense that we start here today a movement, a vast unofficial committee that will sweep the country with planning for how to have intelligent labour unions, work up a list of requirements and recommendations and circulate them everywhere? Does that make sense?

At the workshop in Southampton there were a large number of working-class people and quite a few union members. It was very reassuring. I imagine there will be at least a few in the north when I get there next week. I will try to have this same kind of discussion in the north. I did not in Southampton. I hadn't thought about it enough. It was toward the end of the workshop when I realized how much of the workshop was working-class. In the north, we're going to have to deal with some feelings that they should be preoccupied with northern liberation, but I think we can tie that into the working-class issue pretty well.

Within RC, we are still poorly organized. We have made some beginnings. We have an International Liberation Reference Person for Labour Union Activists. She's pretty good. She took the job with some guilt feelings because her dad had once had a little money but she's been standing in front of a lathe for eleven years now with hot chips getting down her neck and inside her shirt, so she now knows she's working-class. She's done a good job. Some of you here know her. We've had one conference so far with union activists from England, Sweden, The Netherlands, and the United States. There will be a bigger one coming soon.

A number of the people are already fairly influential. We have some union people that have boiled right off the shop floor to positions of influence in the union structure. There could be a lot more.

Inside RC the general working class has hung back, by and large. I've been acting as International Liberation Reference Person for Working-Class Persons, and I've had to neglect that role because I've had just too much else to do. We now have some Apprentice International Liberation Reference Persons for the Working Class. The word "apprentice" was put on there because the people felt much safer to take the job under those conditions than straight out. We don't yet have one individual who is ready to do the whole job. The great majority of the working class is still unorganized, of course. I would like at least two more Apprentice Liberation Reference Persons for the Working Class in Britain. I would appreciate your seeing me privately if you think you should be one of them or if you propose somebody else should be one. Let me know who you think can do the job.

The working class needs support groups everywhere. We

don't need to be fussy about where we organize them. You can organize them at your lunch hour if you are working or you can organize them in the dole office or on the street in front of it, if you're not. The support group is a basic form of organization. Once you have some support groups, bring the leaders together into Wygelian leaders' groups and hold occasional meetings. Let me know who your leaders are. We're going to have some good mailings coming out from now on. The computers are working now and anybody who is taking leadership on these issues whose name, address, and phone number you can get to me—we'll get in touch with through these mass mailings.

Please get on the ball, won't you? Start organizing. The working class is a sleeping giant until you wake up and get things going. A "Wobbly" working-class song in the United States years ago was called "A Little Talk With Jesus." In the song a working-class man is complaining to Jesus about how hard his life is and how "somebody ought to do something." Jesus replies, "I have filled the world with plenty. There is ample for your need. If you want the world, go take it. Have your brains all gone to seed?" Roughly that is the message I think we need to pass on to each other. Grab the ball and run with it—okay?

The Liberation of
Young People and Young Adults

This issue of **Young and Powerful** has been delayed a long while. This is in part the result of some disorganization among young RCers, but in the main it is due to the tremendous amount of work that has fallen on the staff at Rational Island Publishers because of the great expansion of RC in this recent period.

Not all of these articles and letters are very recent but all of them are permanently valuable in that they express brilliant thinking and insights by young people on behalf of young people.

The Young Leaders' Conference in January of 1988 was enormously successful, but required us to face some difficulties connected with young people's liberation that had not been fully faced before. The young people under 21 years of age at the conference were firmly unanimous that they needed a movement led by themselves and that building an international movement outside of RC that would embrace young people everywhere would require leadership of young people by young people. The young adults who attended the workshop who had comprised the young people's leadership supported the young people completely in this and it became a problem to try to provide some continuing leadership and use the experiences that we had gained in the process. The solution was to set up a much more extensive leadership structure for young people than we had ever done before and to provide for resource persons of their own choice for each such young leader so that they would have access to the experience

Appeared in **Young and Powerful** No. 4.

that had been accumulated earlier. The listing of people as apprentices was in an effort to allow them to get some experience leading without being crushed by the sense of responsibility, and the titles will be changed to regular ones as soon as people have a chance to operate and it becomes plain who's most ready to take the key leadership spots. Many of the new young leaders chose young adults who were previous young people's leaders as their resource people, and I'm sure the continuity will be maintained in this way.

I found the young adults who had been young people's leaders who attended the conference to be very impressive. It was plain what it can mean to a young person to be in RC in their teenage or younger years. These young adults were extremely capable as a result of their experience in RC. They thought clearly. They were proud and confident of themselves. They were very clear on young people's issues. They were planning their lives with great confidence and competence. It's plain that the whole RC Community needs to make a great effort to bring the tools of RC to large numbers of young people, for the future of the young people but also for the future of the world. To have RC theory and practice during their young years is going to allow them to be adults who can be trusted to take charge of the world, to prevent nuclear disaster, and to protect the world's population from great harm during the collapse of this society.

It is also plain that young adult RCers, people from 21 to 30, need a leadership structure of their own. Many of them are leading in RC generally, but theirs is a special oppression. It has some of the elements of young people's oppression, but is also different in many respects. A number of these young adults have begun to write about this oppression and begun to establish contact with each other. We have, in effect, a second great young movement waiting to be organized with some splendid leadership already available. There will soon be a Young Adults' Leaders' Conference to set up a structure somewhat parallel to the young people's leadership structure in RC.

Whether **Young and Powerful** will continue to be a journal for both young people (under 21 years of age) and young adults (people from 21 years to 30 years of age) is still an open question. It may be that young adults will need to have their own journal, and the possibility is certainly one that will be entertained by the RC Community as a whole.

(I want to propose that in future issues of **Young and Powerful**, and in RC literature and in RC usage generally, that we stop using the term "adultism" as a synonym for the oppression of young people. We have similarly discarded the term "heterosexism" which was once put forward in many places as a synonym for "the oppression of Gay men and Lesbians" and the term "able-bodiedism" as a synonym for "the oppression of physically disabled people." Both of these terms and, I think, "adultism" imply some fault or guilt for people for being heterosexual, physically not disabled, or being an adult. So, I think the clear terms are "the oppression of disabled people," "the oppression of Gay and Lesbian people," and "the oppression of young people." These are much better terms. *There is nothing wrong with being an adult.* All young people are going to be adults and all artificial separations between people of different ages will eventually be done away with. To use terms which have the effect of implying guilt or wrongness of *who* one is or *how* one is, is, I think, a bad practice. So, I propose that we say clearly "young people's oppression" or "the oppression of young people" instead of ever using the term "adultism" in the future.)

We have established overall International Liberation Reference Persons for Young People with two apprentice persons sharing the position that Gill Turner has held previously. We have also established overall *Assistant* International Liberation Reference Persons for people under 12, for people 13 to 15, for people 16 to 18, and for people 19 to 21. In addition we have established Assistant Young People's Liberation Reference Persons for several *countries* where people were available to assist in all of young people's activities for those particular countries.

One completely new category has been established. This is to have a leader for people born in two particular consecutive years. At this time, we have only one such appointment. This is Alex Saunders, for young people born in 1968 and 1969. The idea is that these leaders will continue to lead the same constituency since they will grow older together with their constituents. They will be available to be young adult leaders as they grow out of the young people's ages, and we will not have to re-train new leaders so fast simply because of the passage of years. These are Assistant Liberation Reference Persons and auxiliary leaders to all of the others. I think that there is a real need for many, many young people's leaders and there's not likely to be any conflict in their functions at all.

Besides these leaders on the international and national level, we ask the RC Communities everywhere to find City-wide Coordinators of young people's liberation (and soon of young adults' liberation also) who will have freedom of initiative to set up young people's support groups in large numbers everywhere in the city, in every Area (where there is more than one Area in the city) and, as they become established and grow, help them prepare new leaders and divide as their numbers become larger, so that we have a constantly expanding network of young people's support groups. The leaders of these support groups and other young leaders will be brought together occasionally in Young People's Wygelian Leaders' groups. This will be the job of the City-wide Coordinators. They can, of course, also organize workshops and gather-ins and other activities in cooperation with the Area Reference Persons and Regional Reference Person of the entire Community.

(All of the above proposals will be paralleled soon for the Young Adults organizational structure as the young adults get together and consult.)

Questions and Answers,
Letters and Replies

Can We "Re-emerge" Organizations?

Dear Harvey,

You have developed something very valuable in RC—very valuable and unique from an organizer's point of view.

Among others, the premises that:

People can take charge of their lives;

That personal, one-to-one communication is the most effective and long-lasting way to communicate;

That people should simply listen to each other, rather than try to claim others' attention;

That people are inherently cooperative; it is only that they have been hurt that stops them from trusting and cooperating.

All these are very helpful in organizing, particularly in the U.S. where television has largely replaced communication for many souls. To recapture any sort of political power more organizers are realizing that people need to communicate personally, develop local leadership, start from the bottom up, etc.

I understand that RC has a basic one-point program of individual re-emergence and nurturing individual leadership. Help and support travels from the group to the individual to enhance that person's leadership and re-emergence.

I wonder in your experience in other organizations (unlike RC) that try to make specific "wide-world" political changes (legislation, state funding, etc.) how do "making friends"

Appeared in **Present Time** No. 76, July 1989.

and uniting many others around a specific program intersect? When you are in the business of changing external reality, as opposed to the business of re-emergence and getting close to others, how have you dealt with the conflicts that arise? Have you found you needed to forsake someone's "leadership" or "re-emergence" in order to take care of business? For instance in your shipyard work during WWII?

It seems to me that to get anything specific and tangible accomplished—real improvements in the lives of people—one needs to change "objective reality" (funding levels for subsidized housing, voter registration laws, etc.). One needs to make decisions about what work needs to get done. And this might mean you stifle someone's individual leadership or ideas.

Part of what seems a little "off" in the RC literature, particularly the Peace journal, is the notion that "anything goes." ("We are all peace activists.") I don't mean to say there needs to be some litmus test (the "you're not good enough" syndrome). But at some time it seems to me there has to be some specific program that people unite around and act *upon.*

This is not the mission of RC, but I wonder if you think that RC ever impedes the development of an objective program because of its focus on "friendship networks," rather than winnable objective victories. (Don't get me wrong; I like making friends as much as anybody. And RC has made more valuable contributions to current political movements than just about anything else I know.)

These ideas are not totally thought through, partly perhaps this is a dynamic, changing issue.

RC is on the "cutting edge" of much good organizing and leadership development, the kind of work that will be long-lasting. How do you think we can best consolidate (institu-

tionalize?) the gains? Is it all done only with individuals, not laws or governing bodies? I wonder what your viewpoint is, having had the opportunity to actively participate in social change over a relatively long period of time.

Our work in Jobs with Peace goes well. People are more ready to listen to talk of cuts in the military budget. The more traditional "peace movement" is trying to focus on the domestic side of the budget, rather than only the elimination of nuclear weapons.

Much of it is not our doing. Part is due to Mr. Gorbachev, who is lessening the fear of nuclear war and decreasing the popular support for increased military spending. Part is due to the declining standard of living and the increasing economic and environmental problems. Even many of the "middle class" in the USA face this decline.

Jobs with Peace is in the process of coordinating demonstrations on "Tax Day"—about April 15, 1989. Part of the project involves getting peace and housing activists to work together. Part involves developing local electoral networks, very much based on individual leadership: people talking to their neighbors—an old idea whose time has come. It has been effective in some areas, increasing voter turn-out and helping turn around some elections.

Michael J. Brown
Jamaica Plain, Massachusetts, USA

Dear Michael,

These are questions that I think about a lot, too, and I don't think I have any final answers to them. I think probably tentatively, at least, that if you make a division among the activities that you carry out, and then develop organizational forms and activities to fit each of the different activities, and eliminate conflicts between them, you'll come out all right.

Basically RC began trying to help people *feel* better, and quickly got into the more basic mode of trying to help people *think* better. We generally call this re-emergence, that is, to the extent that we can dissolve the rigid patterns left by past distress, that thinking is freed up. Almost everyone in RC is agreed upon the goal of re-emergence, of necessity, and once we've faced how much of the distress is the result of oppression, a second goal became, for not quite as many RCers, but most of them, a goal of liberation.

The realization that the lack of policy and the lack of leadership were the principal obstacles to liberation is, I think, leading us in the current period to think that most RCers, at least, will come to have at least a triple goal of re-emergence, liberation, and taking charge. That is, that individual liberations, for completion, are going to require a complete change in the society, and even more fundamental, a complete changing of the accepted or usual relationships between people, so that all relationships are mutually supportive and none of them are exploitive.

I would say that if you and I were working together, for example, in your organization, that we would spend some time Co-Counseling with each other; that we would spend some time in a topic group format discussing, exchanging information in a non-restimulative way, where each person talks once before anybody speaks twice; and spend part of the time in a support group, where all of your fellow workers that can be involved will have a turn with us at being listened to without interruption (whether formally or informally), not only about the insights which constitute RC, but also about the background in which the peace movement operates, the history of society, of war and peace, and any other source of knowledge. I think the things we have learned from having to organize more flexibly in RC would probably turn out to be very valuable for our work in your organization: that every policy statement is a draft policy urging comment and suggestions for improvement from the moment it's issued and periodically re-drafted; that organizational structures would be set up for particular campaigns or periods, based on what we've learned in the simpler forms of organization, but modified for the particular campaign and then not allowed to continue as an ongoing structure except in the areas that after examination will bring convenience and effectiveness for us.

There's an area where other organizations are certainly ahead of RC, which is the area of commitment to each other and commitment to unity and following through around the goals which people share. We have begun to discuss this in RC, and the first discussions have somewhat shocked me at how low a level of commitment people have and how terrified their lives have left them of making a commitment. On the other hand, in the organizations in which I have participated in the past, where the commitment level was high, the commitments were made on the basis of painful emotion, of patriotism or hatred of the class enemy or fear of nuclear arms or something like that, so that I think this whole area needs lots of exploration.

Harvey

Dear Harvey,

*I would be interested in hearing more about the discussion within RC about commitment, unity, and following through around goals that people share. I wasn't sure what further goals we are referring to here, although I have seen in RC an exceptionally high level of commitment of people to each other and to the goals of mutual "re-emergence" and mutual support for the **individual's** goals—clearly more in RC than in any other "organization" in which I have participated.*

I am not surprised that the commitment you have seen in other organizations where the commitment and unity level is high has been based on various sorts of "painful emotion" and targeting some "enemy." It's easy to find a "bad guy" to go hang and rally the troops for that.

In fact, at least in most cases, one of the aspects of Jobs with Peace that I like is that the motivation of the leadership comes from a positive vision—of re-distributing wealth and re-prioritizing our nation's resources in a basic and radical way.

I, too, think it would be important to explore further how to organize people not out of painful emotion, fear, etc.

RC has clearly been very effective in mobilizing the natural inherent power and leadership abilities of many people. The personal counseling, the millions of support groups for every sort of background imaginable, the theory of people's inherent cooperative nature and natural desires to make things right, the excellent literature and the support for the leadership, has been a model of organizational development. Your leadership and personal commitment to make a difference in people's lives has been a critical element.

*The move within RC to focus on liberation has, of course, attracted many "political" people on the "Left." Of course, you have been very smart not to foster the development of RC into another political movement: that would have destroyed its effectiveness and relegated it to another somewhat interesting sect. None of that has happened because of the clear focus on the nurturing of numerous individuals' leadership in a wide variety of spheres. You just have to look at the "information coordinators" in **Present Time** to have your socks blown off. There's nothing like this anywhere else, I am sure. It is a terrific resource.*

The question remains about how to develop a greater level of unity and commitment. Certainly, many have lamented the lack of unity among the "progressive" political forces in this country. It is often hard to tell what is behind this lack of unity: is it a real lack of an intelligent strategy for change? Is it people's personal hang-ups about giving up "turf" or individual "control" over their organization or position? Is it some kind of ego trip? Is it people's fear of cooperation or lack of experience in cooperation? What do you think?

Right now, Jobs with Peace is trying to foster a greater degree of unity among a variety of progressive forces. It is working on bringing together a number of national progressive groups, and attempting to develop some sort of common approach or strategy for our collective work ahead. Our own organization's program of "reducing the military to fund human needs" is one possible "unifying program." One other is a general strategy of encouraging local neighborhood "precinct" networks, with neighborhood leaders who would educate their neighbors, make sure they voted, register new voters in their turf, etc. This is not that "new" an idea, of course. Individual politicians do something like this all the time. What is new, perhaps, is that the loyalty of the leaders is to a program, a set of positive ideas, and an organization that represents those ideas and values rather than an individual politician. More people are doing this around the country. But if this is more widely taken up it would be much more effective. People could learn from each other. It would encourage more and more leadership: there is virtually no limit to the territory that needs to be organized and the number of leaders needed.

My own sense is that this unifying "structure" rather than the Jobs with Peace program would be a more likely basis of unity for many people and organizations. What do you think? Any thoughts you have on proceeding in developing such unity would of course be much appreciated.

Later—

I think the general idea of "information coordinators" is a terrific one, one that shows the breadth of the organization and the trust in many people to take leadership in an ever-expanding way.

I think you are right, of course, in promoting the Wygelian leaders' organization structure. It is certainly an excellent way of people getting together to support each other, get ideas, and see they aren't alone. I have done this informally with "Men in progressive politics" for a number of years: usually a Sunday brunch format, meeting irregularly. Last time, I was surprised how many people showed up, even though I got mostly "maybe's" on the phone. Next time I am going to have to have child care (my fourteen-year-old son can do it: nice to keep it all men) since some of the guys have young children and the wives send them with them on Sundays. "Bowling with the boys" in the 1980's seems to include the little boys.

I received a call from someone who had met me at a January, 1988 Peace Activists' Workshop. He was planning a workshop for peace activists and hoped to approach the issue of "classism" and perhaps racism in the peace movement. He hoped to have people "work on" classism as well as try to develop some ideas for building a more diverse peace movement. The thing that most struck me was the lack of clarity about whether the workshop was to develop new strategies for an organization or organizations, or whether it was to develop ways for individuals *to overcome obstacles they may have personally to developing a more diverse constituency.*

It struck me, from my experience at least, that it would be difficult and confusing to try to do both at the same time. That it would be better to think about and plan for the organization or *the individual, but to try to do both would confuse things. Individuals and organizations are different animals. They operate differently, have different needs, different dynamics, etc. Change within them operates in a different way. It struck me that this may be clear to some of the people who have been successful in RC—or at least it would be helpful for this distinction to be made more clearly, particularly when one tries to go about changing an organization. An organization does not necessarily change because the people within it feel a different way. An organization needs a new program, new fundraising, new membership, etc. to change in certain ways, and these elements need to be addressed in the search for a more diverse constituency.*

At least this has been my experience. When I worked in grass-roots community organizations around basic economic issues (car insurance, utility rates, property taxes, etc.) the constituency was always working-class (the "have a littles, want some mores" in Saul Alinsky's terminology). The peace movement tends to be more upper income, since they already have a decent house, decent job, and want to preserve what they have. They generally have the slack to think about the larger picture: disarmament, etc.

I would be interested in your thoughts on changing organizations vs. changing or supporting individuals. Thinking about your mention of all for one and one for all, I was reminded of that when I read in the paper recently of the rat exterminators in Boston who said this was exactly the way they operated. It struck me that when you have a clear program (getting rid of the rats), this is more generally the case.

Michael Brown
Jamaica Plain, Massachusetts, USA

Dear Michael,

Assisting an individual to get his or her life organized better and assisting an organization to function better are certainly two different things, and I agree they need to be thought of separately. They are intimately connected by the nature of reality, however, and once we have thought of them separately, I think we need to integrate them in our thinking and actions as well.

In the new version of the **Guidelines** which I am proposing for adoption at the November World Conference, I am talking about a three-level (so far) program for Co-Counselors in the Community. The first point is **re-emergence**, and this corresponds to the one-point program which the Communities have had from the beginning, "to use Re-evaluation Counseling to recover one's occluded intelligence and help others to do the same." Large numbers of Co-Counselors, however, out of advancements in their thinking and for practical considerations, have developed and committed themselves to programs of **liberation**. This develops unavoidably as we find that at least a majority of our distresses are installed and perpetuated by oppression of the many varieties that have been used against us. Liberation activity can move our re-emergence up to a "wholesale" level and is a deeply satisfying way of participating in mutual efforts with others.

More and more Co-Counselors are moving towards **taking charge** (sometimes spelled out as taking responsibility, taking power, *and* taking charge in a sort of three-step progression).

The last of our five "frontier" commitments—"From now on I will inspire, lead, and organize all people to eliminate every form of humans harming humans"—not only takes us to an advanced ethical position but also presents a practical progression for action. If we are to "organize" all people in addition to leading them and inspiring them, then we must organize them in organizations, and I conjecture that the several levels of activity will need to be related to each other for any one of them to be maximally effective.

Certainly existing organizations are galvanized into newfound vigor when support groups, "dyads for discussion," and training classes are organized as part of the group's function. Certainly this loose association of people called the Re-evaluation Counseling Communities owes a large part of its excellent functioning to such organizing steps as workshops, conferences, spending of Outreach Funds, City-Wide Coordinators, and Wygelian Leaders' Groups.

I think a common error is to assume that any one organization should attempt all tasks or that "our" organization, which is the one we think about because we belong to it and have been dedicated to it, should take a position and begin activity on all the fronts on which we wish to see action taken. I think this is an organizational mistake and an understandable but self-defeating desire for simplification. People reach mature attitudes on different subjects at different rates, and a wider unity can often be achieved around one-point programs than around complex ones. Thus I think we should be reconciled to belonging to and being active in many different organizations and should be very careful about extending the scope of program of any organization that is functioning well on a single issue. Part of the ease of operation of the Wygelian Leaders' Group is that one may function in several such groups at the same time without the differences in viewpoints on other subjects complicating the work of the particular leaders' group at all.

So, I hope to be in organizations in the future which will allow and encourage individual re-emergence; will be dedicated to the elimination of oppression; and will be seeking "power to the people" for everybody.

I also expect that I will be a relaxed member of various groups that increasingly seek a correct program on *every* issue. I think this is bound to happen as the breadth of our understanding continues to grow.

Harvey

"Decision" Different than "Thinking"?

Dear Harvey,
  About the new Postulates:

*I continue to be confused about the word "decision."
Can you define that word? Or is it something you are assuming to be an undefined term, something we either understand or don't understand?

*How does a "decision" differ from a "fresh, accurate response" to each new moment of living?

If you say we have "complete freedom of decision," does that mean we have complete access to all fresh, accurate responses at all times and under all conditions? If not, then access to which, and how? Or only to accurate responses that do not depend on information which I thought we previously assumed is not really available, having been **mis-stored? (Is the concept of "mis-storage" still useful?)*

*Are you speaking only of "macro"-decisions (as in whether or not to organize a particular revolution) or also of "micro"-decisions (as in mayonnaise or catsup)? How do "micro"-decisions differ from "fresh, accurate responses"?

*What is the relation between "complete freedom of decision" and the presence or absence of information, if any?

*What is the universal value of arbitrarily deciding something before discharging, if, by discharging, information

Appeared in **Present Time** No. 76, July 1989.

could be freed up that would assist in making a good deci-sion?

Or, can we really describe what actually happens as—"first decision, then discharge" or, "first discharge, then decision"? It appears more integrated than that in most micro-decisions, at least—and to separate out the two functions that much could be misleading. Doesn't it often go more like this? —Ac-curate response, discharge, accurate response, discharge, accu-rate response, discharge, accurate response, discharge, accu-rate response (either one can come first). The whole process moving forward in quite an integrated way? Why try and ele-vate one over the other so generally? I don't understand.

K—
USA

Dear K—,

Those are good questions and I am not sure I can answer them satisfactorily yet, but they made me think and I will try to think on paper in response to them. We *could* take deci-sion to be an undefined term, but I think that we can define it in the sense that we are using it in these discussions as choos-ing one possibility where two or more possibilities are avail-able.

I think a "fresh, accurate response to each moment of liv-ing" does involve a decision because in most situations there are components of the situation that cannot be understood or estimated exactly. Typically we could make thousands of dif-ferent responses in any given situation which would be accu-rate enough. To try for the optimum one will involve a deci-sion as to which we think is the optimum one, or perhaps a decision as to how much time we want to spend waiting to come up with a more accurate decision.

To act within our freedom of decision is, I think, a very

high level function and probably requires the complexity of our central nervous systems just as much as does the intelligence.

I have been saying that this complexity of our central nervous systems has allowed the emergence of at least four functions which are qualitatively different than the functions of other forms of life. One is intelligence, the ability to construct a new successful response to any given situation. Another is awareness, which is hard to define, but it is something about noticing what is going on while it is going on or thinking about thinking while thinking. Third is complete freedom of decision. Fourth is complete power, the ability to handle the environment in ways so that it must respond to us in the way we want it to respond. I think these functions are all different from each other. I think that making a decision is a different function than being intelligent.

If one is thinking easily, these perhaps will not seem to be distinct functions. You will respond intelligently and make your decisions all in one flow and not differentiate between the two functions. However, most of us have struggled with the penetration of much of our functioning by distress. We have been surrounded by intrusions of compulsive patterns into the details of our living. Thus the necessity of making a decision often has involved struggling against a pattern, to do the "right" thing.

In such struggling, it's not hard to tell the difference between thinking and deciding.

I have been proposing that decision be used, now that we are aware of our complete freedom to use it, as a more forceful, less delicate, function than intelligence, more directly against our patterns.

(Certainly the effort to think where patterns have dominated us also works to bring discharge. I notice at times when I am challenged or challenge myself to think through a problem that I do not yet have a clear understanding of, that, if I can keep making the effort, it often brings discharge (usually yawns). Yet I think the making of a decision is a more "wholesale," a sturdier weapon for contradicting distress patterns. To use it often contradicts the patterns and forces discharge.)

Put another way, the creation of fresh, accurate responses is the operation of intelligence but sometimes a large number of fresh, accurate responses will be created and considered. Then the function of decision operates in order to choose the one to use. I think the decision function operates even when there are not distress patterns to be resisted or contradicted. I think it operates in unpatterned situations as well.

Certainly we know that adult re-emerging humans, operating in a jungle of patterns and seeking to thread through them to an optimum response, continually make decisions as to which is the *least* patterned response. Often such a decision is to resist a familiar compulsion or addiction.

The concept of mis-storage still holds; any information received during distress that has not been discharged, any information stored under tension which has not been discharged and which has not therefore had a chance to be re-evaluated, is still mis-stored and is still the content of a distress pattern.

I speak here not only of macro-decisions, but of micro-decisions as well.

You say, "What is the relation between complete freedom of decision and the presence or absence of information?" I think simply that lack of information makes the decision more adventurous. There are times when one has no way of knowing for certain which of two decisions is correct. Then one will "play hunches," that is, seek analogies in past situations which might possibly have a bearing on the current situation even if one can't say how close the analogy is.

You asked under what conditions one should decide something before discharging if by discharging one could be freed to think more accurately. The answer, of course, is that we have many pressures and deadlines upon us in many situations. To retire from responsibility "until one has discharged enough" is, I know, attractive to some people. It frees them from the pressure and allows them to go on discharging in the hope that they will not have to make decisions until they are sure of what they are deciding. I think this sometimes can contain a large component of helplessness and irresponsibility. One would have to assume that someone else is taking the responsibility for making decisions for you and that you are trusting that person. To trust someone else to make decisions for you may be very rational in some situations but it is certainly not universally applicable or we would all be helplessly waiting for our dooms.

I don't know if we can totally generalize yet about what happens when we put decision ahead of discharge but by observing it work with some people and from listening to their reports it seems that, if it can be done, it is a more efficient, more wholesale, way of re-emergence.

In practice, we will probably move forward in an integrated way. It is one central nervous system operating. One entity is carrying out all four functions, thinking, deciding, being aware, and reaching for occluded power, but they *are* four separate functions. Current results with people who are taking responsibility seem to indicate that we gain whenever we can put decision first.

In the past we've always done the best we could. When we did not put decision first, we were correctly judging the situation, including our then lack of information. Looking forward, however, we can try to put the decisions first and let them be a contradiction to the distress that will bring more discharge.

Harvey

Don't We Still Need Discharge?

Dear Harvey,

*There is something unclear about the theory for me. It seems to me that it says we can decide to put our attention off our distress or to decide **not** to be restimulated. So if we can do this, **why do we still need discharge?***

I think it is self-evident that the human body is always trying to heal any way it has been hurt. It is this inherent tendency to heal that offers up "restimulation" as a means of access to old hurt. At any moment we can decide to make use of this wonderful restimulation to heal ourselves via the discharge process. This does not always require the presence of another person. More and more I find writings in the RC journals or simply remembered contradictions, photos or music which are enough to get me discharging. Of course the presence of a caring human does contradict isolation which often gives a "fuller," deeper, and more prolonged quality to the discharge.

*If we ignore restimulation, surely the unresolved hurts will damage, or at best limit, our functioning in some way. When we decide not to be restimulated we avoid the **general** shutdown that seems to accompany major restimulation but we do not gain access to the area of thinking which is locked up with the painful experience. Only discharge renews our access to, and flexible use of, this past experience.*

*Even if we can decide not to be restimulated we still **need***

Appeared in **Present Time** No. 76, July 1989.

times at which we can discharge. Does it suggest it is an early issue of our power to control our functions being interfered with? So along with more decisive control of restimulation there might be a more rational and regular programming of sessions in our life!

Stefan Szczelkun
London, England

Dear Stefan,

The notion of deciding not to be restimulated is an important one but does not mean that we stop discharge. The fact that we can decide not to be restimulated puts us in control of the discharge process instead of having long periods of restimulation without discharge, which was what was happening when we were letting restimulation be an unaware process, often taking place because of the accumulated distress in an automatic way.

To take one's attention away from distress in most situations saves most of our lives from shut-down and allows us to bring up distress only when we have the contradictions to it that allow discharge. The distress does not go away without discharge and apparently never will, but the inefficient dragging-on process that was taking place with restimulation assumed to be involuntary is greatly improved by the repeated and successful decision to be in charge of the process. The distress does not go away without discharge, but we get discharge more efficiently and we live more awarely once we take charge of the process.

Does that make sense to you?

Harvey

Correct Policy and Practice
Means Less Effort

Dear Harvey,

My feet hardly touched the ground for a fortnight after the London gather-in in April, where I heard you tell someone: "Being the real you is much less effort. It's not the work that wears you out, it's the dithering."

I always knew this, but I didn't know I knew it until I heard you say it. Just as we all have all the intelligence we can ever need, it seems we also have all the energy we can ever need, the problem is that patterns can make it inaccessible. It's clear to me now that if I can discharge enough (and it seems to need several kinds of discharge) on the distress of weariness and the pattern of time-wasting, I can act in contradiction to the pattern.

I'm finding I can tap into what I now believe to be my innate infinite supply of energy by acting as though I feel energetic when I don't.

A non-RC friend who always seems to fit seventy-two hours' activity into every day once told me, "The secret is not to stop," and there's a lot in that. The lazy pattern re-asserts itself at the slightest opportunity and it's easier not to give it a chance than to let it take over for a while and then have to struggle out of it again.

*I started keeping the "client" and "counsellor" notebooks as soon as I read about them in **Present Time**. I soon found I*

Appeared in **Present Time** No. 73, October 1988.

305

needed a third: "Wide World." Into this go ideas for applying RC theory in daily life, and for spreading knowledge of RC.

My latest project is to organise, through our local Trades Union Council, a day workshop on the theme "A Woman's Place is in Her Union." It will be led by me and an RC woman who is in a white-collar union; I am in an industrial union so that will be a good balance. We will be aiming to organise non-RC women who are not in unions or would like to be more active in the union they are in, and using RC methods to get at whatever's making it difficult for them to get involved.

Recently at a workshop, a man I was counselling threw a lump of very obvious distress at me and I did what I usually do, I thought, "Oh help, I should do something about that," and couldn't think what. The client looked at me expectantly, saw nothing was about to happen, went on talking and the moment was lost. Going home on the train the next day I thought of a brilliant contradiction! This happens to me all the time. I have no trouble with steps 0 and 1, adopting the correct attitude to the client, and identifying the distress, but when I get to step 2, thinking of every possible way to contradict the distress, I often have trouble thinking of one possible way.

Thinking of good contradictions takes time, which is what you don't have in a session. What am I supposed to do? Tell the client, "I see what your distress is, just go and make us some tea while I think of some contradictions?" Or make a note of the distress and tell the client I'll phone or send a letter telling how to contradict it? I can't seem to "think on my feet."

Partly it feels like fear, or more accurately, panic. I feel as though I'm on one of those TV quiz shows where you have to answer as many questions as you can in two minutes. Only this matters so much more.

We aren't supposed to remind a client after a session of what they've been talking about. So if I think of a good contradiction some time later, is it in order to tell the client about it, by phone or letter, or do I just hope they'll come back to it in another session? In a workshop situation it could be someone I'm not likely to have another session with.

I realise the long-term answer is to counsel on my panic reaction and my fear of not being a good enough counsellor, and attack whatever it is that shuts down my intelligence in that situation. But that could take a long time, and I'd like your suggestions for how to deal with the problem meanwhile.

I was interested in Pamela Haines' proposals in **Present Time** *April 1988 for a clear transition from fundamentals classes to a more purposeful and committed level of counselling. I shall try and get my clients to think and tell me about what they want out of our sessions and what their long-term goals in counselling are, so we can approach each session with a clearer view of our common purpose.*

In the Brighton RC Community we have recently established the habit of ending each fundamentals course with a day workshop which anyone in the Community can come to and they and the new people can get to know each other. The topic for the day will be something the fundamentals class wants to work on, or something the teachers think the Community as a whole will find useful. This workshop could be the occasion for the sort of major decision work that Pamela was talking about, and for choosing partners to carry it forward with.

Sue Jones
Haywards Heath, West Sussex, England

Dear Sue,

Thanks for your neat letter. I appreciate it a lot and am pretty sure that experience and discharging your panic will make you fast on your feet. It's quite all right to ask a client in the next session if they would like to tackle that subject again because you think you've thought of a better contradiction, and generally I think they'll agree. You don't have to be completely formal, you can always ask.

I like the way you are thinking, and thanks for writing to me.

Harvey

How Does Oppression Start?

Dear Harvey,

*In **The Upward Trend**, you write, about oppression, "The principal individual means for the perpetuation of oppression is the feeling of wanting to switch roles in a distress recording of mistreatment, to accept the more 'comfortable' role, in a re-enactment of a mistreatment recording, of being the mistreator rather than being the mistreated, and to settle for co-operating in oppressing someone else rather than ending all oppression." I have heard you say similar things several times and have never felt really comfortable with that way of putting things. I don't disagree with what you say, but I want to put it in another way, and that leads to some interesting implications.*

You and others in RC have stated many times that all oppression starts with being oppressed yourself. This has been demonstrated over and over again in demonstrations in workshops and, of course, in individual sessions. But that still does not answer one important question: Why do human beings start to oppress other humans? Even if our intelligence were temporarily damaged, it seems strange that we would actively start oppressing others just because we got hurt or oppressed ourselves.

My hypothesis is that humans start oppressing because:

1. We are oppressed ourselves.

2. We are shown oppression of others.

3. We are told more or less directly, "If you don't take

Appeared in **RC Teacher** No. 22, 1988.

*part in oppression we will oppress you in the same way."
This scares us into taking part in, or at least not opposing,
the oppression.*

*4. We try to get rid of our hurts in this area. Because we do
not know how to do this, we instead act them out on the
oppressed.*

*We have found out that it is a bigger hurt not to be allowed
to show your love than not to be loved. In analogy with that,
I suspect that seeing the oppression of others (whether you
belong to that group or not) is as hurtful as being oppressed
yourself. Because of the hurts that we receive from being oppressed and seeing the oppression of others, it is possible to
scare us with a threat of being oppressed again. If we hadn't
been hurt in this way, we would probably just laugh at such a
threat. But, as we are already hurt, we can be scared into taking part in the oppression. One example of this is that, when
boys get to that age when they are conditioned to do oppressive things to girls, the worst insult from another boy is being
called a "girl." The message is: "Do as the other boys do, or
we will treat you in the same way as we treat the girls."*

*Still, I think that these threats are not the real driving force
of active oppression. Because we have a strong, strong desire
to get rid of all our distress, we try to work on our experiences
of oppression. We very early acquire the habit of focusing
our attention on the distress, for the obvious reason of not
being listened to. Without the information about how distress, discharge, and re-evaluation work, we work on our distress in ways that are often oppressive. I think that the real
motive behind any oppressive action is a misdirected attempt
by a person to get rid of some distress around oppression.*

*If this thinking is correct, there should be a common fear
of belonging to an oppressed group, for example, men being
afraid of being a woman. A direction for a man of pronounc-
ing loudly, "I am also a woman," should challenge that fear
and bring discharge. Working on the feeling of seeing others*

being oppressed should also be possible. The first memory of seeing somebody else being oppressed should bring discharge if the story is told and the guilt contradicted.

I have applied these directions to myself as a client, and they work. As a counselor, I had hoped to be able to test my hypothesis, but (perhaps fortunately for my clients) I cannot design experiments the way I do in chemistry. I had hoped to gain more experience with time, but it just doesn't happen, so I decided to write about it anyway.

Elis Carlström
Göteborg, Sweden

Dear Elis,

I agree with much of your thinking about oppression, but perhaps not in every detail. First, there are many hurts besides the hurts of oppression, and though oppression only operates on the basis of a distress pattern, there are many distress patterns which are not in themselves oppression (we have defined oppression as "the systematic one-way mistreatment of a group of people with the mistreatment supported and enforced by the society"). Thus, I don't think that all oppression necessarily starts with the person being oppressed himself or herself but certainly starts with the person being hurt himself or herself. In most cases, the hurt would be the oppression, but not necessarily always, or oppression would never have gotten started in the first place.

When people have asked me how the suppression of discharge started, I have offered a fantasy of a tribal people hiding in the thicket during a raid by an enemy tribe and a baby being fiercely quieted when it begins to cry, for the safety of all the people who are in hiding. This would leave a recording which would lead the baby when grown up and a parent to shut off the discharge of his own child without any current reason except the restimulation. You can think of many other possible examples.

I agree that we are hurt not only by being oppressed ourselves but also by witnessing the oppression of others. It is almost a truism among experienced counselors that the person who is not beaten but had to passively observe the beating of others tends to be much more frightened than the person who was actually beaten.

I agree with you that the acting out of the oppression stems from the attempt of the original victim to discharge their own hurt. I think this is true of every dramatization or rehearsal. Unfortunately, however, understanding it does not by itself heal the distress. Discharge of the pattern is necessary, even though a decision not to rehearse the pattern can prevent the dramatization during the interim period when discharge is being achieved.

I think you are right that people tend to be afraid of belonging to any other group which they see being oppressed.

I look forward to hearing from you more.

Harvey

Keep Clarifying Classist Oppression

Dear Harvey,

I attended two of your open question nights at Groton-wood, Massachusetts this week. It was a great experience and gave me lots to work on and think about. One area that you counselled people on was class issues. You had four or five people stand before the audience holding hands, and had them speak about their experiences (what they liked and what was crummy) about being in their respective economic classes. I learned a lot from the working-class people, who discharged and took great strength in making their commitments to working together and moving into the future to change the world.

*As I watched the middle-class group (among whom I have historically counted myself) and the owning-class group, I felt that although I was learning about their **experiences**, I wasn't necessarily learning about their oppressions as fully as I did with the working-class group. The second and third groups also did not easily discharge with the commitments. I have been thinking about this, wondering why, and coming up with some observations I'd like to try out on you.*

Although theory seems to be trying to equate the experiences of these classes, saying that there was/is the good and the crummy in each (i.e., that we all have been hurt because of the economic castes we have been placed in), it seems to me that the hurts of working-class people are more concrete, immediate, visceral, tangible, and nameable. Of course I am

Appeared in **Present Time** No. 70, January 1988.

generalizing, but let me pursue this further nonetheless. Issues like being hungry, being cold, being unsure of shelter and of livelihood produce a unique sort of distress. The focus in counseling working-class people is on trusting one's thinking and on discharging about the despair of changing and of ever leading oneself and others into improved conditions. These conditions are very clear, concrete, and observable.

Middle-class distress seems to be largely about confusion, an abstract and muddy proposition, at best. Isolation is part of this as well. It seems that useful directions would not so much involve talking about the oppressions of the daily experience (because **comfort** is the daily experience for middle- and owning-class people, and **comfort** is not an oppression). It would start with the most **simple, clear, unconfusing, unequivocal** statement about one's class position. "I am wealthy," "I am middle class," "I am owning class," "I have money"—all seem to be strong contradictions to confusion. When these simple, **concrete** directions were used in the demonstration I saw, people began to smile, shake, make sounds. **Simple** seems to be a way to go forward with this issue for middle- and owning-class people.

One further thought that really hit me as I watched the demonstrations: working-class oppression is its own animal. Middle-class and owning-class oppressions are actually other oppressions and distresses. Alcoholism, drug abuse, sexual, physical and psychological abuse, abusing money, workaholism—these are all **different** than and separate from one's class. They are not caused by being middle- or owning-class, and members of the working class suffer with these as well. My point is that counseling on middle- and owning-class distress may be about some other areas and issues, whereas working-class distress seems to have its own identity. Certainly issues such as guilt and shame and isolation may be part of owning- and middle-class distress, but again, these are more abstract distresses and may need different counseling strategies than the working-class counseling strategies.

I see a problem here in dividing the classes again (as economic distress seems to do already). I just think some acknowledgement needs to be made about how different these distresses are, for more effective counseling for all.

Martha Glaser
Littleton, Massachusetts, USA

Dear Martha,

I appreciate your letter of November 5th. Thanks for thinking about the demonstrations. I think that most of what you say is exactly right, but I think there ARE basic characteristics of middle-class and owning-class distress. Just off the top of my head, of course the middle-class position is one of confusion; they are actually a section of the working class, and are bribed and confused and coerced into acting against their own interests and the interests of their own class. The guilt, shame, and confusion is an essential part of it. The middle class are also oppressed economically just as all the rest of the working class is, in that they produce, on the average, far more value than they will ever receive for their work. They just get a little more than the working class does as a bribe.

The owning class are essentially complete humans, hate oppression, hate exploitation and yet are bribed and coerced and lied to in order to play that role. It is a deep oppression even if it doesn't arise out of hunger and cold and over-fatigue. It is a destructive oppression, and I think it needs to be worked on, but your attitude of clarifying that there is a difference in being on which end of the stick when one person is beating another, is excellent.

Harvey

Acting, Not Suffering, Where We Care

Dear Harvey,

I hope that all is well with you and that you are continuing to feel encouraged and empowered by the tremendous progress we are making throughout the world in relation to our ideas about the nature of human beings, the nature of distress, and our workable ideas about how to contradict same.

I am writing because I need your clear thinking about an issue which is currently causing me much distress. I recognise that I am unable to think clearly myself about the issues, so I am looking to you for some guidance, and/or contradictions to help me unjam my current difficulties and feelings of powerlessness.

I am greatly distressed to hear of news about current events within South Africa. I have been distressed for some considerable time. I was distressed at the time of your last workshop in Leicester, and for a long time before that. The problem is that I feel so powerless. I don't know what to do. I want to stand behind such leaders as Bishop Desmond Tutu yet I don't know how to do this. If I write, he will probably not receive my letter (in any case I do not know where to write). I want to offer my support and encouragement to Re-evaluation Counsellors within South Africa, yet I do not wish my letters to expose them to government action nor to discrimination.

I am uncertain about whether any action I might be able to take would merely ease my sense of distress or would actually

Appeared in **Present Time** No. 71, April 1988.

*help black people within South Africa. My thinking to date is
that letters would simply ease my distress, but could cause
physical distress and worse to those at the receiving end. Am I
right in this?*

*Within my own country I can and do talk to people about
South Africa and about the whole issue of racism. I made up
my mind some time ago that* THE *most important issue for
me to tackle was anti-racism. Accordingly, I offered to participate in the work to be carried out within my professional
organisation on the multi-cultural issue. I wrote the enclosed
article for* **Social Work Today** *(much of which, as you will
see, was "cribbed" from articles produced by Re-evaluation
Counsellors) and in so doing I managed to turn the thinking
within the professional practice committee from ideas about
multi-culture to ideas about anti-racism. I am now leading
the sub-group, which has been established to produce policy
and practice guidelines on this issue. I find my role extremely
scary, because I feel that my knowledge base is so limited.
Nevertheless, I am determined to contribute much effort to
this task. My professional organisation is extremely racist,
sexist, classist, etc. Yet it could (and does) offer such a lot to
those involved in the social care profession. The better we
make the organisation, the better we are able to offer support
and care to children, disabled people, elders, mentally ill people, etc. I have thought of putting some effort into becoming
the president of my organisation, say within the next two or
three years. I know that it is possible for me to do this. I
know I will do the job really well, yet I am afraid of my ambi-
tion and wonder whether I am deluding myself in claiming
self-disinterest. I know I want to propagate the ideas of Re-
evaluation Counselling, yet I also know I will enjoy holding a
powerful position.*

*Racism and the surrounding problems seem of such magni-
tude that whatever I do will be insignificant and nowhere near
enough. I feel confused, not knowing whether my expectations of myself are unrealistic or too low. I am sorry to pre-*

sent you with such a "distressed" problem. I know you can help.

Marilyn Hambly
Radcliffe-on-Trent, Nottingham, England

Dear Marilyn,

I am very moved by your letter and the enclosure. I am glad that you care. I am sorry that you are distressed, but you are by no means powerless. Writing to people in South Africa might be a little helpful but you are right, it can sometimes be dangerous. What we will do is communicate through RC to the people we can and the others will know and benefit mostly from what we can do in our own countries. Your writing the article is a very, very good move. Planning to become president and influence the policies of your organization is excellent and becoming acquainted with your members of parliament and the political party leaders of your choice and seeing that all of the organizations that you can join adopt your policy against racism and publicly do something, is a very powerful thing and will be more help to the people of South Africa (and the people of England) than anything else you can do.

Your distress about the racism at present is, in a way, not justified. As bad as the situation is in South Africa, it is very good compared to what it has been in the past. People are dying in battles that used to die without being able to fight back very much. Probably more deaths occurred without publicity, simply because of the oppression, than are now occurring with publicity because of the rebellion against it. Things are better than they were in every way and your alliance with the people against racism is very important.

Thank you for taking the initiative and thank you for writing me.

Harvey

Mothers, Choosings, and Cultures

Dear Harvey,

I think you are right about people being buds on the same branch. I think you might have trouble convincing some mothers of that, however, especially ones who have given a baby up for adoption. I was also thinking that the babies and toddlers of my acquaintance do seem to be very attached to their mothers and get upset when they are left with other people. It may go back to the expectations that we are probably born with—that we are the center of the universe and that other people will love us and pay attention to us. In our culture it seems that mothers are the only ones who are not only allowed, but expected, to have that kind of unconditional love for their children. If we all spen the time and attention with young ones that mothers do, the n maybe it wouldn't be upsetting to be separated from Mom. Absent distress, we all might be everyone's "parents" and "children."

Another thing you mentioned was the idea that everything we do is a matter of our own choosing. I have been aware for a year and a half or two years that I am continuously in the process of choosing what I do and who I am. I think it comes as a result of asking myself why I was doing a particular thing or other. The only answer that made sense to me was that I chose to do so or that I chose to be a certain way. My distaste for the idea that I might be helpless in any situation and unable to make a choice may have helped that idea along. You did say that you thought perhaps people should carry out their agreements. I think that there is no logical reason

Appeared in **Present Time** No. 69, October 1987.

for that exception to the, "There are no shoulds in the world" idea. I think that carrying out your agreements is as much a choice as anything else. I would like to think that it's one of those things that we would all choose to do more and more as we climb more and more out of our distresses. It is not clear to me how a society could function, however, without establishing some sort of responsibility for carrying out, or not carrying out, agreements. An externally imposed responsibility for fulfilling agreements could be part of the equation that people balance when choosing whether to do what they've agreed to or not.

Another sketchy thought has to do with culture and the various commitments, brought about by the visit to our Community of an Irish leader. The thought has to do with each of us being proud of our culture. I am only groping my way through this one, but it seems to me that the pride in our various cultures and the commitments are useful for as long as we carry around the negative effects of our particular culture. But that I have every right to be as proud of anyone else's culture as I do of my own background, for the parts of all of them that allow people to remain human in whatever ways they do so. It sometimes seems that people can limit themselves by adopting the good things about their own culture as the only way that they can be. My thinking about this gets muddied by the way that cultures get destroyed by outside cultures seeking to dominate a "native" culture, whatever that is anymore. I believe that every culture should be able to decide its own solutions to its own problems, but I don't know how you decide what group of people is a self-determining group. Do you simply say that all countries in existence on a certain date are the units of self-determination?

Mary Ruth Gross
San Jose, California, USA

Dear Mary Ruth,

I think the question of our not being ancestors or descendants is going to have more and more importance for us, the more we think about it, and your speculations are very similar to mine. I think you have thought more about freedom to choose everything than I have, but I would feel that agreements that are entered into must be honored and kept, as being very important; that they not be violated without notice; and wherever possible a new agreement negotiated to replace them. But I think to violate them without notice is a lack of integrity and would be very harmful of our relations with each other.

As far as the taking pride in our cultures, I agree with you that taking pride in them as opposed to anyone else's culture is at most a very temporary step, and that as RCers we need to remember that every culture is composed of useful lore that needs to be respected and honored and treasured and shared with everyone else in the world, and a set of patterns which arise understandably, but are nonsense in the present, and which need to be sorted out and rejected, and certainly not passed on to anyone else. What dᵒ you think of that?

Harvey

The Harm of Hypnosis

Dear Harvey,

A friend of mine was at the therapists' workshop and found it very helpful. From my conversation with her I have a question. Apparently the question of hypnosis came up and you spoke of it quite negatively. I recall that you have talked about that before, but don't remember what you said. I would appreciate hearing your thinking on the subject sometime when you have a moment.

Jean Baierlein
Portland, Connecticut, USA

Dear Jean,

Hypnosis is the artificial shutting down of the mind in order to install a rigid pattern. The effects of it are exactly the same as the shutting down by distress, with the little extra danger that the agreement to shut down can become recorded and the person can become victimized by that. The effects of hypnosis are *always* harmful, always. Discharge is necessary to get rid of the pattern and sometimes it's very difficult to get rid of it.

The claims for benefit from hypnosis come down pretty much to (a) that occluded material can be recalled under hypnosis. (This is true, as it is for narcosynthesis, but it is always, always, always harmful and sometimes very harmful. You occluded the material for good reason and it will come up spontaneously when you are ready to handle it. To bring it up or

Appeared in **Present Time** No. 71, April 1988.

force it up ahead of time with hypnosis or drugs is very damaging.) (b) That you can suppress symptoms that one does not like by putting in a counter-command during hypnosis. (This is also true. You *can* suppress a symptom by setting up a hypnotic distress pattern counter to the effects of the existing distress patttern, but you set up a deep conflict within the person and the distress will always come out in some other form. It is always harmful.) Any hypnosis that a person has had needs to be discharged thoroughly.

Harvey

How to Get Started in Ethiopia

Dear Harvey,

I want to give you an idea of how things have been going here and ask for your help, if you're able. I'm in the midst of a very religious group of Ethiopian teachers who have been very welcoming and friendly to me. They go out of their way to make me comfortable, and many of their customs, though not shared by my culture, are a blessing to me. Men here have no qualms about walking hand-in-hand or arm-in-arm, for one thing. A great deal is made of respect for the teacher from both parents and students, which is a relief. And general hospitality for all, but especially for guests or visitors, is highly valued.

Thus far I've made some advances in making a difference in life here. I've made strong, unshakable friendships with three men here (two teachers and one high-school graduate). I've shown myself to be dedicated to my job and to the long- and short-term welfare of children, while at the same time being relaxed and fun-loving.

The relationship with the high-school graduate is the deepest, and we've had several deep discussions. He seems receptive to RC theory, although actually discharging is going to be a hard step for him to make. But I'm at the point of sharing time with him informally at first. My challenge will be not to get too heavy with him too soon, yet not be weird about avoiding it.

I've received the copy of your last book. Though I've en-

Appeared in **Present Time** No. 73, October 1988.

joyed it and get excited and inspired about leadership while reading it, there seems to be a step missing for me—mainly, how to get started. There must be a million ways, all of them capable of being blocked by my timid patterns. But let me just run through them and if you have the time tell me if any of them are notably flawed or recommended. Would it be best to go for an RC class first and gain respect that way? Should I get into the inner workings of school administration and policy making? Should I get one or two solid "believers" behind me first? Should I make it a priority to listen to and gain the trust of those with titles? Should I concentrate on encouraging and bolstering the courage of the rank and file? Should I initiate a new committee to think through school policy and propose changes?

All of them I've mulled over and in writing them down I can see that there are some that are preferable. For one thing, I think I'm going to need a solid base for myself and developing some one-to-one conscious listening and sharing relationships comes first. Some of the other ideas rather hinge on my demonstrating courage and clear thinking before any group would agree to come together with me.

But I don't understand how leadership emerges from a situation where a person has close friends, is well informed on the basics of human interaction, lives zestfully, and is well liked by almost everyone he comes in contact with. I've discovered that leadership doesn't just rise up to greet such a person. Somehow I've got to make a move and I just don't know how. I imagine it probably has to do with timid and indecisive patterns, but could you give me another hand with them? I'd really appreciate it.

Chris Kurtz
Addis Ababa, Ethiopia

Dear Chris,

It sounds to me like you are doing fine. I think you probably have some unrealistic notion of transforming usual relationships into RC relationships. Personally, I would do just
about what you have been doing. I would act like an RCer in
every way; I would arrange every meeting of two or more
with you to be a taking-turns meeting, in other words a support group; and I would loan people scrolls or pieces of RC
literature or particular articles and ask for their comment.
But basically, listen and like and validate people at every turn
and then when they tell you one day that you are totally admirable and they wonder how you manage it, you say, "Well,
I have studied at this and I would be very glad to tell you what
little I have learned." There's no big jump from a friendly
relationship to RC, it's just doing what comes naturally.

It sounds like you have done just fine so far.

Harvey

Too Much "Tolerance"?

Dear Harvey,

I had a fine time at the Midwest USA Teachers' and Leaders' Workshop in Chicago last June. Although I could get away only for two days during the week, I got a lot out of it. I wanted to let you know what I appreciated. I also have a concern.

First, the panel you did with the people of color was first-rate. It constantly amazes me when I hear that information again. I've heard it before yet it still sounds like I'm hearing it for the first time. I am committed to discharging all my hurt around incorporating racism. When that happens, maybe it won't be a problem remembering how people have been abused.

Next, the concern. I have to confess I was troubled by having a psychic support group. You seemed delighted that it was raised as an issue. Now, I understand that you would welcome almost any area around which people can organize. And maybe there's no obvious reason to discourage a psychic support group and encourage one for Jews or Catholics. Maybe you read the whole thing as a "discharging on psychic issues support group" anyway. But it seems to me that it's useful to make some judgments about what's appropriate in RC. Especially when the legitimacy of the workshop and RC as a whole lend support to a concept that is alien to what we are trying to do. We are trying to empower ourselves, are we not? Any energy we put into psychic or paranormal phenomena is that much less energy we have to devote to the meaningful issues around which we are striving to organize.

Appeared in **Present Time** No. 77, October 1989.

Would you have no objections to, let's say, a Satanic support group? An animal sacrifice support group? A witches' support group? Certainly, you would at least make careful distinctions about the wording of these groups.

So my concern is that by letting a psychic support group go, we have implicitly valued it on equal footing with all the worthy groups organized. In all fairness, I'm not sure how you could have objected without threatening the convener, but it would be plausible to assume that she was asking for a contradiction in the first place when she suggested the topic. Where in the inherent reality is there a legitimate place for psychics? What powerlessness or sense of doom are psychics desperately attempting to address?

I'm gratified that there were few takers for such a group and that it never got off the ground. There were repeated attempts to convene a topic group table for psychics at dinner with the convener being especially vocal about announcing the time and place.

At any rate, let me be direct with my question. Have you ever vetoed a suggestion for a support group? What logic do you apply? I'd appreciate any thoughts you have about what I've said.

John Kador
Geneva, Illinois, USA

Dear John,

I'm glad you enjoyed the workshop, and I certainly enjoyed your letter. Let me see if I can answer some of your concerns about having someone report on the oppression of "psychics." I hesitated before appointing an Information Coordinator for psychics for some time.

All of us are distressed. All of us walk around partly rational and partly a mound of distress patterns, and our most elegant functioning so far is almost certainly colored a little bit by the chronic patterns which we have not emerged from yet. It's easy to get caught in arguments where one person points at another person and says, "Your behavior is patterned where I disagree with you," and the pointed-at person replies, "No, *your* behavior is patterned where we disagree," and an interminable shouting match be set up. I have found myself in this position, where my policy in leadership has been challenged, many, many times.

I have worked out a procedure for myself, in which the first thing I do when challenged in this manner is to question, "Is there a possibility that I am just reciting a pattern?" If I can't see that I am, I check with thoughtful people who have disagreed with me in the past and been right, and ask them if my position seems to be out of a pattern. If they do not all agree that it is, or better yet, if none of them agree that it is, then I try to get into communication with the person who is insistently condemning my position. If I finally fail and some action is necessary, I tell him, "Well, I can't absolutely say that you are wrong and that I am right, but if anyone's pattern is going to guide me in this situation, it's going to be mine and not yours," and that has worked fairly well.

It seems to me that we must be against *all* oppression, including the oppressions that are directed against people with the excuse that they have a particular kind of pattern.

I would say the usual manifestations of "psychicness" are easily duplicated by any expert magician, who will tell you he's not doing anything supernatural, and they are easily understood in the ability of a pattern to present things with impressive "reality" as they aren't really to careful observers. But I don't think you are any help to the persons who are psychic by deriding them, and I think that if they are listened to, they will discharge and come to their own good judgment about the matter. Coincidence can appear amazing, particularly if you don't know the realities of statistics and probability. Any roomful of people is very likely to have two people with the same birthday in it, which seems incredible to the people in the room, who say, "Why, there's only thirty of us and there are 365 days in the year," but this is because they do not understand the math and because everybody wants to believe something exciting beyond their present knowledge, wants to be thrilled by something they don't understand yet.

So, I think it would be good for all the people who feel they are "psychic" who are in RC to communicate with each other, and if they reinforce each other's beliefs, fine, there are lots of clubs and magazines and so on doing it in the wide world anyway. I think much more likely, they will find some safety to discharge and come to a rational, much less afraid viewpoint than they had before. And, if they don't wind up agreeing with me completely, what the heck. I may be in the middle of a skeptic's pattern, that I equate with being rational.

How does that grip you?

Harvey

Organizing

Let's Really Reach
For the Working Class

I propose that every Community or fledgling Community move directly and promptly to establish a regular monthly one-day workshop **FOR WORKING-CLASS PEOPLE**, that this be determinedly organized and continued in spite of any difficulties encountered, and that help be sought from the RC leadership locally, regionally, and internationally, to solve any difficulties.

1) This one-day monthly workshop (almost certainly needing to be held on weekends or holidays) shall be open only to people who are *presently* working-class.

2) The cost shall be low, affordable even by people who are unemployed or on welfare. (I propose that funds be collected by a box being on display at the beginning of the workshop, with a sign on it saying, "Put in $5—or equivalent—towards the cost of the workshop if you can; if you can't spare it, you are completely welcome anyway.")

3) Someone takes responsibility for these workshops over a period of time who is either presently working-class herself or himself, or committed to bringing RC tools to the working class. This overall leader can ask other leaders to lead particular workshops.

4) That these monthly workshops shall be viewed as equivalent to fundamentals classes or to ongoing classes. That attendance at a fundamentals class previously not be required for admission to these workshops. That working-class people be

Appeared in **Present Time** No. 74, January 1989.

invited who are sponsored by someone already using RC who has at least attempted to explain RC to the person and given them an introductory session.

5) That the agenda for these workshops include the following items:

a) Quick introductions.

b) A class. In this, some theory will be presented and questions answered, problems solved, and short demonstration sessions done.

c) Support Group meetings.

d) Lunch. Good bread, a stew or salad, and milk or juice such as can be prepared easily and paid for out of the contributions, should be available for people who do not bring their own lunches.

e) Individual sessions.

f) A leaders' meeting. Every person at the workshop is a leader. Each person speaks in turn on: (1) how I have used RC to lead people, (2) what the situation for working-class people is in our locality, what the opportunities are, what the difficulties are, and(3) what I propose to do about it.

6) Cleaning up and leaving the premises neat and spotless.

7) A closing circle: Announcement of the next workshop and the leadership. Each person says what was best for her or him about the workshop.

I propose that these be held in people's homes if other premises are not available, that they be held regularly, and that they be given the Community leadership's full attention to guarantee that they are attractive and successful.

Please write directly to me or to Dan Nickerson, the International Liberation Reference Person for Working-Class People, on how this project is proceeding. Request help when needed from the general RC leadership on all levels.

The Effective Use of Literature

We have used the term "re-emergence" to summarize the reclaiming of our inherent natures and abilities into operational use again. The oppressive society and the accumulation of distress patterns have placed confusion, occlusion, misfunction, and indoctrination into false concepts and assumptions upon us. We have assumed that individual re-emergence is possible because to assume otherwise seeems to confine us to assumptions of powerlessness or hopelessness or helpless dependence on someone else's initiative. Yet we have been fairly clear that, practically, re-emergence depends on cooperation between individuals, and therefore necessarily on communication between them. *Decision* plays a powerful role in making Co-Counseling effective, but communication and clarity of concepts are even more fundamentally important.

Our treasure, our working capital, and, in some respects, our greatest achievement has been the accumulating insights into the actual nature of reality which we have extracted from the confusion in which we started and from which we are re-emerging. To communicate these insights to each other in effective ways has been, of necessity, a principal preoccupation. In pursuit of this we have convened and reported on innumerable topic groups. We have exchanged directions, sung songs, taught classes, given lectures, and tried to communicate in every other possible way we could imagine.

A constant difficulty with all of these kinds of communication has been contamination of the authentic insight by patterns. This contamination stems from two principal sources.

Appeared in **Present Time** No. 76, July 1989.

First, the patterns of the communicator which lard his or her speech with meaningless phrases, misleading tones of voice, and facial expressions that have no connection with the present scene. Second, the patterns of the person communicated to, who hears things that are not being communicated at present but echo from past distresses restimulated by some similarity in the present. Often, too, either the communicator or the communicated-to quickly forget what was said or what was heard and substitute for it, in their perception, a patterned message from a persisting chronic pattern.

We have sought to find ways to combat these difficulties and we have had outstanding success in one area. This is our written and recorded literature.

The written word contradicts all three of the pseudo-abilities of the distress recording. The distress recording can persist, can confuse one, and can make one forget, but the written word can out-persist the pattern; it can clarify, re-clarify, and re-clarify by its continuing existence; and it can remember and remember and remember (and remind one) no matter how many times forgetting has intervened. Most of these characteristics and this effectiveness are shared by the audio- or video-recording.

Our literature is a remarkable compilation of creative and inspired thinking by a very large number of people of the most diverse backgrounds and interests. Many of the most crucial and central generalizations have appeared under my authorship, but even these, in almost every case, are summaries of the thinking of a large number of people. The way in which the many relationships between Co-Counselors which we summarize in the word "Community" have arisen has provided an unparalleled opportunity to promote, gather, and be inspired by the thinking of this vast variety of people.

A voluminous correspondence from all over the world has developed (which requires several hours of each day to reply to). A vast array of workshops are held in every part of the globe and centered on every conceivable topic. Thousands and thousands of topic groups report on issues about which the contributors are deeply motivated and concerned.

The development of our many journals represents a completely new kind of people's journalism. In these, people write about the subjects that concern them most, about the details of their own lives and struggles, on the topics about which they are actually experts out of their own experiences. They are inspired by and respond to each other's writings. Good editing strains out patterns and sloppiness from these writings and meets the goal of helping the contributor "say what he or she was trying to say."

Thirteen books, fifty-six pamphlets, two hundred separate issues of twenty-nine journals, sixty-two videocassettes, and twelve audio-cassettes have been published and mostly remain in print. Very little of this treasure-trove ever goes out of date.

The use which Re-evaluation Counselors have made of this treasure and the extent to which it has been implemented as an avenue for wide and rapid communication to the world is another matter. Here, obviously patterns have interfered with and limited the effectiveness of our publications drastically.

There are hopeful signs. There is now a growing group of *aficionados* who eagerly await each new publication, who call their friends in excitement to urge them to read particular articles, and who order twenty copies of each new journal to distribute to their growing circle of friends who look to them as wonderful sources of these exciting ideas. However, the full use of our literature has only begun.

Certain patterns can be perceived in this slowness (which I think it is time we challenge decisively). One seems to be a kind of general embarrassment, which the oppressive society has put on us, over being *meaningful*. (We were probably be-littled when we spoke as small children with wonder and feel-ing about important things because this contradicted the sleazy apathy, into which many of the adults around us had resigned themselves, and made them feel uncomfortable.) We were re-buked and belittled and called childish or naive for caring about things, for openly enjoying beauty, for marveling at the wonder of the world around us.

We communicate the precious insights of RC in many ways. Our modeling of them by the way we live and relate to others is basic. Our attentive listening, our careful oral communica-tion, our asking of insightful questions, all serve as channels of communication to the people around us.

Now that we have our printed literature, our videocassettes, and our audio-cassettes available, it makes very good sense to use them to the fullest. To sell (or, if necessary, give) a sub-scription to **Present Time** to a friend requires a small amount of energy and then the journal will continue to communicate for hundreds of hours. To establish a lending library of all the literature in beginning Communities lays a far better foundation for the Community than the traditional hit-or-miss contact with the theory only through classes and work-shops. To offer audio-cassettes to people, as companions for time spent driving in one's car or for relaxing company be-fore sleep, can have a long-lasting effect.

To purchase videocassettes for an Area library and allow classes to view them for a very small fee (but sufficient to pay the cost) can bring much of the benefits of top-notch work-shops to the nine-tenths of our Communities who don't get to workshops.

The thoughtful, systematic use of our literature can bring very satisfying results and enhance all of our other efforts.

Commitments

Commitments

TO BE YOUR OWN ELEGANT, WISE, AND POWERFUL SELF

From this moment on, the *real* (your own name)! This will mean _____.

AGAINST PRETENSE

I am obviously completely incompetent and completely inadequate to handle the challenges which reality places before me.

However, (fortunately or unfortunately), I happen to be the best person available.

TO RECLAIM POWER

From now on I will see to it that everything I am in contact with works well, and I will not limit or pull back on my contacts. This will mean _____.

AGAINST IDENTIFYING ONESELF WITH PATTERNS

Recordings of past distress experiences have no power of their own at all.

They only contrive to give the appearance of power and influence to the extent that I slavishly submit to letting them use *my* power and *my* influence.

(If I think of them as pieces of recorded tape, they have, at most, a trifling historical significance, *unless* I insert them in the tape recorder that is myself and allow them to play me, an action which I am completely free to decide to do or not to do.)

Therefore, I now decide to deny any past distress any credibility in the present, or any influence or operation in my life.

And I will repeat this decision as many times as necessary to free my life completely from the influence of past distress.

TO UNITY OF ALL HUMAN ASPIRATIONS

From now on I will inspire, lead, and organize all people to eliminate every form of humans' harming humans. This will mean _____.

A PROPOSED NEW FRONTIER COMMITMENT

Since thinking is necessarily fresh thinking, I hereby decide that I will never again let anything from the past influence the way I act in the present or future

and

I will repeat this decision as many times as necessary to achieve the clear-cut results that I want.

TO END PREOCCUPATION WITH DISTRESS

It is logically possible and certainly desirable to end the ancient habit of paying attention to past distress and replace it by a new attitude or posture of paying attention to interesting and rewarding concerns, including the present-time situation, and so I now decide to do this and will repeatedly so decide until the ancient habit is broken.

BLACK PERSONS

For the complete liberation of my beautiful, wise, strong, and courageous black people, I solemnly promise I will always remember our/my own goodness and strength. I will fight against every division that tends to separate us from each other and from other people. I will settle for nothing less than complete liberation, complete equality, complete opportunity, and complete respect for everyone.

JEWISH

For the long-range survival of my people, I solemnly promise that, from this moment on, I will treat every person I meet as if she or he were eager to be my warm, close, dependable friend and ally, under all conditions. This will mean that _____.

CHICANO/A

In respect for my beautiful land and the enduring and proud people that inhabit it, I promise that I shall cherish my culture and language, unite my people, and in alliance with all peoples of the world, see that all oppressions are ended.

PILIPINO/A

For the real freedom and unity of my beloved people, I solemnly promise that I will take pride in myself and the Pilipino Nation under all conditions.

I will work to wipe out the last vestiges of colonialism.

I will strengthen the bonds between all Pilipino people of whatever religion, language, or background, including the Philippines' sons and daughters overseas.

FOR A UNITED, FREE PHILIPPINES WITHOUT OPPRESSION.

IRISH

For the long-range encouragement of my brave and noble people, I joyfully promise that, from this moment on, I will never again demean myself, or permit myself to be demeaned, not permit any Irish person to be demeaned by anyone, including the person herself or himself, but shall stand as a proud example of the beauty, nobility, and wisdom of my wonderful people.

ISRAELI

From now on I will see to it that everything I am in contact with works well. However, remembering that the person and the pattern are completely different and separate, and that the pattern is reinforced and the person is hurt by criticism, I promise that from now on I will never again speak or act critically to, or about, another person, including myself, but instead in every contact with every person I will find and express some appreciation of that person and of myself.

(in Hebrew)

```
מטחה והלאה אדאג לכך שכל דבר שאני במגע איחו יעבוד היטב . עם
זאת,  בזכרי  שהאדם והדפוס נפרדים ושונים זה מזה לגמרי , ושהדפוס
מחוזר על ידי ביקורת בעוד האדם נפגע ממנה,  אני  מבטיח/ה שמטחה
והלאה לעולם  לא  אדבר  או אפעל בביקורתיות כלפי או אודות אדם
אחר,  כולל עצמי .  במקום זאת, בכל מגע עם כל איש איש אמצא ואבטא
הערבה כלשהיא לאיש/ה זו ולעצמי.
```

CANADIAN

I promise to always treasure our beautiful land and waters and our vast spaces and thriving cities, and to love every Canadian, celebrating our diversity, our Native hosts, and our anglophone, francophone, and other guests, and remembering our stamina and boldness now and throughout our history.

The True North, Strong and Free!

ARAB

In total respect for the beauty and wisdom of my people, I cheerfully promise that I will cherish my culture and language, and remember how delightful and important we are to all human beings.

ENGLISH

If the entire situation is taken into account, we English people have always done the very best that we could. And it wasn't all bad. The future, however, is going to be extraordinarily better. England expects every Co-Counselor, led by the working class, to model rapid re-emergence with full respect, equality, and support for every other human being.

NORTH ENGLAND

We northern English were colonized. We have been forced, for our survival, to oppress other folk in the name of English freedom and superiority. We resisted. We kept our pride and identity. Now, led by the working class, we can win the freedom of the North, from which to lead the liberation of all England.

SCOTTISH

I promise always to remember that my ain beautiful Scotland was betrayed, colonized, and impoverished to the present day by England. Partly we endured to stay alive. Partly we were occupied and colonized. Partly we were scattered around the world in order not to die. Now, however, our freedom can be redeemed. With the support of the working classes of the neighbouring countries, Scotland will be free. I promise to think, plan, and work unceasingly to that end. From now on Scotland will have at least one voice: MINE.

SCOTTISH OWNING-CLASS

Bribed, bamboozled, moulded, and manipulated, we have remained 100% Scottish (with English accents). Now every privilege and advantage that was pushed on us will be turned to the support of Scotland's freedom. Head on, working class! We will follow! Whae hae!

SOUTH AFRICAN

I promise to remember to be proud of every tribe and race and its contribution to the history of South Africa, our rich and beautiful land, and our brilliant and promising future.

I promise to fight without pause for the elimination of racism, fear, greed, special privilege, and all other oppressive factors from the life of South African peoples and for the achievement of a just South African society based on equality and opportunity, sisterhood and brotherhood of all people living in South Africa.

For a united, peaceful, and prosperous South Africa for everyone! (said in Bushman, Zulu, Xhosa, Sotho, Afrikaans, and English).

JAPANESE-AMERICAN

With all my honor, I solemnly promise that from this moment on I will never again be less than fully visible as a proud, strong, beautiful, and dignified Japanese-American—Hi!

LES QUÉBÉCOIS

Pour moi, pour mon peuple, et pour mon beau pays je permets solennelement de toujours être fier(ère) de ma langue, de ma culture and de mon héritage, et d'exprimer cette fierté en tout temps.

D'éliminer tous les effects de l'oppression intériorisée sur moi-même et sur les autres québécois.

De travailler sans relâche à construire l'unité entre les québécois et à établir le respect et l'amitié entre tous les peuples d'Amérique du Nord. Je me souviens!

Vive le Québec libre!

QUÉBÉCOIS

For my own sake, and for the sake of my beautiful country and people, I solemnly promise that I will forever express pride in my heritage, my language, my culture, and my nation.

I will resist and eliminate all the effects of internalized oppression, upon myself and upon other Quebecois and shall work unceasingly for unity among us and for respect and friendship between all the peoples of North America. I will remember!

We will be free!

LES ACADIENS

Sous le joug de l'éxil et de l'oppression, avec un coeur plein de confiance, d'espoir and de détermination, je promets de toujours chêrir mon héritage et ma culture. De toujours être fier d'être acadien(enne) et toujours être de tous les Acadiens où qu'ils soient. D'éxige le respect pour tous les Acadiens de tous les autres peuples et d'offrir le respect en retour à tous les autres peuples, de favoriser la sororité entre tous les francophones du monde. Pour l'unité entre nous où que nous soyons!

Pour la fin de l'éxil!

Pour une Acadie libre!

ACADIANS

Out of exile and oppression with a heart full of faith, hope, and determination, I promise that I will forever cherish my heritage, my language, and my culture, that I will forever be proud that I am an Acadian and forever be proud of all Acadians everywhere, that I shall require respect for Acadians from all other peoples and shall offer respect to all other peoples in return. That I shall advance the sisterhood and alliance of all French-speaking people in the world.

For unity among us wherever we are!

For an end to exile! For a free Acadie!

SWEDISH

Som en stolt svensk vägrar jag att acceptera några gränser för min kärlek eller för mitt inflytande på världen. Jag kommer att visa fullständig respekt och förvänta mig allt av mina medmänniskor men aldrig låta snällhet eller omtanke om andra hindra mig från att ta de djärvaste initiativ.

SWEDISH

As a proud Swede I refuse to accept any limit for my love or my influence on the world. I will show complete respect and expect everything of my fellow beings but never let kindness or caring about others prevent me from taking the boldest initiatives.

SWEDISH

From now on I promise that I in every situation will remind myself and others in a bold, self-assured, and enthusiastic way about what a special, unique, and unusual human being I am.

UNITED STATESER

For the survival and cleansing and long-range flourishing of my beloved United States, I promise that, from this moment on, I will speak out and act against every injustice, no matter how long-established. I will insist that the ideals and goals which inspired the founding of our country and for which our people have repeatedly striven and fought and sacrificed, shall be lived up to.

The United States is my country. I shall forever claim her with pride in her every good quality and with determination to correct any of her past, present, or future wrongs. My United States! With freedom and justice for all!

SOUTHERN UNITED STATESER

I sincerely promise that, from this moment on, I will never falter in my pride in being a Southerner, in my love for the beautiful Southern land, for the thoughtful courtesy and caring of its people, for their often-obscured but always-persisting resistance to oppression, for all our proud heritage and our brilliant future. I shall never lose sight of the fact that *all* people of the South are my sisters and brothers, nor allow any slight against any Southern person to go uncorrected, not even if voiced by Southerners themselves. The *real* South will rise again!

U.S. MIDWESTERNER

I promise that from this moment on I will be proud of the strong cities, beautiful corn fields, lakes, and forests which are my home. I will remember that my people are special and worth every effort it takes to reach them. I will boldly lead all humans from the solid center of my country, firmly trusting my thinking and speaking my mind. The world can depend on my power and intelligence for its survival.

PERSONS OF MIXED HERITAGE

Recognizing that we are the people of the future, and that every one of our cultures and our heritages is valuable and to be respected and appreciated, we proudly proclaim ourselves to be 100% universal humans, and we invite all human beings to join us in this claim.

"DISPLACED" PERSONS

We have endured loneliness and exile and have survived. We have struggled to keep our roots in the culture of our homeland. We have tried to be excellent guests and win a permanent place in the land of our exile. Now, realizing the common goals and common interests of all humanity, we proclaim ourselves and all other people citizens of our beautiful planet Earth, welcome wherever we abide or travel. The world is our home!

DISABLED PERSONS

I cheerfully promise that from now on I will always remember that my body is wonderful and that I am fully human, that I am totally admirable and lovely to be close to, and I will confidently expect to be cherished exactly as I am by all human beings.

WOMEN

I solemnly (fiercely, cheerfully) promise that, from this moment on, I will never again settle for anything less than absolutely *everything*. This means that _____.

MEN

I promise that, from this moment on, I will be proud to be male, and will seek closeness and brotherhood with every other man of every age, race, nation, and class.

I will permit no slandering or disrespect or blaming of any man for the hurts which have been placed upon him and I will seek to restore safety to all men to discharge these cruel hurts.

I will fight to end and eliminate the burdening of men with over-fatigue, over-responsibility, and coercion into armed service in which we have been brutalized, and forced to kill or be killed.

I will cherish my birthright of being a good, intelligent, courageous, and powerful male human.

YOUNG PEOPLE

I solemnly promise that, from this moment on, I will never again treat any young person, including myself, with anything less than complete respect. This will mean that _____.

YOUNG ADULTS

I joyfully promise, from this moment on, to never give up my dreams and goals. I choose to remember always that the whole world is mine, and I need never be alone in figuring it out and making it just right.

ELDERS

I promise that I will never die, that I will never slow down, and that I will have more fun than ever.

ELDERS

I promise that from this moment on, I will live my life with unabashed delight and confidence, using my full wisdom, creativity, love, and energy to ensure that the world around me proceeds exactly the way I want it to and envision that it can.

I will do this by inviting and encouraging others to join with me, think with me, and act in all of our best interests.

As a basis for living this fully, I will pay loving and thoughtful attention to the needs of my body, mind, heart and soul, and welcome other people's love and attention when it is freely given.

I will respect and honor other elders and never permit anyone, including myself, to invalidate or stereotype elders again.

ALLIES TO ELDERS

I promise that from this moment on I will invite, encourage, and expect elders to live their lives with unabashed delight and confidence, using their full wisdom, creativity, love, and energy to ensure that the world around them proceeds exactly as they want it to and envision that it can.

To this end, I will persist in inviting them to notice what is good in the present moment, what their strengths and contributions are, and how deserving they are of my love and attention, as well as the love and attention of others.

To assist them in attaining and maintaining a full and vigorous life, I will listen lovingly, respectfully, and attentively to past and present experiences, triumphs, hurts, and disappointments, encourage them to notice and discharge their feelings, and invite them to think about how the world should proceed, how they can be effective in making the world right, and what help they need from me and others to move things along.

I will also encourage them to take loving and thoughtful care of themselves and to make and maintain strong relationships with others based on mutual attention, interest, and affection. I will never again permit anyone to invalidate or stereotype elders.

PARENTS

I promise to remember always that I am a *good* parent, that I always have done the best I could, that I have passed on to my children as few of the hurts that I endured as a child as I could possibly manage, and that some day I'll get a little rest.

PARENTS

I am a good parent. I love my child/ren. From this moment on, I will relish my excellence as a mother/father, enjoy my precious, resilient child/ren, and discharge my every regret.

I hold myself and my fellow parents blameless for the struggles we still face due to our heavy oppression. I am proud of the goodness and commitment of all parents, and am proud of the vital work we do. As a mother/father, I will remember that there will be time to pursue every goal that is dear to my heart.

WORKING CLASS

I solemnly promise that, from this moment on, I will take pride in the intelligence, strength, endurance, and goodness of working-class people everywhere.

I will remember to be proud that we do the world's work, that we produce the world's wealth, that we belong to the only class with a future, that our class will end all oppression.

I will unite with all my fellow workers everywhere around the world to lead all people to a rational, peaceful society.

I am a worker, proud to be a worker, and the future is in my hands.

MIDDLE CLASS

I cheerfully promise from now on to stand proudly visible, to be my true self without caution or pretense, to work for the unity and liberation of all working people, and never to be quiet again.

OWNING CLASS

I promise that, from this moment on, I will refuse to feel guilty or accept blame or isolation for the class position in which my birth or other events placed me, but will instead take full pride in my complete humanness. I will recognize and remember my close ties to all other human beings. I will treasure and appreciate the favorable factors in my background which allowed me to keep much of my humanness and abilities intact and functioning. I pledge that this humanness and these abilities and advantages will be used, with zest and joy, for the complete liberation of every human being from every oppression.

OWNING CLASS

I promise always to remember that I and my people are completely good, and I never need pretend again. No matter how frightening it feels I will give up the control of wealth and the justification for it. And I will come home and humbly take my own place with working-class people in setting the world completely to right.

LESBIANS

Because I am good, and belong, like every other woman, at the center of all matters, I promise never again to accept any limits on my loving, my relationships, or my abilities. I am completely good, I am fully feminine, I am a Lesbian.

GAY MEN

Beloved brothers, because of our supreme importance to the world now and forever, I promise to always remember that my love is good and my manhood is complete and without limits.

RC LEADERS

I promise that, from this moment on, I am in complete charge of *absolutely everything*, including the entire RC Community. Ha! Ha! Ha! Ha! (In tones of triumph, satisfaction, and power.) This means that _____.

CATHOLIC

I pledge to never again demean or apologize for myself, my family, or my church for being Catholic, but to esteem them all as beloveds of God and all the universe.

GEREFORMEERDE BEVRIJDING

Ik geloof oprecht dat ik goed ben geboren en gebleven als mens en als gereformeerde.

Ik ben heel gewoon en evenveel waard als ieder ander.

Ik mag uitrusten zonder dat ik iets heb gepresteerd en tevreden zijn over wat ik doe.

Ik beloof dat ik altijd van mezelf zal houden en dat ik nooit zal vergeten dat mijn leven mijzelf toebehoort en dat ik ervan mag genieten.

Ik ben gereformeerd en geschapen naar Gods beeld en Zhij zag dat het goed was en dat geldt ook voor mij. Dat betekent _____.

CALVINIST LIBERATION

I sincerely believe that I was born and have remained good, as a human and as a Calvinist.

I am just an ordinary person and I am worth just as much as anybody else.

I may rest without having achieved a thing and I may be satisfied with the things I do.

I promise that I will always love myself and that I will never forget that my life belongs to me and that I may enjoy it.

I am a Calvinist, created after the image of God, and S/He saw that it was good and this also applies to me. This will mean _____.

AGAINST RACISM

I resent and will fiercely oppose racism's crippling limits to the progress of my beloved human race. Always keeping in mind my proud heritage of fighting oppression, and wanting to enrich my present and future, I will engage and join with others to smash racism so that we all may live in a free world.

CLASSROOM TEACHERS

As a proud worker in the liberation of all human intelligence, I cheerfully promise that I will always treat every learner and every teacher, including myself, with complete respect.

ARTISTS

I promise to always remember my power, love, and intelligence as an artist, and the vital role that artists have played in every culture and time. I will never again invalidate any artist, including myself, or any work of art, but rather ally myself with all artists to end our economic oppression, and enthusiastically encourage the creativity of every human.

COLLEAGUES

As a full-fledged human being, I promise to think and to respect thinking, to allow no invalidation of any scholar or teacher, including myself, to refuse to be isolated from my colleagues or to act as an agent of oppression, and to boldly apply my full knowledge and power to the creation of a just world.

WORLD CHANGERS

I have chosen to change society, but I also choose to be intelligent in the way I go about it.

The future needs *me*, well-rested, well-nourished, and well-exercised.

The past is useful as a source of information, but never as a substitute for my own fresh thinking. Mao (or any more recent leader) respected Marx (or any more previous leader), but did his own fresh thinking. I will respect all past thinkers but my thinking will necessarily be more brilliant than theirs because I stand on their shoulders.

If I am not enjoying what I am doing, then there is something wrong with how I am doing it and I will correct it.

VETERANS

I promise that never again will I allow my country to wage war.

RANK AND FILE

I have decided and do repeatedly decide to ensure that everything around me will go well. I am just one of thousands of ordinary RCers who use ordinary tools which now belong absolutely to every one of us. I will be in charge of the world I am in contact with, and thousands more will be doing the same.

THERAPISTS

I promise always to remember that I am no more than an assistant to the person I am seeking to help; that nothing I do that strains my survival can be of real, long-range assistance to another; that everything I do will be directed to enhance the power, the independent thinking, and the humanness of the person I am assisting; and that the factor of approval by authority will never sway my judgment in what I do to assist.

RAISED-EXPATRIATE

Knowing that we are at the centre of all wide-world matters, we will confidently expect to be welcomed and cherished exactly as we are by everyone.

We promise to take pride in the position in which events placed us, the strengths this has given us, and the close ties we have with all people. The world is our home!

AGAINST CRITICIZING

From now on I will view each person in the light of his/her value to me, to the RC Community, and to the world. I will under all circumstances *think* no critical thoughts of anyone; and I will under all circumstances notice and comment on the slightest contribution, service, and evidence of growth; because no matter how slight these actions feel to me, they are immense if they lead toward the re-emergence of me and my students. And I will repeat this as often as necessary until the ancient habit pattern of criticizing has been broken.

CIVIL SERVANTS

From now on I will take complete responsibility for the liberation of Blankville.

With my excellent leadership, Blankville will become a beacon of peace and progress to the rest of Blankland and the world.

AGAINST MONEY DISTRESS

I will do everything necessary to arrange ample funding for all my projects. I will discharge completely any of my patterns that gets in the way, and I will counsel anyone who needs to think differently in order to help me accomplish this.

I promise that I will never again let money stand in the way of accomplishing my goals.

Reports

The October 1987 Trip to China

I left Seattle on October 2nd for Honolulu. I worked that evening with a group of leaders in the Hawaiian RC Community at April Sasaki's house, and the next day did a workshop at a very special United Churches of Christ Church that had once been an army barracks. We had a fine workshop; twenty-six or twenty-seven people were present, some from several of the islands other than Oahu. It's very plain that the Community is coming to life and has a good future ahead of it. Some Native Hawaiians were at both meetings, and we began work on Hawaiian liberation. One of these also plans to become a youth leader and will be in touch with the international youth leaders. It was a very satisfying workshop. It was a pleasure to be back with the Hawaiian Community, especially as it's showing so much life and vigor under April Sasaki's leadership.

On Sunday morning, Tim and Mary Ni came from San Francisco and joined me at the airport. Their plane was late and we had very tight connections to our plane to Tokyo and Hong Kong. Their bags caught up with us in Guangzhou two days later.

GUANGZHOU

When we arrived in Guangzhou (which used to be known in the West as Canton), we were met by representatives of the Women's Federation of the city.

We were there for four and a half days. We grew very fond of the leaders of the Women's Federation.

Appeared in **Present Time** No. 70, January 1987.

The first day we gave talks to an audience of 700 women leaders assembled in the Women's Federation headquarters, which is a very large and well-furnished building. The director, Li Bi Xian, was at that meeting and joined us at lunch later. At lunch also the secretary of the Party for the province of Guangzhou sat with us, Wu Xiao Feng. I was impressed by these two women. They seemed very aware of problems, very competent in their work, very caring about people, and very direct. We began a friendship that I hope can continue over a long time. We sat on a huge dais on a stage in front of this enormous body of women, all of whom had very comfortable upholstered seats and desks in front of them. Li Mei Ge translated for us as she did throughout the journey. She did a totally admirable job, always seeming at ease, keeping up well, and seeming to be understood well by all the women.

I gave a short talk on the essentials of counseling, stressing what a dominant role women and women leaders have played in the Communities since they began. Mary Ni spoke more at length on her experiences with women's work. Tim spoke briefly on the work with children. There was some formal appreciating back and forth.

Then we were asked if we would like to see their new children's center. We were eager to do so and were taken to where the huge center is still under construction. Twenty-one million yuan are being spent on this structure, about half contributed by the government, about a third being raised by popular subscription donations, and the rest coming from overseas Chinese, particularly from Hong Kong.

It consists of a tall building (it looks like about twenty stories) with an astronomical observatory on top, and classrooms and office space filling the rest of the building. Beside it is a kind of a children's palace done in very unusual architecture with many smooth, winding ramps and a host of the most delightful features you could imagine. There are small railways, tunnels with fairytale scenes abounding on each side, two dance pavilions, a huge maze where mirrors and clear walls confuse the passer-through thoroughly, great stuffed animals with little theaters in their stomachs that children can work themselves, a computer room, a ballet studio, singing and music studios, every part ingeniously done. It's still in construction, none of it is in use yet. We were surrounded by construction workers as the director of the center guided us through. It took a long time to simply glimpse even part of the features. It's the most impressive building for children's use that I have ever heard or, or ever dreamed of. It certainly sets a standard for all of us parents in the West for the kind of thoughtful regard a society can pay to its small children. Five hundred children are expected to use it every day. It will undoubtedly be a place of delight for children to visit over and over again whenever they have a chance.

Lunch at a Cantonese-style restaurant had what seemed like thirty-two courses one after the other. I was able to ask many of the women leaders at the table with us (and the male chauffeur who had been driving) the stories of their lives. Each seemed eager and relaxed about taking a turn, and talked freely about their backgrounds (which were extremely varied). Some of them discharged in laughter or a few tears as they spoke. A number of them said that they had learned things about each other that they had never known before. It was a pleasant and congenial time and one of the happiest first meetings with people that I have ever experienced. I feel very good about the caliber of the women's leadership in the city after this contact with them.

That afternoon we were taken to Hua Nan Sho Fan Da Xua, a Normal University, where professors of psychology, other teachers from the college, and graduate students and undergraduates listened to a short introduction to RC. Our host was Li Jucai, the chairman of the Psychology Department. A psychiatrist was an eager participant in the discussion afterwards. I rather think from the questions he asked and from the communication we had with him the next day that he will be enthusiastically helping to get RC started in that particular academic atmosphere.

We returned there the next day for a discussion session with professors, the psychiatrist, and graduate students only. Here we attempted some demonstrations in spite of the awkwardness of the translation step.

I also conducted a small support group. This worked very well. People eagerly took their turns, talked and discharged a little. When I asked at the end if they had enjoyed the experience, each of them turned a reproachful face upon me and said, "But I still have my problem!" Since they had a five-minute turn, mostly talking, I could not keep from bursting into laughter at their expectation that in five minutes their "problem" would have been solved. But we all parted in good order. We left bundles of literature there, not only the literature we had rough translations in Chinese for, but also a copy of each of the books in English. There were many promises to keep in touch and to let us know of their experiences in attempting to continue Co-Counseling with such a quick beginning.

The second morning we returned again to the Women's Federation of the city of Guangzhou to a smaller group. Twenty-four women were present besides the officials. This time there were many questions and great interest was shown in what we had to say. Follow-up questions occurred two or three times in many cases.

On the third day, we visited the headquarters of the Provincial organization of women for the whole Province of Guangzhou. We met in the hall in which the Provincial Congress meets. Again we were on a very impressive dais with big chairs and many microphones. I talked again and so did Mary and Tim, and this time the questions, which came fairly thick and fast once they got started, were almost entirely directed to Mary and Tim. The one they gave me to handle was what should a wife do when her husband is taking a mistress. I did my best by suggesting that they help get the wife and the mistress together, saying that together they could certainly straighten out the erring male.

We had dinner on our own that night and enjoyed it and did a little Co-Counseling in between and a long series of lessons began with Pi Xiao Ming where she began to recover her lost English and I began to try to get at least a few phrases of Chinese. We got to bed early that night, were up at 5:30, and caught the plane for Kunming, which is a city of about two million, still in South China, but a two-hour flight inland from Guangzhou and about a mile high in altitude.

KUNMING

There we were met at the airport by the Women's Federation representative and taken to our hotel. Some small trouble developed in that our tickets for our departure had not been arranged for, but after some negotiations this was straightened out.

On Saturday morning we went to the Yunnan Shi Fan Da Xue, the Normal University in Kunming. There was a large meeting of students, I think about 200, in a big hall. The former president of the university and the psychology professors gave us a most warm welcome and seemed to enjoy the talks and questions a great deal. Here the students had very personal questions and we answered them for over an hour. Tim answered some, but I answered most of them. Any anecdotes about my own experiences as a client or about clients in my past were received with great enthusiasm. There was much laughter, and at first they said to continue going as long as we wanted and then the word came in that it was time to quit (5:00 pm), so they announced to the students that we would be speaking again at 9:00 Monday morning and suggested that the students skip their classes so they could be there. It was a very live afternoon.

On Sunday a trip to the Stone Forest was scheduled. This is an area of about a hundred acres, some distance from Kunming, of very unusual stone formations. I didn't go; I took the day to rest up.

I slept in late and then went through the busy streets of stores, looking for a switch for my reading lamp and some bread so that I could have a bread and milk snack instead of going out to eat late. It was very pleasant to walk among the crowds. Sunday is not the given day of rest, but more people than usual, I think, have that as their day off and there were many people with their children. Everyone would meet my glance briefly and then look away, except people with children. If I would smile at their children, they would stop and smile with me and we would join in appreciation of the marvelous little children. The children are so obviously well cared for and loved and happy.

I found a place that sold ice cream cones and had one, and a group of children in the seven to ten year range came and surrounded me to watch me eat it. One of them finally began trying her English on me, at which they all tried a few words and laughed mightily at my replies and accompanied me for thirty feet or so before their adults called them back.

We had a discussion that night as to how we could best enhance the spread of RC in China and came up with some preliminary ideas.

We met again with Dr. Wan and with Dr. Lu. Dr. Wan is a psychiatrist in charge of a big hospital but also has intimate connections with the Normal University. Dr. Lu is the former president of the university who is now in charge of a research project in psychology. He is the one who had asked if his project could take over the translation of *all* the RC literature. We left a set of books with him. The room had a large number of students in it and a considerable number of faculty with possibly some visitors. More students kept arriving and more chairs were brought in. There were still some standing outside with their heads craned in when we began answering questions. We had the written questions from the meeting two days before, and I started out answering those. Finally Dr. Wan objected that these questions were "old." I agreed that we would answer questions from the floor but said that I first wanted the audience to experience Co-Counseling. So I asked them to choose partners and do a three-minutes-each-way mini-session. They were shy and hesitant to do it at first, but Dr. Wan and Dr. Lu and the dean of the college urged them and encouraged them until almost all of them did choose partners. Then of course they talked eagerly. The din was enormous. I timed the turns. When I noticed that the faculty end of the room was not Co-Counseling, I insisted they do it too. The leaders very enthusiastically said, "Yes, of course, we too." So they all participated.

Then Tim and I took questions from the floor. Tim answered a number of questions that were directed to work with children. Mary did not receive any questions this time. Then there was a talk by Dr. Wan, summarizing what I had said, relating it to many Chinese traditions and saying (very brilliantly, I thought) that RC fit many Chinese traditions but that it did not fit others and that they must learn the parts that did not fit Chinese tradition. He was saying, in effect, that they had a great deal to learn in RC. We could not have imagined a more effective endorsement by a person of greater authority and presence. He's a very magnetic character, laughs easily, communicates well with the students and apparently has excellent relationships with the other faculty people as well. He became our "sponsor" to a considerable extent in that meeting. We left feeling the meeting was enormously successful.

We were presented with gifts of hand-painted pictures with our names and descriptions that had been done especially for us. They were beautiful pictures and we hope to have them fastened to parchment to become durable scrolls. Mine was a crane, Tim's was a horse, Mary's was a rabbit, Li Mei Ge's was flowers, and Pi Xiao Ming's was flowers and a bird.

After the meeting, we had to wait a bit for transportation. Dr. Wan said to me, "Could you come back next year and do a workshop? If you would be willing to do a three-day workshop, I will fill it with psychiatrists and psychologists." I said I would certainly be interested.

We had the rest of the day to ourselves. We conducted a class among the five of us, and we did some Co-Counseling. Then three young staff members from the Mental Health Association came and took us out for noodles that evening. We were able to talk somewhat. The reporter who had interviewed us before for the Kunming newspaper came back and took pictures. She promised to send us copies of the articles. Three or four other classmates of Pi Xiao Ming also showed up late when I was trying to get to bed. We were up very early the next morning and, after about two hours at the airport, caught a very full 7:37 a.m. flight to Shanghai.

The flight was beautiful, with beautiful weather and clouds. We crossed over a great deal of rough country, making it very plain why agricultural survival is so crucial for China. With its huge population only a small part of the land is actually able to be cultivated. We passed hundreds of miles of hills and valleys that were obviously too rough to be cultivated. As we came out into the plains areas approaching Shanghai, we could see the great rivers and an enormous canal system that carried water from the river in all directions for the paddies.

SHANGHAI

When we landed at Shanghai we were met by a leader from the Women's Federation and were taken for a long ride to the Park Hotel, which is across the street from a very large park, the People's Park. On the way traffic was difficult and we took some detours. The outlying streets were full of bicycles. The ones closer in to town were full of pedestrians. The taxis and trucks travel through these great crowds of pedestrians and bicyclists with their horns blowing much of the time.

The hotel was of ancient British imperial design and pleasant enough. We tried eating at a number of places in Shanghai. My favorite was a "fast food place" where you get a stainless steel metal tray with one or two very limited choices of menu and a great block of steamed rice. Tim's and my skills with chopsticks were improving. I'm quite relieved to notice that the way I eat noodles with chopsticks is exactly the way that the Chinese eat noodles with them. I had thought that if one were skilled enough one could be dainty while eating noodles with them out of a bowl of broth, but apparently that can't be done.

We had no meetings the first day, but the second day was very full. Early in the morning, about 8:30, we appeared at the Women's Federation. A long room with tables was filled with some very impressive women. I gave a talk, Tim gave a talk, Mary gave a talk, and we answered many questions. The women took voluminous notes and seemed very, very interested. Quite a number of them apparently had enough English that when I said something that pleased them, they often laughed or smiled animatedly before the translation. Li Mei Ge as always did a marvelous job of translating expertly, and when questions were asked that took what seemed like four or five minutes in Chinese to ask, she would hand them to me in six words. We were presented with a gift of a hand mirror and a comb in elaborate enamel and embroidery and a beautiful scarf as well.

After a bite to eat, we taxied to the huge Shanghai Mental Health Center No. 1. This is affiliated with the World Health Organization. It is a huge mental hospital with a thousand beds and a satellite in the suburbs with another thousand beds. Li Mei Ge and Mary Ni got separated from the rest of us and had trouble finding another taxi. The head of the hospital, Dr. Xiu, after waiting a little, apologized and said, "Do you mind if I begin to tell you about the hospital?" In very good English, he gave us a description of the entire hospital, the wards, the basis of their work, and how they operate and supervise out-patient clinics all over the city. There are a thousand out-patient clinics staffed part-time by a physician. On the hospital staff itself there are eighty psychiatrists and four psychologists. Psychologists do psychometry and some research, but all the work with the patients is supervised by the psychiatrists and they train nurses and orderlies and occupational therapists who come there from the various universities in the hospital itself. Dr. Xiu was a very human, kind, and good man. He took us around the hospital and showed us several of the wards, an assistant running ahead to unlock them. The "mildly distressed" people were doing occupational therapy, putting bobby pins on cards or other tasks, or were watching television. Some of these wanted to talk to me. They were all asked to applaud us when we came in and we were briefly introduced. The patients who wanted to talk sometimes acted a little wild and seemed somewhat embarrassing to the staff. Some of the party laughed at them, but I noticed that Dr. Xiu did not, and Tim and I of course did not. Dr. Xiu translated their questions and I answered them as best I could and shook hands with a number of them. They were just like the people in mental hospitals in the United States, frustrated, bored, and very eager for human communication.

We were taken to a "seriously ill" women's ward, where a smaller number of people lay sedated and drugged in various ways and were simply watched over as if they were living corpses.

Then we met with Dr. Xiu's staff. There were about forty of the psychiatrists present, mostly young, quite a few women. Since Li Mei Ge was not there yet, one of the assistants began translation. We were about fifteen minutes into the talk when Li Mei Ge and Mary Ni showed up (to every-body's great relief). Dr. Xiu had been helping his assistant in the translation and seemed to follow it very well. After the talk we answered questions and left.

That evening Mary's uncle, George Wu, who is eighty-three years old and a longstanding Christian leader and leader of the YMCA in China, had arranged for us to come to the YMCA to meet with the staff, interested friends of his, and members of the English classes that were being conducted at the YMCA. It was a very full room. It was suggested that we not do translations since it was good for people to practice their English. I did a short lecture which seemed to be largely understood and there were many, many questions. I was able to do several demonstrations, some of them quite effective, and with very bright people. One was with a young man who said he could not tell the meeting but confided to me privately that he had been considering suicide many times in the last few days over a rejection by a young woman. I recommended that he immediately fall in love with four new women and tried to get four young women to stand up as models. This was too great a hurdle for the women, but I finally managed to get three young men to stand up, appealing to their bravery to pretend to be women, and I was the fourth woman. He made romantic overtures to each of us, which helped him to laugh quite a bit. He was eager to continue to be client and asked all kinds of sad and probing questions, but I finally managed to get him to sit down and answered some other people's questions. Later when we were leaving the building, he followed me outside and said, "I cannot know how to thank you enough. I think you have saved my life. And can I ask one more question?" And I said, "No, I'm going home to bed." And he laughed at that. I felt we had terminated the relationship well.

We asked people to choose a partner and do mini-sessions and I followed Tim's earlier suggestion that they decide who went first by having the older of the two persons be the first listener. At first, only a few seemed able to do it because of the universal shyness, but as the few began to talk animatedly and I encouraged the others, eventually, in some form or other, the whole room was participating. The noise of the talking was extraordinarily loud. Our impression was that if we could maintain contact a lot of these people would be very eager to take a Co-Counseling class. Some of them promised to keep in touch with us. We left a set of literature there.

On Thursday, the 15th of October, we went to Fudan University. George Wu had arranged this contact as well. The University is an old one, pre-liberation, fairly independent, and has some good traditions. George Wu said that many foreign students attend there as well as Chinese students and there is a graduate school. We didn't see anyone except Chinese at the groups that were gathered for us. The first group were sociology faculty and sociology graduate students. The undergraduate students present were from psychology classes. It was a large room and it was full of close to 200 people. The head of the department escorted us in and introduced us. I did all the talking, Li Mei Ge translated. I gave a short introductory lecture. Quite a few of the students seemed to have enough English that they laughed at jokes before they were translated. Particularly with the graduate students who tended to sit up front, there was considerable liveliness in their response. A number of written questions came in as well. Altogether we spent about an hour and three quarters with them. I thought it was a good interaction.

We had been told we would have an hour's discussion with the graduate students and faculty of the sociology department afterwards, so we climbed a few flights of stairs to a different room and had some more tea and answered questions there. One of the questions was about our research. I explained that our research was not done in a laboratory but took place in people's lives. I explained that a great deal of research is being done under all kinds of conditions and that we had evolved our publications so that people could share their results and their discoveries and their knowledge with each other through the publications. I went through the October 1986 **Present Time** (which we happened to have along) for about a third of the magazine, indicating how the articles reported people's discoveries in many countries.

We were presented with three books on philosophy in Chinese as a parting gift and little medals, done in metal and porcelain, of Fudan University. No cabs were available at that time, so we rode the university bus to a central point across People's Park from the hotel. Mary and Tim went with George Wu to visit his family, who are Mary's relatives. They had a wonderful dinner, many, many courses long. Li Mei Ge and Pi Xiao Ming and I spent the evening in serious discussion.

On Friday the 16th, four of us went to the Bund, the great river waterfront of Shanghai. On our side of the river there is a promenade for people to walk up and down and have their pictures taken. We saw a tea garden with a very fine collection of Chinese scrolls and paintings on silk and parchment in its upstairs. The water, which I think is tidewater for the Wampoo River, was very, very busy with strings of barges and all sizes of powerful tugboats, shuttling back and forth. We walked up it to where a tributary river comes into it in the middle of Shanghai, and then spent some time at the Friendship Store, looking for mementos to take home. Mary, Tim, and I left for the plane about noon to go to Jinan. Li Mei Ge and Pi Xiao Ming stayed another day before flying to Beijing where we met them on Sunday.

We were very late leaving Shanghai because of fog and our plane was several hours late to Jinan. It was a small propeller plane and stopped at Nanjing on the way. There had been a meeting of about 300 people waiting for the lecture that night in Jinan, but we got there about 11 o'clock at night, much too late. Sun Jian Min met us with a friend and a car, but also the Women's Federation people were there.

JINAN

The hotel was a massive one. Sun said it was an old one, but it has certainly been re-furbished lately because the fittings were the most modern we experienced in China. We got to bed and early the next morning, at 9 o'clock, we spoke to the faculty of the Sociology and Social Work schools at the Technological Institute. We circulated a roster and it turned out there were many people from various kinds of engineering among them also. They had a lot of questions and it was a pleasant meeting.

Afterwards, we went sightseeing. We saw the most famous of the springs that make Jinan known as the "City of Springs." Then we drove around the lake which is fed by the biggest spring and which is a popular feature with many parks and crowds of people. The park around the spring had an excellent monument to an artist who died a decade or so ago and three pavilions full of his paintings. They were traditional-type paintings, but very fresh and lively with a profusion of birds.

Sun's friends had passed the word to some of the people who had been disappointed the night before and in the afternoon at three we had about eighty people out for a lecture. This was a lively group and had many questions. We set them up for a mini-session. In every case on this trip where we organized mini-sessions, people were at first very shy to turn to each other. We would go through the audience and turn them to each other. Sometimes we would take singles by the hand and move them down to where another single was sitting. Always, once they started to talk, the noise was deafening. Not everyone would do it, but the ones who did chattered loudly and well. We actually did a demonstration or two here also.

In the evening we had a banquet-type dinner at the hotel with the Secretary of the Polytechnic Institute. This had been arranged by Sun with great persistence. The assistant secretary and the assistant's assistant secretary and a couple of others had been at the afternoon lecture and seemed pleased with it.

The meal itself was the most formal we had in China. Everything was done formally. Every time anyone took a drink out of their orange pop or their red wine or their white wine or their vodka, whichever it was, everybody else had to drink at the same time. We left after the final toast to prepare for the train to Beijing which left late at night.

We had a "soft" sleeper's compartment with four beds to a compartment. The three of us had three of the beds and a Chinese man had the fourth. It was quite comfortable. All of us slept better than we usually did at a hotel. The motion of the train was very pleasant, the beds were firm, the coverlets were heavy and warm. It became cooler during the night as we moved north, and when we got to Beijing it was quite cool.

BEIJING

We arrived in Beijing at 7:30 in the morning. Music had been playing for about an hour interspersed with a monologue by a friendly female voice, reminding us to be well-behaved citizens and don't spit and get our luggage organized and perhaps other things. Mary didn't translate much of it for us. Li Mei Ge and Pi Xiao Ming were waiting for us as was the man from the travel bureau of the Women's Federation.

Our hotel, the Hua Du Bin Guan, was a smaller, very pleasant one. After having a bath, we decided to go out and try to do some shopping, but we had a great deal of trouble finding a taxi. They all refused at first to take us where we wanted to go because the Beijing International Marathon was being run that day and the crowds, they said, would make it impossible to get there. We started out to walk and finally managed a taxi.

Back at the hotel Li Mei Ge brought a number of her friends. Chen, whom we met last year and who has been very active, had started a women's support group of single women and has accomplished good things with it. Professor Jiao, who has taught English for many years, teaches the group a class once a week in English. He also is facing retirement and wants a more meaningful life than translating for a commercial company, which is what he's doing now. He asked, in effect, if he could become part of Re-evaluation Counseling and assist with the translating, and we welcomed him most enthusiastically. After a while, Professor Jiao left to go to the Beijing Roast Duck Restaurant to be sure that the meal that he was preparing for us was correctly done.

A Dr. Sun, who had taken some translation tasks on last year even though he was blind, had found it difficult and had asked his daughter to help him. She came over that afternoon to ask some questions about the translation. She said that certain phrases, such as "the world is going to hell in a bucket," puzzled everyone that she asked. I had to explain that my books were written in my dialect and often in slang, not in standard English. I was able to explain most of the puzzling phrases. She seemed very pleasant and pleased to be able to do the translation. She said that she got a great deal out of the ideas in the books. She brought me a present, a pair of "health balls," which are stone balls that you learn to twirl in your hands and are supposed to relax you. We had seen, in the Friendship Store, some pictures of President Reagan being given a pair to twirl. I don't think he's used them very much.

At the Beijing Roast Duck Restaurant, we had a real banquet. The food had been very carefully chosen and it was very pleasant to see how gracious Dr. Jiao was about it. It was a real contrast to the formal dinner in Jinan. So we wound up back at the hotel somewhat late and stuffed.

The next morning we went to the United Airlines Office for Mary to change her flight and then to Kao Yi's home (Kao Yi is another uncle of Mary's). There we met Kao Yi and his children, Mary's cousins, Kao Yue, Kao Zhong and Kao Xiang, who has a new baby who can cry very lustily. The time went by very rapidly. Kao Yi had carved a seal for me last year and this time he had carved one for each of my children and prepared a sheet translating what the characters that approximated the sounds of their names meant in each case. Kao Yue went with us to the street market which I had enjoyed so much last year. There are delicious fried foods sold there, and I bought many, many belts and many, many back scratchers and some tweezers and everything else I saw. I loved shopping at the market.

We got back to the hotel just in time to change our clothes and be picked up by the Women's Federation to go to their big central office and school, where 200 women were gathered to listen to us. The secretary of the National Federation was a very impressive cadre and we liked her very much. Mary, Tim, and I each gave a talk. I spoke on RC, Mary on women's oppression, Tim on working with small children. We had people do a mini-session but ran out of time to answer questions.

We were given some beautiful presents there. One was a beautiful picture of peacocks worked out in colored shells, and framed behind glass. There was also a set of dolls and two sets of three books on psychology of women in Chinese. When we got back to the hotel, Chen and Li Mei Ge came and Co-Counseled with Tim and Mary much of the evening. Kao Yue came later and had a long talk with Mary.

I tried to call Aquiles Cordiero and could not get him at home, but when I called the Brazilian Embassy, Aquiles was the voice that answered. He came over and we had a long talk and he told of visiting with Sung See Whai in Hong Kong. We examined a lot of his philosophical ideas. Finally, when the Co-Counseling was through, the others came in and met him. We worked out a way that he would keep in touch with Li Mei Ge to their mutual advantage.

We finally got to bed, were called at 5:15, and were ready to leave the hotel at 6 a.m. The second car was in trouble, but by holding suitcases on our laps, we got to the airport in time and managed all the formalities. We flew to Shanghai and then to Tokyo. I had hoped to briefly see some of the Tokyo Co-Counselors at the airport, but we missed connections. We parted company with Tim there, who flew to San Francisco. Mary and I got to Seattle after a twenty-eight-hour trip.

SUMMARY

The whole trip was far more successful than we had dared to hope. We have hundreds of good new contacts, several groups of people trying to learn to Co-Counsel from the literature and by practicing, two accredited teachers of RC, Li Mei Ge and Sun Jian Ming, and a couple of dozen new warm, close friends.

Li Mei Ge has shown good judgment as a future Reference Person and did a superb job of translating everywhere.

The translation of the literature is well underway.

East Coast USA, Latin America, Ireland, and California Conferences and Workshops

MEN

I was at home in Seattle for two days before leaving for the Men's Conference at Hebron, Connecticut, USA. This was a very successful conference. Men were there from Germany, Sweden, Israel, Ireland, England, and Canada, besides the U.S. Men from each nation had a chance to talk about the difficulties in attending a predominately U.S. conference, and relationships seemed to go extremely well. There were over 110 men there.

Charlie Kreiner was much appreciated by the men for the inspiring workshops that he has been doing in so many places. In his time for self-estimation and reconfirmation as the Men's International Liberation Reference Person, Charlie committed himself to more intense organization and more frequent circular letter contact with the local men leaders. Organizationally, the plan is to set up many men's support groups which will divide and multiply rapidly followed by men's Wygelian-type leaders' groups focused around the leaders of the support groups and men who are playing leading roles in other ways. The men were clearly at ease in RC. There is obvious re-emergence from the past feelings of being criticized and somewhat unwelcomed by the women. Men are moving forward into leadership and taking pride in their full humanness in very fine ways.

NEW ENGLAND USA TEACHERS AND LEADERS

Next was a teachers' and leaders' workshop at Groton-

Appeared in **Present Time** No. 70, January 1988.

wood near Boston. This is a yearly institution that has always been a very solid and productive workshop. This year was no exception. People are growing very rapidly in confidence and in influence in the wide world here. Because of the economics, the very large weekend workshop was expected to shrink to about twelve people, but enough people felt they couldn't leave it so that it never got smaller than twenty-five. A workshop of twenty-five allows for some intense work that was thoroughly enjoyed by those who were there.

NEW YORK CITY

The following night I met with Emma Ramos-Diaz and part of her Puerto-Rican leadership group in New York City. Here too, gains were very evident even though only about half of the leaders could attend. They were an impressive, substantial group and were taking leadership on their own in many ways. Commitments were made for reaching Puerto Ricanos in many other places on the mainland and in Puerto Rico.

ANTI-RACISM

The next day, Judy Ennes and I traveled down to Appel Farm in New Jersey for the Anti-Racism Workshop. This was a workshop for whites who have been leading anti-racism work and was led by me with the coaching of Barbara Love, Tommy Woon, and Emma Ramos-Diaz, the International Liberation Reference Persons for black persons, people of Chinese heritage, and people of Puerto Rican heritage.

We zeroed in on the phenomenon of whites leading anti-racism work and doing workshops away from home when their own circle of close friends and intimates, their circle of work mates, their Areas and Regions, do not include a representative number of people of color. This led to a good examination of why white people of such good will, in practice, still accept the distorted isolated lives that not having people of color as intimate friends, saddles them with. It led to a commitment for all white RCers to actively seek out people of color in all the circles of their lives, become active friends and allies with them, fall in love with them, develop close friendships, and in practice furnish the extra support and alliance which every person of color needs as a contradiction to the extra oppression which they endure because of the racism in the culture. I think this will clarify for many people why "nice" well-meaning approaches to people of color based on our fears, timidities, and embarrassments have not worked and have been, in effect, racism. Any distress which a white person exhibits, called forth by the non-white color of another person's skin, is in effect white racism. The immediate remedy is to aggressively take the initiative to surround oneself in every level of one's life with people of color.

An article in the October **Present Time** by Eileen Hayes about correct counseling of people of color at a large workshop was a helpful starting point in the discussions.

I anticipate a real breakthrough in our anti-racism work following this workshop and, as a result, a real fleshing out of our Communities with adequate numbers of our many wonderful kinds and cultures and nationalities of people of color.

BUENOS AIRES

I flew directly from New York City to Buenos Aires, changing planes in Rio de Janiero. Argentina was not only in the middle of spring weather, which was nice, but is obviously flourishing as an RC Community. There is a large amount of literature already translated and more in the process of being translated (and being circulated in photocopied form). The Community in Buenos Aires is still small, but the strength of the leadership is, in my opinion, about five times what it was a year ago. Francisco Lopez-Bustos is still very much the leader in charge, but there are many other people leading around him and some new forces that are opening up the way to new populations very quickly. We had one person from the provinces there for the first time and just missed having someone there from Montevideo, Uruguay present. Also, our upcoming leader from Spain, Dr. Eneko Landaburu and friend, had arrived just the evening before and participated in the workshop.

The workshop was just excellent. The work in the working-class barrios is going forward. The leadership taken by the religious sisters is multiplying rapidly. We have academic, young people's, Gay men's, and Lesbian leadership developing as well.

LIMA

From Buenos Aires, I flew to Lima. Here there were some conflicts with other activities the first day of the workshop, but by the second day, a very solid group had formed. A Wygelian-type leadership group was set up to guide the development of the Community. The director of the center in which we met decided to add himself to the group of RC leaders after participating in the workshop. A very splendid leader of the only nation-wide black organization in Peru, also is taking leadership in RC. Sofiana was away at school in the United States, but both her parents participated actively in the workshop and I think will be important forces in the future.

The desperate economic situation and the growth of violence in the country as a result, present difficulties, but I am quite confident that things will work out well. Susan Collett deserves a great deal of credit for her responsible persistence in bringing the Community together there.

MANAGUA

From Lima I flew to Managua where our active Community has consisted for some time of exactly three people—all of them leaders in the Baptist Church and leaders in the Baptist seminary there. The four of us spent a good deal of time working together. Later, Brenda arranged that I speak to the staff of the Baptist Hospital. About eighty people attended that meeting. The doctor who is the director of the hospital turns out to be a Palestinian, which was a welcomed acquaintance. I promised to put him in contact with other RC Palestinians. Later I spoke to the students at the seminary. Before we left there was agreement that Brenda, Roger, and Jerjis would each start a fundamentals class within the next month. When we came out from the meeting where we had decided this, many of the students of the seminary were hanging out by the door and called out to Brenda, asking her when the class would start. I am quite sure that the possibilities for RC in Nicaragua are very good.

There is some feeling of relief in Nicaragua that the destructive military action of Reagan's contras is being inhibited by the resistance of people in the United States. There is still a great deal of fear and anxiety, however. It is certainly plain that whatever we can do to eliminate this threat to the people of Nicaragua would be most welcome. The Baptists among whom RC is starting are a small percentage of the population, but they are a highly respected group and play a good role in the development of representative government there.

MEXICO

From Managua, I flew to Mexico City and met Rogelio Acosta, our Apprentice Regional Reference Person for Mexico. He drove me up over the rim of the great plateau in which Mexico City (now estimated to be over twenty million people) sits, to a place called Topaztlan, near Cuernavaca, where we had a lovely workshop site in a kind of Catholic retreat center. Here the leaders from Cancun, Puebla, and Irapuato, and new contacts from Mexico City, had an excellent workshop. The work of translation was, as always, arduous, but here, as in all the other places in Latin America, volunteer translators did excellent work and the feeling at the end of the workshop was one of confidence and great enthusiasm. Some USers attended and played a becomingly modest role and thoroughly enjoyed themselves. Some people who we would have liked to have been there could not come, being abroad or otherwise occupied. I don't think there is any question that there will be a substantial Mexican Community growing under Mexican leadership and suiting Mexican conditions admirably.

DUBLIN

I had a little trouble getting home from Mexico because of plane delays, and I was very, very tired by the time I made it. Two days later I left for Ireland and by far the best Irish workshop that we've ever had. I spent one day with the Dublin leaders and then the weekend with 130 leaders from all over Ireland. The spirit and attitudes were fine. Some confusion attached to one leader was pretty well dealt with, and two new Regions were set up—one for the Republic of Ireland outside of Dublin, one for Northern Ireland (the part still under British rule), so we now have three Regions in Ireland.

The tone of the work was just excellent. There were many people who could not come and whom I missed seeing, but it was lovely being with the great throng who did attend. There were many priests and nuns, our first working farmer, many working-class people, and people from the provinces. It was a very representative all-Ireland workshop.

THERAPISTS

The next weekend was the second Therapists' Workshop for Psychiatrists, Psychologists, and other Therapists. This was held north of the Golden Gate in the San Francisco Bay area. This, too, was an excellent workshop; Jane Bunker, the ILRP, did a fine job of organizing it. We had people there from all over the United States and some Canadians. An excellent commitment was worked out and the revision of the program and policy for therapists' liberation was begun.

SECOND WOMEN'S CONFERENCE

My last stop before this issue of **Present Time** goes to the printer was at the second of the three great Women's Leaders' Conferences planned for 1987-88. This was near Hebron, Connecticut, USA. (The first was in Santa Cruz, California last summer and the third will be in England [for Europe, Western Asia, and Africa] in the summer of 1988.)

About 180 women attended this conference. It was organized by Beth Edmonds and led by Diane Balser, with my assistance.

It was a *marvelous* conference. Most women attending were leading in the wide world as well as within RC and had obviously grown greatly in clarity, confidence, and influence in the recent period. Diane's leadership was profoundly correct and inspiring. There was almost uniform eagerness to share leadership and closeness in the world with the burgeoning men's movement.

Women leaders were there from Argentina, Mexico, Chile, Puerto Rico, Canada, and every part of the eastern half of the USA. Sisterly representation was also present from England, Israel, and the western and west coast USA.

My role at the conference was to clarify policy and organization, demonstrate counseling on the internalized forms of sexism, and lead on the relations between women and men.

More Traveling and Workshops

My travels and workshops in the months of January and February have been reported in part in other places in this issue. However, I note that the Netherlands' Leaders' Workshop between Christmas and New Year's was a very, very encouraging workshop. There was a large group of leaders there, and the growth and re-emergence and responsibility and power were very evident. The Netherlands Community is doing well and they have some fine new leaders who are taking hold very responsibly in addition to the ones with more experience.

There's much on the Young Leaders' Conference in other articles and something on the first workshop in Hungary, but I would say that I am quite impressed with the caliber of the people who are exploring RC in Hungary and I think we have an unusually capable leader in Molnar Gabriella. She took a train after the workshop to join Robert Zarkovic and me in Yugoslavia for additional experience. Some of the plans there had to be changed. The television interview, for example, was postponed because the interviewer was interviewing some Soviet leaders, but we did travel from Beograde to Osieki, then to Novosad, finally back to Beograde, speaking to groups of psychologists in each of the three cities, or people who were mostly psychologists. In each place we found some individuals, often old friends of Robert's, who were very eager to follow up on their first acquaintance with RC.

The second peace activists' workshop near Boston was very impressive. A broad spectrum of the important peace organizations in the United States was represented, with some fra-

Appeared in **Present Time** No. 71, April 1988.

ternal and sororal delegates from Europe and Australia also present (there will be a European peace activists' conference later on this year).

The points that stood out for me about the workshop were:

1) unanimous agreement that members of the peace organizations must be encouraged to enter political parties, trade unions, and business organizations to win them over for effective peace policies instead of the activists only remaining in their own organizations and talking to each other and their unorganized contacts;

2) agreement that peace activism so far deserves a great deal of the credit for the missile treaties and the disarmament negotiations that have been achieved and are proceeding;

3) agreement that the "internalized oppression" of peace activists has been a major difficulty in the effectiveness of peace forces. This was tackled at the workshop in demonstration after demonstration, and effective techniques were pretty much in the possession of all of the delegates by the end of the workshop. (One of the most effective is the use of the "frontier commitment"—"From this moment on, the *real* me, and this means _____" as a beginning for the *exchange* of commitments, alternating every few minutes between a pair of committed Co-Counselors);

4) the realization that almost all the delegates at the conference regard themselves as "middle class." This brought home to me very sharply that we need to explore and develop policy on middle-class liberation and we will have our first middle-class liberation workshop at Appel Farm, near Philadelphia on May 20-24 this year. Charlotte Lowrey is the organizer.

I then flew to Trinidad. Waveney Richards has gotten RC started in a good way. The population is generally very alive and alert. It reminds me of Hawaii in the tendency to have attention out and be so positive. Waveney has a fine group of friends around her and the workshop was quite satisfactory.

The meetings and workshops in Scandinavia in February were also very joyous occasions. The Danish Community is still small but its leaders are widely respected and the tone of the group is very, very solid. I had a little chance to rest in Copenhagen and enjoyed it very much. Then I spent an afternoon and evening with the Community in Gothenburg and did a four-day workshop at Fiskebadde near Stockholm, an open question evening for the RC Community, and an introductory lecture and demonstration evening with a wide-world organization which presents "new thinking" to the public.

What pleased me a great deal was that we have the beginnings of contact with people of Samer (Lapp) heritage in Denmark and Sweden. There is a Finnish support group organized in Stockholm which intends to travel to Finland and begin classes and support groups there in cooperation with, I think, a lot of other ex-patriate Finns in other countries. We have a Spanish RCer who has been active in Stockholm and is planning on returning to Spain to teach RC sometime soon. It was very gratifying to me that Cathrine Hansen of Siljan, Norway and Anne Helgedagsrud of Bergen, Norway were both able to be at the workshop. They are people that I am very fond of, and the possibilities they represent for Norwegian RC to again begin flourishing are very gratifying to me.

I had the rest of February at home and will have all of March.

Quick Report from the Continental Conferences

At the 1985 World Conference of the Communities in Montreal, Quebec, Canada, it was decided that the International Community was becoming too large for its outreach funds to be able to any more finance such a representative World Conference with delegates from all over the world, and that it would be more economical to have Continental Conferences in 1989 with larger and more economical participation, followed by the election of a small number of delegates to meet as a World Conference either late in 1989 or early in 1990. A few guidelines were set up about this, the main requirement being that the delegates from the continental conferences were expected to represent approximately a thousand Co-Counselors for each delegate.

Each of the Continental Conferences, except the North American (French- and English-speaking) one, asked to expand the conference into a workshop, seeing this as a more important need than the deliberative or legislative aspects of the conference for the Communities on that continent.

The Continental Conferences this year began with the conference for Australia and New Zealand. This was held from May 25th to 29th near Sydney, Australia. There was a good representation, with ninety-one delegates from many different Communities in Australia and sixteen delegates from New Zealand. What was especially noteworthy about the New Zealand delegation was that it was almost evenly divided between the Maori people and the whites of New Zealand.

Appeared in **Present Time** No. 77, October 1989.

The Australian RCers had asked ahead of time to put the emphasis of the conference on beginning work against racism. The New Zealanders had asked that Native North Americans attend to begin a linkage of indigenous peoples. This had been planned but was frustrated at the last minute by the inability of the North American Native RCer to attend. This was later compensated for in some degree by a Maori delegation attending workshops in the United States and becoming acquainted with American Native leaders at that time.

The Australian Communities had registered a very significant growth over the past years and showed very sound and capable leadership. There were delegates there from Brisbane, from Newcastle and the North Coast, Blue Mountains, the southern coast, and Sydney from New South Wales. There were people there from Canberra, the national capital, and Adelaide, from Melbourne, from Perth and the two strong Communities in Hobart, Tasmania. Probably the highlight for all Australians was the panel in which five Aboriginal people became acquainted in the process of speaking to the white delegates and registered the beginnings of a clear policy of Aboriginal liberation with the support of white allies.

Jonathan Shaw was recommended to be continued as Regional Reference Person for continental Australia. Anne Smith was elevated to Apprentice Regional Reference Person for Tasmania, and Diane Shannon was confirmed as Regional Reference Person for New Zealand with the Apprentice designation dropped. These three Regional Reference Persons were chosen as the delegates to the World Conference.

The next Continental Conference, of English-speaking and French-speaking North Americans, was held at Bryn Mawr College in Pennsylvania in the United States. It was held June 10th through the 14th. There were a hundred and seventeen delegates, including a fraternal delegate from Mexico. This Continental Conference represented at least three-quarters of all the Co-Counselors in the world today since Co-Counseling began in this section of North America and has been growing there much longer than in other places.

It was a spectacular occurrence. It astounded me and other experienced and senior leaders in the picture it gave us of how soundly Co-Counseling has developed and how well it has spread. We had never had such an opportunity to realize it before. I personally am in regular touch with much of the world Community but a great deal of what I hear is the nature of problems to be solved, difficulties to be managed. This was a new view.

Much of the work at the conference was conducted through caucuses—caucuses by country, by age group, by occupation, by race, by liberation perspectives. The delegates were quite representative of the geography and the various divisions of the population. The people-of-color caucus, which met every day and had substantial input in all the deliberations of the conference, was fully a quarter of all attendants. Thirty-three caucuses met and reported as panels and it was in these reports that the enormously reassuring picture emerged of how well Re-evaluation Counseling has put down roots everywhere and how solidly it is based in almost every section of the people.

When the caucuses reported as panels, each member of each panel was asked a series of four questions. The first question was: What has been "just great" about being the kind of person you are? (physician, black person, working-class person, woman, etc.). Second: What has been hard about being this kind of a person? Third, has RC been useful to you as this kind of a person, and if so how? And fourth, how does your special branch of RC, and RC in general, need to improve to be more helpful to you as your kind of a person?

In the answer to the third question, "Has RC been useful to you, and if so how?" the full impact of our growth and development came through. Each person in each delegation responded with great enthusiasm. The replies sounded something like:

"It certainly has!" "It changed my life completely," "It saved my life," with each person proceeding to detail several crucial ways in which his or her life had been changed for the better.

When all the reports were done, a number of things were very plain:

(1) We have gathered together in RC the crucial insights, the unoccluded knowledge that humanity needs to re-emerge to its full functioning and to preserve the world from destruction. Even though we are gaining new knowledge all the time, what we have already is adequate.

(2) It was plain that RC can transcend any barriers of language, nationality, age, race, economy. Wherever we have presented it well, people of every group have been able to hear it.

(3) People of every group have made and are making it their own. The roots are down deep everywhere. This group of insights is uniting and can unite all humanity.

It was extremely thrilling to me, but all the experienced leaders in RC who were there expressed the same amazed realization that we had come so far and we had achieved so much, while being preoccupied with the difficulties that we had to solve.

We elected ten delegates and eleven alternates to the World Conference from this Continental Conference. The delegation chosen in this case omitted most of the experienced and geographically well-known leaders in RC, including most people who have been outstanding leaders of the Community. This was done on the decision to have the delegation more representative of the different Wygelian groups within these advanced Communities.

The third Continental Conference took place in Tepoztlan, Mexico. This was the conference of Latin America, which included all of South and Central America and Mexico as well.

Fraternal delegates were present from Puerto Rico, from the Chicano/Chicana nation within the borders of the United States, and from Spain. The number of delegates was five from Argentina, two from Spain, one from Puerto Rico, seventeen from Mexico.

The delegates from Colombia had been denied visas, so were unable to attend. Emergency surgery kept the Nicaraguan delegate from attending. Other difficulties kept the Peruvian delegates from being there.

Nevertheless, it was an excellent conference and the ties for inner Latin American solidarity were strengthened greatly and preparations made for much participation in the translation of RC literature into Spanish. Katie Kauffman attended from Rational Island Publishers to coordinate this work. Rogelio Acosta was recommended to be confirmed and continued as Apprentice Regional Reference Person for Mexico. Francisco Lopez Bustos was similarly recommended and confirmed, and the "Apprentice" portion of his title was dropped. He is functioning now as a full Regional Reference Person for Argentina.

Fifty delegates from twenty-two countries attended the European and West Asian Continental Conference held at Budapest, Hungary, August 4th through August 8th. This was a most remarkable conference. The amount of translation that had to take place was astounding. Everything was done in at least English and Hungarian, but often seven other languages were being translated, following the two main ones, with amazing efficiency and effectiveness.

The people there were thrilled to be crossing the barriers that have divided Europe for so long and many of the newer countries to RC, such as Spain and Hungary, reported rapidly accelerating growth. Again, panels were made use of and most national delegations spoke through the panels to the rest of the delegations with excellent effect. For the first time in such a conference, we had representatives of the Same people (the reindeer herders of northern Scandinavia/Finland), from the Finnish people, from the Turkish people, and from the Basque people. Palestine, Israel, Italy, Greece, The Netherlands, Flanders, France, Yugoslavia, Norway, Sweden, Finland, Spain, Friesland, Hungary, Turkey, Belgium, Poland, Ireland, Scotland, England and Wales were all represented.

The special feature of this conference was that it was followed after a one-day interim by an East/West workshop, for which many of the conference delegates remained. This was a long-standing dream of the organizer of the conference, Molnar Gabriella of Budapest, to begin to heal the schism that has divided Eastern and Western Europe since the end of World War II. To this workshop came two delegates from Russia, one from Estonia, one from Lithuania, two from East Germany, two from Yugoslavia, ten from Poland, twenty-two from Hungary, two from Turkey, and so on.

Here again, panels played an important role. Outstanding was the one-man panel of the delegate from Estonia. He had witnessed an extremely enthusiastic panel of the Hungarian delegates the evening before. Many of them had not previously met each other since they work in different parts of Hungary, but as they listened to each other were more and more enthusiastic and declared a huge organizing campaign to take RC into every part of their country. When the delegate from Estonia spoke, he said, "I did not come here to participate, I came as an observer. It is not my habit to become involved in things, certainly not emotionally involved, but I must tell you that after listening to the Hungarian panel last night I went to my room and cried for a long, long time. I think I must tell you I am emotionally involved in RC."

It was very thrilling to see the healing of the cold-war wounds taking place before our eyes, very warming to see how eagerly the theory was grasped and understood. The momentum that was generated there for the growth of RC in many European countries is impossible to doubt.

The Continental Conference for Africa was held September 1st to 4th at Harare in Zimbabwe. We had five delegates from Kenya, about twenty-two from Zimbabwe, and seven from South Africa. Four of these were black Africans and three were white. The delegates from Uganda found it impossible to make the journey although they are working actively in Gulu using RC towards ending the terrorist campaigns in the province. As a result of the conference, organized Areas have been established in Nairobi in Kenya and in Harare in Zimbabwe. These are under black leadership with separate white leadership occupying a junior role to the black leaders in the black Communities.

Following the conference I went with some of the delegates to South Africa and held a series of workshops in Durban. We established black RC leadership and white RC leadership, independent but cooperating with each other, there, established the beginnings of black leadership in Johannesburg, and both white and "colored" leadership in the Cape, Western Cape and in Cape Town. Workshops were held there, too.

The World Conference delegates from the African conference are Melphy Sakupwanya, the black leader of the Zimbabwe Community, and Wanjiku Kironyo, a black woman leader of the Nairobi Community. The alternate delegate if one of them cannot attend is Thembe Nene, who is a black South African woman.

The Southern and Eastern Asian Continental Conference was held in Kodaikanal in Tamil Nadu, India. We met in a great stone convent built during British imperial times, high in the mountains of Southern India. The location was over a mile and a quarter high and it was amazing to see bananas growing in such cool climates. People were there from many parts of India, from Andhra Pradesh, from Karnataka, from Maharastra, from Pune, from Tamil Nadu, from South Arcot, from Pondicherry, Trichy, Satyamangalam, from Dindigul, Kodaikanal, Madurai, Kanyakumari, and from North India.

There were three delegates from the People's Republic of China, there were four delegates from Malaysia, two from the Philippines, one from Hong Kong. This conference functioned almost entirely as a workshop. A great deal of work was done with the frontier commitments and the delegates found the deliberate use of contradictions to be fascinating.

Three delegates to the World Conference were chosen because of the huge populations involved. (India and China together have a third of the world's population.) Li Mei Ge from Beijing, who was not able to attend the Asian Conference because of recent surgery, Subbaraman, the Regional Reference Person for India, and the leader of Malaysia, Noraini Kassim, were chosen as the delegates. Usha, a very powerful woman from the very articulate Bombay Community, was chosen as an alternate if any of these could not come.

People were delighted to be together across the old national boundaries of Asia. Sister Rebecca and Justino Cabazares from the Philippines agreed to build a Community in that country. Sister Rebecca has been an ally of ours for a long time and has decided to commit herself to RC and her peer counseling foundation, which she had founded, will be teaching RC from now on.

The conference was almost dominated by a large number of Indian nuns and priests who were present. There were Muslims as well from more than one country, but the great preponderance of social worker/religious people undertaking monumental projects against the poverty of southern India was quite outstanding. These are lovely women and men and RC is greatly cherished by them as a tool for making their religion effective and for carrying out their goals with the people of India and in the Philippines.

The World Conference will take place November 3rd through the 7th near Orlando, Florida. We will have about twenty-six delegates.

Both Tim and I attended all of the Continental Conferences except the Asian one. Tim had to return to his job after the African one. I was present at all of them. All the Continental Conferences recommended that we be continued in our jobs.

A number of International Liberation Reference Persons were invited as special guests to some of the Continental Conferences where their expertise and leadership were felt to be especially needed by the people in these continental areas. All the International Liberation People were invited to the Bryn Mawr North American Conference in order to have them all be present at one place. Almost all of them were able to attend, and a good deal of clarity about the Liberation Reference People and their functioning with each other was attained as a result of their being together.

The world Community has grown greatly since 1985. It is in a very healthy state of affairs except in a very few European Communities where the disruption initiated by Daniel Le Bon has temporarily made work difficult for some of the people there. The number of workshops being held and led in a very good way is several times as many as a very short period ago. Translation is proceeding apace and the use of modern technology—of computers, facsimile machines, long-distance telephoning, express mail service, and computer typesetting—is making a great improvement in the inter-communication for all of us.

All of us, of course, look forward to the World Conference, but even more, I think, to the steady expansion and improvement of our lives, our communities, and our contact and influence with the rest of the world. We plan to take advantage of the gains we have won against the nuclear threat, to take advantage of the ending of the Cold War divisions, to take advantage of our much enhanced skill at communication and organization. We plan to play an influential part in helping the world move forward to a safer, child-appreciating, classless, mutually supportive society.

A feature of the African conference was the advanced work against racism, which moved my understanding forward a long way. At the conference were seven white women living in Zimbabwe, a number of whom were exiles from South Africa. It was very clear to me and to the black delegates there that Zimbabwe had to be organized into two Communities, a black-led Community and a subordinate-but-associated white-led Community, because of the obvious unaware racism of the white RCers.

(There are many white residents still in Zimbabwe; they dominate much of the economy and they still live apart from the blacks mostly still in old colonial attitudes. The blacks refer to them as "Rhodies," meaning that they still think they're living in Rhodesia, which was the imperialist name for the country when it was ruled by whites.)

The seven white women were all anti-racist activists. Several of them were refugees from the racism of South Africa. They could not understand why they must be organized separately. The black delegates said to me privately, "They haven't the slightest notion of what's going on, but the minute they come into a meeting with us they start telling us what to do, they start trying to dominate everything, and we can either fight them or out of long habit keep quiet and let them do what they want. It makes it impossible for us to work." The white women could not understand this. Some of them had been exiled from South Africa because of their opposition to apartheid, and one at least had been imprisoned and tortured. It seemed to her that her position against racism was clear. She could not believe there was any problem with her joining the black RC group. We managed to do some good work on this.

I was asked to demonstrate how to work against internalized oppression and chose sexism. I said it operates three ways: against the victim herself, against another woman, and between groups of women. I worked with one woman against her internalized sexism and then got one of the white women and a black woman from Nairobi to come up together and pushed them to be friendly with each other. At each push the white woman was delighted, shook, laughed, was obviously pleased that she was being pushed into a relationship with the black woman. The black woman welcomed her very well. I finally made them hug each other. The white woman shook and sweated, and then I asked them to kiss each other. Again, the white woman was delighted. For a while they were very close to each other and stood next to each other and laughed together. When I said I must go to the third stage of internalized oppression and excused them, and the black woman sat down, the white woman moved ten seats away and sat by herself. I made her get up and come sit by the black woman and hold her hand, at which she sweated and smiled and laughed again. She had a hard time understanding what was wrong with her separating herself from the black woman immediately the demonstration was over. After I talked about it, some of the whites began to understand. I would now say racism is installed by making people afraid of other people, on the pretext of some difference, and usually when we are very young.